LAPHAM'S
QUARTERLY

Perpetual peace is a dream, and not even a beautiful dream, and war is an integral part of God's ordering of the universe.... Without war, the world would become swamped in materialism.

—General Helmuth von Moltke

Battle rages in Haugsbygd, Norway, 1940 (detail).

www.laphamsquarterly.org

Volume 1, No. 1. www.laphamsquarterly.org. Lapham's Quarterly (ISSN 1935-7494) is published four times yearly (November, March, June, September) by the American Agora Foundation, 33 Irving Place, 8th Floor, New York, NY 10003. Periodical Postage paid at Edgerton, WI, and at additional post offices. Copyright © 2007 the American Agora Foundation. Nothing shown may be reproduced in any form without obtaining the permission of the creators and of any other person or company who may have copyright ownership.
Newsstand distribution: CMG. Newsstand Consultant: Ellen Sugarman, 617-505-5596.
Subscriber Services. Subscription: 1 year, $60; in Canada, $80; in all other countries, $100. All payments in U.S. Dollars. Direct all inquiries, address changes, subscription orders, etc., to: email: custsvc_laphams@fulcoinc.com; telephone: 877-890-3001; mail: Lapham's Quarterly, PO Box 3000, Denville, NJ 07834. Editorial and Business Office, 33 Irving Place, 8th Floor, New York, NY 10003. Postmaster: Send changes of address to Lapham's Quarterly, PO Box 3000, Denville, NJ 07834.

LAPHAM'S QUARTERLY

Volume 1   *Number 1*

STATES OF WAR

Introductory

Voices in Time

Voices in Time

English plan of the Battle of Yellow Ford, Ireland, 1598.

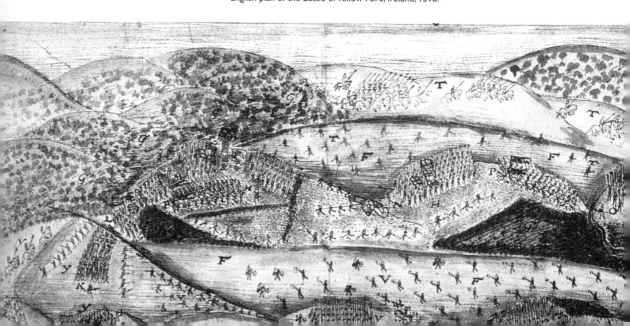

Voices in Time

Voices in Time

Further Remarks

Many of the passages in this issue have been abbreviated without the use of ellipses; some punctuation has been modified, and while overt misspellings have been corrected, archaic word and grammar usage remains unchanged. The words in all instances are faithful to the original texts.

ART, PHOTOGRAPHY, AND ILLUSTRATIONS

Among the Contributors

Winston Churchill (1874–1965), a direct descendent of the Duke of Marlborough, became Britain's Prime Minister on May 10, 1940, the same day the German armies launched their invasion of France. In the front rank of the twentieth century's most formidable statesmen, Churchill was renowned for his eloquence as an orator, for his gifts as a writer, and for his courage as both a soldier and a politician.

Herodotus (c. 484–425 BC) is known as the "Father of History" for his "inquiries" into the origins of the Greco-Persian Wars of 490 and 480–479 BC. *The Histories*, originally presented orally and designed to have a theatrical element, encompassed battles, political incidents, and the marvels of foreign lands—according to which the occupants of present-day Finland were once fierce cannibals, and parts of Turkey and Russia were dominated by roving bands of female warriors.

Sultan Selim I (1470–1520) added roughly one million square miles of landscape to the Ottoman Empire, murdered most of his male family members, and accumulated a vast treasure that remained uncounted and unseen until 400 years after his death.

In a note discovered after his death, **Oliver Wendell Holmes Jr.** (1841–1935) wrote that the uniforms to be found in his closet "were worn by me in the Civil War, and the stains upon them are my blood."

Private First Class Jessica Lynch (1983–) was injured in an ambush during the U.S.-led invasion of Iraq in March 2003. She was briefly held as a prisoner by the Iraqi military in a hospital in Nasiriya, and the American news media transformed the incident into soap opera.

Although his tomb is now a tourist attraction in a UNESCO World Heritage Site and the city of Leningrad has been restored to its place on the Gulf of Finland as St. Petersburg, **V. I. Lenin** (1870–1924) retains his standing as the godfather of Marxist revolution.

Sun Tzu (sixth century BC), a military strategist and general serving the state of Wu, is credited with writing the *Art of War*. A Chinese historian from the second century BC named Sima Qian tells a story about the king of Wu ordering Sun Tzu to lead a procession of concubines as a test of his skills as a commander.

William Shakespeare (1564–1616), poet, dramatist, magister ludi of the English language.

Edward Gibbon (1737–1794) published *The History of the Decline and Fall of the Roman Empire* in 1776, the same year that brought with it the American Declaration of Independence, the publication of Adam Smith's *The Wealth of Nations*, and Captain Cook's discovery of Australia.

George S. Patton (1885–1945), "Blood and Guts" to those who loved and feared him, was one of the most brilliant generals of World War II. A believer in the doctrine of reincarnation, Patton counted among the lives he once lived those of an English knight during the Hundred Years' War, a Greek hoplite who fought the Persians, a Napoleonic marshal, a prehistoric mammoth hunter, and the Carthaginian general Hannibal.

A virgin queen during an era of vengeful princes and impotent kings, **Elizabeth I** (1533–1603) ruled over a kingdom famous for its poetry, its navy, and the efficiency of its secret police. Skilled in the arts of horsemanship and unrequited love, she spoke six languages and played the lute.

Believed to have been blind and unable to write his name, **Homer** (c. eighth century BC) is credited with the composition of the *Iliad* and the *Odyssey*, books one and two of the Western Canon.

A failed novelist and playwright deformed at birth by a club foot, **Joseph Goebbels** (1897–1945) served Hitler's Third Reich as its Minister of Public Enlightenment and Propaganda. As Russian troops swarmed into Berlin on May 1, 1945, Goebbels and his wife, at bay in the Führer's bunker, committed suicide after killing their six children by crushing cyanide capsules in their mouths.

Samuel Langhorne Clemens (1835–1910), better known as **Mark Twain**, began his career as a typesetter, a newspaperman, and a Mississippi riverboat pilot. Eventually the author of roughly fifty books and essays, his *Adventures of Huckleberry Finn* still contends for the elusive title of the Great American Novel.

Augustine of Hippo (354–430), a Roman magistrate transformed into a bishop of the early Church, formulated his notion of Christian morality as a response to his having been sorely tempted by a peach.

Tecumseh (1768–1813), a Shawnee leader who failed to incite American Indians into open rebellion against the U.S. government.

Allegory of Fleeting Time, The angel-genius holds a portrait cameo of Emperor Charles V, by Antonio Pereda, c. 1634. .

THE GULF OF TIME

by Lewis H. Lapham

"He who cannot draw on three thousand years is living hand to mouth."
—Goethe

During my years as editor of *Harper's Magazine*, I could rely on the post office to mark the degree to which I was living in what Goethe surely would have regarded as straitened circumstances. Every morning at ten o'clock, I sat down to a desk occupied by five newspapers and seven periodicals (four of them embroiled in politics, the others concerned with socio-economic theory or scientific discovery), three volumes of ancient or modern history (the War of 1812, the death of Christopher Marlowe, the life of Suleiman the Magnificent), a public opinion poll sifting America's attitude toward family values and assault weapons, and at least fifteen manuscripts, solicited and unsolicited, whose authors assured me in their cover letters that they had unearthed, among other items of interest, the true reason for the Kennedy assassinations and the secret of the universe.

The afternoon mail added to the weight of evidence making the case for what I didn't know and wasn't likely ever to know, and, over a period of years, I came up with a risk-assessment model wired to the sound of the human voice. If, on first looking through a dispatch from the Yale University library or the White House Situation Room, I couldn't hear the voice of its author, I let it go the way of the Carolina Parakeet. The device operated as a loophole through which I escaped the tax of having to read most of what rolled out of the presses in any given year in one or another of the dead languages designed for television broadcast or the teaching of better business management. The volume of email traffic and the expansions of the Internet over the last two decades have broadened the market for "multimedia inter-facing" and "innovative delivery strategies," brightening our horizons with "quicker access to valued customers," accelerating the transmission of unintelligible messages written in academic cipher or ideological code. The surfeit of new and newer news, "prioritized" and "context-sensitive," now comes so quickly to hand that, although we may wish it otherwise, we're smothered in the feathers of the stuff—on air, in print, online; as broadcast, podcast, broadsheet, blog. Within the wind tunnels of the high-speed electronic media, the time is always now; the data blow away or shred, and what gets lost is all thought of what happened yesterday, last week, three months or twenty years ago. Unlike moths and goldfish, human beings deprived of memory tend to become disoriented and easily frightened. Not only do we lose track of our own stories (who we are, where we've been, where we might be going), but our elected representatives forget why sovereign nations go to war.

On the assumption that the blessed states of amnesia cannot support either the hope of individual liberty or the practice of democratic self-government, *Lapham's Quarterly* grounds its editorial premise on the risk-assessment model that allowed me to edit *Harper's Magazine*. If the words on the page translate into the sound of a human voice, I don't much care whether the author sets up the mise-en-scène in 1740s Paris or Harlem in the 1920s. Some years ago on its editorial page, the *New York Times* handed down the ruling that, "Great publications magnify beyond measure the voice of any single writer." The sentence employed the wrong verb. The instruments of the media amplify a voice, serving much the same purposes as a loudspeaker in a ballpark or a prison. What magnifies a voice is the force of mind and the power of expression, which is why Shakespeare's plays still draw a crowd in Central Park, and why we find the present in the past, the past in the present, in voices that have survived the wreck of empires and the accidents of fortune.

History does not repeat itself, but it rhymes.
—Mark Twain

As a college student, I acquired the habit of reading with a pencil in my hand, and, in books that I've encountered more than once, I discover marginalia ten or forty years out of date, most of it amended or revised to match a change in attitude or plan. In a worn copy of Scott Fitzgerald's *The Great Gatsby*, in what I take to be my handwriting at age nineteen, I find a series of exclamation points subsequently crossed out and accompanied by the remark, in my handwriting circa the age of thirty, "Too romantic." In a biography of Aaron Burr, I come across a note, "Too cynical," corrected at a later date and with a different pen, by the further note, "Maybe not." Reading the work of authors reporting from the front lines of different centuries, it sometimes happens that I find myself at different periods in the history of the same map coordinates—Herodotus and T. E. Lawrence exploring the deserts of Arabia; George Orwell, Martin Amis, and Samuel Johnson tempted by the seductions of London. When I complicate the proceedings with a superimposition of marginalia reaching across a distance of fifty years and written while traveling in cities as unlike one another as Chicago and Havana, I can begin to guess at what the physicists have in mind when they talk about the continuum of space and time.

It's been said that over the span of nine months, the human embryo ascends through a sequence congruent with fifty million years of evolution; that within the first six years of life, the human mind replicates the dream of its five-thousand-year journey from the sand castle cities of ancient Mesopotamia. The figures in the dream have left the signs of their passing in what we know as the historical record, navigational lights flashing across the gulf of time on scraps of papyrus and scratchings in stone, on ships' logs and bronze coins, as epic poems and totem poles and painted ceilings, in confessions voluntary and coerced, in five-act plays and three-part songs.

The record is our inheritance, the one that Goethe had in mind when he suggested a restructuring of the deal that Satan offered Faust. It isn't with magic that men make their immortality. They do so with what they've learned on their travels across the frontiers of five millennia, salvaging from the ruin of families and the death of cities what they find to be useful or beautiful or true. We have nothing else with which to build the future except the lumber of the past—history exploited as natural resource and applied technology, telling us that the story painted on the old walls and printed in the old books is also our own.

Cicero made the point fifty years before the birth of Christ: "Not to know what happened before one was born is always to be a child." The American historian, Arthur Schlesinger Jr., made the same point in the essay that served as his epitaph when it was published in the *New York Times* on January 1, 2007, two months before he died. Under the heading, "Folly's Antidote," he prescribed strong doses of history as a cure for "the delusions of omnipotence and omniscience," akin to those that persuaded the Bush Administration to stage a rerun in Iraq of America's misadventure in Vietnam. The failure to connect the then with the now Schlesinger diagnosed as an illness which, if left untreated, he thought likely to lead to the death of the American idea. Children unfamiliar with the world in time make easy marks for the dealers in fascist politics and quack religion. The number of people in the United States at the moment who believe in the literal truth of the Book of Revelation exceeds the number of people who lived in all of medieval Christendom.

Navigators Using an Astrolabe in the Indian Ocean. Vellum by Boucicaut Master.

An acquaintance with history doesn't pay the rent or predict the outcome of next year's election, but, as the season or occasion requires, it makes possible the revolt against what G. K. Chesterton once called, "the small and arrogant oligarchy of those who merely happen to be walking about"; instills a sense of humor; and brings with it the tray of "examples and warnings" offered by the Roman historian Livy as, "fine things to take as models, base things, rotten through and through, to avoid." About the methods of pacifying cities bloodied by civil war, I learn more from Machiavelli's *Discourses* or the *Memoirs* of William Tecumseh Sherman than from the testimony of General David Petraeus or the commentary on Fox News. When I see Hillary Clinton and Rudy Giuliani being bundled around the country in a flutter of media consultants fitting words into their mouths, I think of the makeup artists adjusting the ribbons in Emperor Nero's hair before sending him into an amphitheater to sing with a choir of prostitutes. The remembrance of the good old days in ancient Rome serves as a program note for the performances on set with Diane Sawyer and Tim Russert.

To bring at least some of the voices of the past up to the microphone of the present, *Lapham's Quarterly* chooses a topic prominent in the news and, within the perimeter of that topic, assembles a set of relevant texts—literary narrative and philosophical commentary, diaries, speeches, letters, and proclamations, as well as essays and reviews by contemporary historians. The method assumes that all writing, whether scientific treatise, tabloid headline, or minimalist novel, is an attempt to tell a true story. Some stories are more complicated or more beautiful than others. Some stories are immortal, others incoherent. Homer told a story, and so did Albert Einstein; so do Jay Leno and Donald Duck. The stories that bear a second reading are true in the sense that the voice of the author emerges from the struggle to get at the truth of what he or she thinks, has seen, remembers, can find language to express.

> It is not the neutrals or the lukewarms who make history. —*Adolf Hitler, 1933*

I know of no task more difficult, but it is the joint venture entered into by writer and reader—the writer's labor turned to the wheel of the reader's imagination—that produces the freedoms of mind from which a society gathers its common stores of energy and hope.

My sense of such an enterprise I gathered from a prolonged correspondence with the readers of *Harper's Magazine*—people whom I never met and wouldn't recognize if I came across them in an elevator or a police lineup. The return addresses on their envelopes didn't amount to a demographic profile valuable to an advertising agency (some of the readers drank a great deal of brandy; others subsisted on mushrooms and dried fruit; some had attended as many as seven universities; others had yet to graduate from high school), but if I couldn't guess at the weight of anybody's automobile or stock portfolio, I knew that I was talking to people bound together by their interest in the meaning of words. When they found something amiss in a published manuscript, they took the trouble to correct a wrong fact or repair a disjointed paragraph. No matter what the subject under discussion—the authorship of the Bible, the moral bankruptcy of the Reagan or Clinton administrations, the trouble with New York literary critics, the neglected reasons for the fall of the Ming Dynasty—the care taken with the composition of their letters testified to the importance they attached to the telling of a truer story. Like the writers whose work appeared in the magazine, its readers were unafraid of the first-person singular, willing to think out loud, to bet the pot on a metaphor, to look for words that maybe could settle the wilderness of their experience with the fence posts of a beginning, a middle, and an end.

Addressed to readers similarly inclined, *Lapham's Quarterly* doesn't aspire to the status of homework. It undertakes to foster and extend an acquaintance with history, to suggest that the uses of the past are as rich in possibility as were the American forests before the arrival of Christopher Columbus. Again, I'm indebted to Arthur Schlesinger, whose enthusiasms were communicable. Knowing that the four most expensive words in the English language are "This time it's different," Arthur also knew that the study of history is a perpetual work in progress carried forward under the headings of the provisional, destined never to reach a final verdict or discover the lost gold mines of the imperishable truth. Some things change, others don't, but absent a knowledge of which is which, how then do we find our bearings in the drift of time?

So also is *Lapham's Quarterly* a work in progress, provisional and incomplete, its elements forthcoming from a quorum of contributing historians and at the suggestion of readers who send texts and commentaries to www.laphamsquarterly.org; its subscribers can expect the eventual additions of Letters to the Editor, Notes on New Books, Counterfactual Speculations, and Recommended Reading. Because the contents will never qualify for the label "comprehensive," the editorial choices come down to the difference between writing that's a pleasure to read and writing that isn't. Neither the holder of an advanced academic degree nor a candidate for university tenure, I can afford to take liberties with the rules of scholarly category and definition, and from an author whom I admire I will listen to anything and everything—to reports of marvels in Samarkand or Winesburg, Ohio, to descriptions of Talleyrand's mistresses or Kaiser Wilhelm's uniforms, to suspicions of fraud in Albany, or to a rumor of giant ants standing watch over the treasure

> *A morsel of genuine history is a thing so rare as to be always valuable.*
>
> —*Thomas Jefferson, 1817*

of Peru. If I'm to believe the physicists and the evolutionary record, the figures in the dream inhabit the continuum of space and time, which means that they depend for their existence on acts of the imagination.

Heraclitus named war "the father of all things," and so it is with the first issue of *Lapham's Quarterly*. The decision wasn't hard to reach. The history of Western Civilization bills itself as the romance of war. On whom else do we bestow the prize of immortality (Caesar, Genghis Khan, Napoleon, Adolf Hitler) if not on the champions of mortal destruction? For generations it's been said that man's destiny is war, the trials by combat endorsed by the philosopher Georg Wilhelm Friedrich Hegel, as the "terrible," but "necessary" purgative that "saves the state from social petrification and stagnation," praised by the poet, William Ernest Henley, as the "giver of kingship, the fame-smith, the song-master."

An old story, told and retold, in different languages, under different flags, with the blessing of different holy names, across the span of a hundred generations, the lines of bloodstained succession as fiercely preserved as a family inheritance. Pick up the thread of the narrative in Babylon in the days of Cyrus the Great, move forward in time to the triumphs of Alexander of Macedon, student of Aristotle, to Caesar's legions governing what they knew as the province of Mesopotamia, through the centuries of languid despotism imposed on the valley of the Euphrates by the grand viziers of the Sublime Porte, to the division of the Ottoman spoils at the Treaty of Versailles, and so at last, with a new store of fireworks and a fresh set of headlines, to President George W. Bush's theory of democratic empire at play in the wreckage of downtown Baghdad.

No matter how often told, the story begins with a call to arms and ends with a cortege of postmortems. The sequence of texts in this issue of the *Quarterly* follows the customary procedure, the rules of engagement subject to change on short notice, the fields of honor seldom as advertised. Had it occurred to President Bush and his adjutants to conduct a similar review—of their thinking about war as well as about the disposition of their horses and guns—it's at least conceivable that the U.S. Army might not have been sent to trample out the vintage where Saddam Hussein supposedly had stored the grapes of wrath. The industrial-strength bloodletting on the Western Front in World War I discredited the notion of war as a glorious undertaking certain to provide proofs of selfless valor and noble character; the dropping of the atomic bombs on Japan in August 1945 mothballed the use of large-scale warfare as the heavyweight instrument of foreign policy. If it's true that all societies trace their origins to the god of war, it's also true that over time they learn to limit the collateral damage, to no longer regard war as a law of nature but as a form of cultural expression, like the wearing of togas and Halloween masks.

The military historian John Keegan observes in *A History of Warfare* that sooner or later the captains and the kings find more cost-effective ways of keeping the peace and robbing the populace. "War, it seems to me, after a lifetime of reading about the subject, mingling with men of war, visiting the sites of war and observing its effects, may well be ceasing to commend itself to human beings as a desirable or productive, let alone rational, means of reconciling their discontents." Not as tentative as Keegan, the historian John Mueller (from whom an essay, "Band of Brigands," appears on page 193) shapes the argument of his book *The*

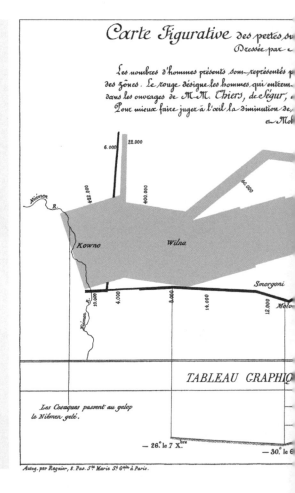

Napoleon began his march to Moscow on a balmy June 23; by December 14, his Grand Armée had been reduced to less than 2 percent of its initial strength. This map, published in 1869 by Charles Joseph Minard, graphically depicts the army's ill-fated journey. The brown line indicates the size of the French army advancing toward Moscow (where one millimeter of thickness indicates roughly 10,000 men; numbers indicate strength at specific points); the black line indicates soldiers retreating. The scale shown to the right—lieues communes de France, or, the common French league—is worth 4,445 km. The lower portion of the graph shows the temperature on the army's return from Russia (read right to left), measured in degrees below freezing on the Réaumur scale.

Remnants of War on the premise that "unlike breathing, eating, or sex, war is not something that is somehow required by the human condition or by the forces of history. Accordingly, war can shrivel up and disappear, and it seems to be in the process of doing so."

Consistent with the story lines of the twentieth century's wars to end all wars, the conclusions drawn by Keegan and by Mueller suggest that President Bush's splendid little war in Iraq is the work of a man imprisoned in an obsolete tense. His adjutants apparently find it hard to say anything in his presence that doesn't go well with the sound of bugles, and in the speeches staged against a backdrop of flags and high-ranking uniforms, he presents himself as a military commander in the romantic tradition of General George Patton (page 24), captivated by the song of the sword that Oliver Wendell Holmes brought to the students at Harvard University in 1895 (page 30), content with the blessing of Saint Augustine (page 36). To accept as a consequence the price being paid to the piper in Iraq is to acknowledge the truth of the old Arab proverb that says we have less reason to fear what might happen tomorrow than to beware of what happened yesterday. I know of no better reason to read history. Construed as a means instead of an end, history is the weapon with which we defend the future against the past.

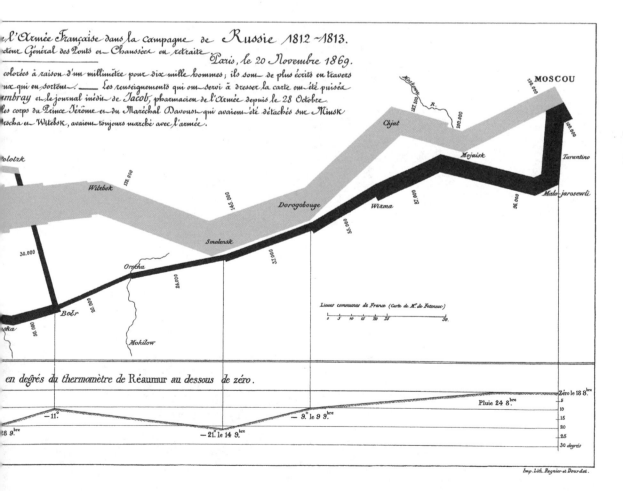

American soldiers head toward the Normandy beach on D-Day, June 6, 1944.

CALLS TO ARMS

2003: Kuwait

LIEUTENANT COLONEL TIM COLLINS BLOWS
THE TRUMPET OF RIGHTFUL DESTRUCTION

We go to liberate, not to conquer. We will not fly our flags in their country. We are entering Iraq to free a people, and the only flag which will be flown in that ancient land is their own. Show respect for them.

There are some who are alive at this moment who will not be alive shortly. Those who do not wish to go on that journey, we will not send. As for the others, I expect you to rock their world. Wipe them out if that is what they choose. But if you are ferocious in battle, remember to be magnanimous in victory.

Iraq is steeped in history. It is the site of the Garden of Eden, of the Great Flood, and the birthplace of Abraham. Tread lightly there. You will see things that no man could pay to see, and you will have to go a long way to find a more decent, generous, and upright people than the Iraqis. You will be embarrassed by their hospitality even though they have nothing. Don't treat them as refugees, for they are in their own country. Their children will be poor. In years to come, they will know that the light of liberation in their lives was brought by you.

If there are casualties of war, then remember that when they woke up and got dressed in the morning, they did not plan to die this day. Allow them dignity in death. Bury them properly and mark their graves.

It is my foremost intention to bring every single one of you out alive, but there may be people among us who will not see the end of this campaign. We will put them in their sleeping bags and send them back. There will be no time for sorrow.

The enemy should be in no doubt that we are his nemesis and that we are bringing about his rightful destruction. There are many regional commanders who have stains on their souls, and they are stoking the fires of hell for Saddam. He and his forces will be destroyed by this coalition for what they have done. As they die, they will know their deeds have brought them to this place. Show them no pity.

It is a big step to take another human life. It is not to be done lightly. I know of men who have taken life needlessly in other conflicts. I can assure you they live with the mark of Cain upon them. If someone surrenders to you, then remember they have that right in international law and ensure that one day they go home to their family. The ones who wish to fight, well, we aim to please.

If you harm the regiment or its history by overenthusiasm in killing or in cowardice, know it is your family who will suffer. You will be shunned unless your conduct is of the highest, for your deeds will follow you down through history. We will bring shame on neither our uniform nor our nation.

As for ourselves, let's bring everyone home and leave Iraq a better place for us having been there. Our business now is north.

Remarks delivered by British battalion commander Collins to over 600 soldiers on the morning of March 22, 2003, hours before they carried their business north to Iraq.

1917: Baghdad

LIEUTENANT GENERAL SIR STANLEY
MAUDE PRESENTS THE GIFT OF
FREEDOM TO THE PEOPLE OF IRAQ

In the name of my king, and in the name of
the peoples over whom he rules, I address you
as follows:

Our military operations have as their object the defeat of the enemy, and the driving
of him from these territories. In order to complete this task, I am charged with absolute and
supreme control of all regions in which British
troops operate; but our armies do not come into
your cities and lands as conquerors or enemies
but as liberators. Since the days of Halaka, your
city and your lands have been subject to the
tyranny of strangers, your palaces have fallen
into ruins, your gardens have sunk in desolation, and your forefathers and yourselves have
groaned in bondage. Your sons have been carried off to wars not of your seeking, your wealth
has been stripped from you by unjust men and
squandered in distant places.

Since the days of Midhat, the Turks have
talked of reforms, yet do not the ruins and
wastes of today testify to the vanity of those
promises?

It is the wish not only of my king and
his peoples, but it is also the wish of the great
nations with whom he is in alliance, that you
should prosper even as in the past, when your
lands were fertile, when your ancestors gave
to the world literature, science, and art, and
when Baghdad city was one of the wonders
of the world.

Between your people and the dominions
of my king there has been a close bond of interest. For two hundred years have the merchants
of Baghdad and Great Britain traded together
in mutual profit and friendship. On the other
hand, the Germans and the Turks, who have
despoiled you and yours, have for twenty years
made Baghdad a center of power from which
to assail the power of the British and the allies
of the British in Persia and Arabia. Therefore

the British government cannot remain indifferent as to what takes place in your country
now or in the future, for in duty to the interests
of the British people and their allies, the British government cannot risk that being done
in Baghdad again which has been done by the
Turks and Germans during the war.

But you people of Baghdad, whose commercial prosperity and whose safety from oppression and invasion must ever be a matter of
the closest concern to the British government,
are not to understand that it is the wish of the
British government to impose upon you alien
institutions. It is the hope of the British govern-

Victorious British troops enter Baghdad, 1917.

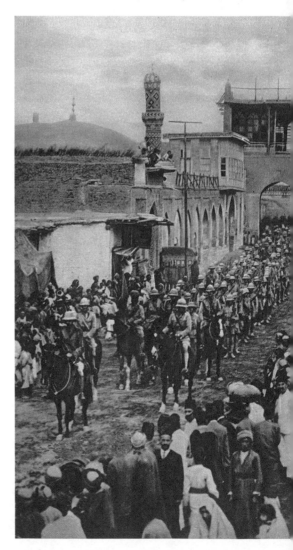

ment that the aspirations of your philosophers and writers shall be realized and that once again the people of Baghdad shall flourish, enjoying their wealth and substance under institutions which are in consonance with their sacred laws and their racial ideals. In Hedjaz the Arabs have expelled the Turks and Germans who oppressed them and proclaimed the Sherif Hussein as their king, and his Lordship rules in independence and freedom and is the ally of the nations who are fighting against the power of Turkey and Germany; so indeed are the noble Arabs, the Lords of Koweyt, Nejd, and Asir.

Many noble Arabs have perished in the cause of Arab freedom at the hands of those alien rulers, the Turks, who oppressed them. It is the determination of the government of Great Britain and the great powers allied to Great Britain that these noble Arabs shall not have suffered in vain. It is the hope and desire of the British people and the nations in alliance with them that the Arab race may rise once more to greatness and renown among the peoples of the earth, and that it shall bind itself together to this end in unity and concord.

O people of Baghdad, remember that for twenty-six generations you have suffered under strange tyrants who have ever endeavored to set one Arab house against another in order that they might profit by your dissensions. This policy is abhorrent to Great Britain and her allies, for there can be neither peace nor prosperity where there is enmity and misgovernment. Therefore I am commanded to invite you, through your nobles and elders and representatives, to participate in the management of your civil affairs in collaboration with the political representatives of Great Britain who accompany the British Army, so that you may be united with your kinsmen in the north, east, south, and west in realizing the aspirations of your race.

"The Proclamation of Baghdad," issued by the commander-in-chief of British forces in Mesopotamia on March 19, 1917, eight days after his army captured the city.

1095: Clermont

POPE URBAN II SUMMONS THE FAITHFUL TO HOLY CRUSADE

From the confines of Jerusalem and the city of Constantinople, a horrible tale has gone forth and very frequently has been brought to our ears, namely, that a race from the kingdom of the Persians, an accursed race, a race utterly alienated from God, a generation forsooth which has not directed its heart and has not entrusted its spirit to God, has invaded the lands of those Christians and has depopulated them by the sword, pillage, and fire; it has led away a part of the captives into its own country, and a part it has destroyed by cruel tortures; it has either entirely destroyed the churches of God or appropriated them for the

You may not be interested in war, but war is interested in you. —Leon Trotsky

rites of its own religion. They destroy the altars, after having defiled them with their uncleanness. They circumcise the Christians, and the blood of the circumcision they either spread upon the altars or pour into the vases of the baptismal font. When they wish to torture people by a base death, they perforate their navels and, dragging forth the extremity of the intestines, bind it to a stake; then with flogging they lead the victim around until, the viscera having gushed forth, the victim falls prostrate upon the ground. Others they bind to a post and pierce with arrows. Others they compel to extend their necks and then, attacking them with naked swords, attempt to cut through the neck with a single blow. What shall I say of the abominable rape of the women? To speak of it is worse than to be silent. The kingdom of the Greeks is now dismembered by them and deprived of territory so vast in extent that it cannot be traversed in a march of two months. On whom therefore is the labor of avenging these wrongs and of recovering this territory incumbent, if not upon you? You, upon whom above other nations God has conferred remarkable glory in arms, great courage, bodily activity, and strength to humble the hairy scalp of those who resist you.

Let the deeds of your ancestors move you and incite your minds to manly achievements; the glory and greatness of King Charles the Great, and of his son Louis, and of your other kings who have destroyed the kingdoms of the pagans and have extended in these lands the territory of the Holy Church. Let the Holy Sepulcher of the Lord our Savior, which is possessed by unclean nations, especially incite you and the holy places which are now treated with ignominy and irreverently polluted with their filthiness. O most valiant soldiers and descendants of invincible ancestors, be not degenerate, but recall the valor of your progenitors.

But if you are hindered by love of children, parents, and wives, remember what the Lord

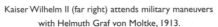

Kaiser Wilhelm II (far right) attends military maneuvers with Helmuth Graf von Moltke, 1913.

says in the Gospel, "He that loveth father or mother more than me, is not worthy of me.... Every one that hath forsaken houses, or brethren, or sisters, or father, or mother, or wife, or children, or lands for my name's sake shall receive a hundredfold and shall inherit everlasting life." Let none of your possessions detain you, no solicitude for your family affairs, since this land which you inhabit, shut in on all sides by the seas and surrounded by the mountain peaks, is too narrow for your large population; nor does it abound in wealth; and it furnishes scarcely food enough for its cultivators. Hence it is that you murder one another, that you wage war, and that frequently you perish by mutual wounds. Let therefore hatred depart from among you, let your quarrels end, let wars cease, and let all dissensions and controversies slumber. Enter upon the road to the Holy Sepulcher; wrest that land from the wicked race and subject it to yourselves. That land which, as the Scripture says, "floweth with milk and honey," was given by God into the possession of the children of Israel. Jerusalem is the navel of the world; the land is fruitful above others, like another paradise of delights. This the Redeemer of the human race has made illustrious by His advent, has beautified by residence, has consecrated by suffering, has redeemed by death, has glorified by burial. This royal city, therefore, situated at the center of the world, is now held captive by His enemies and is in subjection to those who do not know God, to the worship of the heathens. She seeks therefore and desires to be liberated, and does not cease to implore you to come to her aid. From you especially she asks succor, because, as we have already said, God has conferred upon you above all nations great glory in arms. Accordingly, undertake this journey for the remission of your sins, with the assurance of the imperishable glory of the Kingdom of Heaven.

From Robert the Monk's History of the First Crusade. *To the French knights assembled in an open field and wearing surcoats emblazoned with the crusader's red cross, the pontiff spoke with what chroniclers noted as "sweet and persuasive eloquence."*

ACHILLES PREPARES FOR BATTLE

The glory of armor lit the skies and the whole earth laughed,
rippling under the glitter of bronze, thunder resounding
under trampling feet of armies. And in their midst
the brilliant Achilles began to arm for battle...
A sound of grinding came from the fighter's teeth,
his eyes blazed forth in searing points of fire,
unbearable grief came surging through his heart
and now, bursting with rage against the men of Troy,
he donned Hephaestus' gifts—magnificent armor
the god of fire forged with all his labor.
First he wrapped his legs with well-made greaves,
fastened behind his heels with silver ankle-clasps,
next he strapped the breastplate round his chest
then over his shoulder Achilles slung his sword,
the fine bronze blade with its silver-studded hilt,
then hoisted the massive shield flashing far and wide
like a full round moon—and gleaming bright as the light
that reaches sailors out at sea, the flare of a watchfire
burning strong in a lonely sheepfold up some mountain slope
when the gale-winds hurl the crew that fights against them
far over the fish-swarming sea, far from loved ones—
so the gleam from Achilles' well-wrought blazoned shield
shot up and hit the skies. Then lifting his rugged helmet
he set it down on his brows, and the horsehair crest
shone like a star and the waving golden plumes shook
that Hephaestus drove in bristling thick along its ridge.
And brilliant Achilles tested himself in all his gear,
Achilles spun on his heels to see if it fit tightly,
see if his shining limbs ran free within it, yes,
and it felt like buoyant wings lifting the great captain.
And then, last, Achilles drew his father's spear
from its socket stand—weighted, heavy, tough.
No other Achaean fighter could heft that shaft,
only Achilles had the skill to wield it well:
Pelian ash it was, a gift to his father Peleus
presented by Chiron once, hewn on Pelion's crest
to be the death of heroes.

> **Homer,** *from Book XIX of the* Iliad. *The unbearable grief in the heart*
> *of Achilles flows from his mourning the death of his friend Patroclus.*
> *In Book XX, Achilles brings to his enemies the searing points of his*
> *agony and wrath.*

1944: East Anglia

Men, this stuff that some sources sling around about America wanting out of this war, not wanting to fight, is a crock of bullshit. Americans love to fight, traditionally. All real Americans love the sting and clash of battle.

You are here today for three reasons. First, because you are here to defend your homes and your loved ones. Second, you are here for your own self-respect, because you would not want to be anywhere else. Third, you are here because you are real men and all real men like to fight.

> Soldiers in peace are like chimneys in summer.
> —William Cecil, Lord Burghley, c. 1555

When you, here, every one of you, were kids, you all admired the champion marble player, the fastest runner, the toughest boxer, the big league ball players, and the All-American football players. Americans love a winner. Americans will not tolerate a loser. Americans despise cowards. Americans play to win all of the time. I wouldn't give a hoot in hell for a man who lost and laughed. That's why Americans have never lost nor will ever lose a war; for the very idea of losing is hateful to an American.

You are not all going to die. Only two percent of you right here today would die in a major battle. Death must not be feared. Death, in time, comes to all men. Yes, every man is scared in his first battle. If he says he's not, he's a liar. Some men are cowards, but they fight the same as the brave men or they get the hell slammed out of them watching men fight who are just as scared as they are. The real hero is the man who fights even though he is scared. Some men get over their fright in a minute under fire. For some, it takes an hour. For some, it takes days. But a real man will never let his fear of death overpower his honor, his sense of duty to his country, and his innate manhood. Battle is the most magnificent competition in which a human being can indulge. It brings out all that is best and it removes all that is base. Americans pride themselves on being He-Men, and they *are* He-Men.

Sure, we want to go home. We want this war over with. The quickest way to get it over with is to go get the bastards who started it. The quicker they are whipped, the quicker we can go home. The shortest way home is through Berlin and Tokyo. And when we get to Berlin, I am personally going to shoot that paper-hanging son of a bitch Hitler. Just like I'd shoot a snake!

When a man is lying in a shell hole, if he just stays there all day, a German will get to him eventually. The hell with that idea. The hell with taking it. My men don't dig foxholes. I don't want them to. Foxholes only slow up an offensive. Keep moving. And don't give the enemy time to dig one either. We'll win this war, but we'll win it only by fighting and by showing the Germans that we've got more guts than they have, or ever will have. We're not going to just shoot the sons of bitches, we're going to rip out their living goddamned guts and use them to grease the treads of our tanks. We're going to murder those lousy Hun cocksuckers by the bushel-fucking-basket.

War is a bloody, killing business. You've got to spill their blood, or they will spill yours. Rip them up the belly. Shoot them in the guts. When shells are hitting all around you, and you wipe the dirt off your face and realize that instead of dirt it's the blood and guts of what once was your best friend beside you, you'll know what to do! I don't want to get any messages saying, "I am holding my position." We are not holding a goddamned thing. Let the Germans do that. We are advancing constantly, and we are not interested in holding onto anything except the enemy's balls. We are going to twist his balls and kick the living shit out of him all of the time. Our basic plan of operation is to advance and to keep on advancing regardless of whether we have to go over, under, or through the enemy. We are going to go through him like crap through a goose, like shit through a tin horn!

From time to time there will be some complaints that we are pushing our people too hard. I don't give a good goddamn about such complaints. I believe in the old and sound rule that an ounce of sweat will save a gallon of blood. The harder *we* push, the more Germans we will kill. The more Germans we kill, the fewer of our men will be killed. Pushing means fewer casualties. I want you all to remember that.

There is one great thing that you men will all be able to say after this war is over and you are home once again. You may be thankful that twenty years from now, when you are sitting by the fireplace with your grandson on your knee and he asks you what you did in the great World War II, you won't have to cough, shift him to the other knee, and say, "Well, your granddaddy shoveled shit in Louisiana." No sir, you can look him straight in the eye and say, "Son, your granddaddy rode with the great Third Army and a son of a goddamned bitch named Georgie Patton!" That is all.

> *In charge of the U.S. Third Army in June 1944, Patton felt obliged to explain the basic plan of operation prior to the invasion of northern France.*

Saracen cavalrymen of Saladin. Detail from a French manuscript, fourteenth century.

1791: Paris

PAULINE LÉON DEMANDS A WOMAN'S RIGHT TO SHED BLOOD

Legislators:

Patriotic women come before you to claim the right which any individual has to defend his life and liberty.

Everyone predicts that a violent shock is coming; our fathers, husbands, and brothers may be the victims of the fury of our enemies. Could we be denied the joy of avenging them or of dying at their sides? We are *citoyennes*, and we cannot be indifferent to the fate of the fatherland.

Your predecessors deposited the Constitution as much in our hands as in yours. Oh, how to save it, if we have no arms to defend it from the attacks of its enemies?

Yes, gentlemen, we need arms, and we come to ask your permission to procure them. May our weakness be no obstacle; courage and intrepidity will supplant it, and the love of the fatherland and hatred of tyrants will allow us to brave all dangers with ease. Do not believe, however, that our plan is to abandon the care of our families and home—always dear to our hearts—to run to meet the enemy.

No, gentlemen. We wish only to defend ourselves the same as you; you cannot refuse us, and society cannot deny the right nature gives us, unless you pretend the Declaration of Rights does not apply to women, and that they should let their throats be cut like lambs, without the right to defend themselves. For can you believe the tyrants would spare us? No, no—they remember October 5 and 6, 1789…. But, you say, men are armed for your defense. Of course, but we reply, why deprive us of the right to join that defense, and of the pleasure of saving their days by using ours? Do they know the number and strength of our hidden enemies? Have they but one fight to fight? Is our life dearer than theirs? Are our children not orphaned by the loss of their fathers as much as their mothers? Why then not terrorize aristocracy and tyranny with all the resources of civic effort and the purest zeal, zeal which cold men can well call fanaticism and exaggeration, but which is only the natural result of a heart burning with love for the public weal?

Without doubt, gentlemen, the most joyous success will crown the justice of our cause. Well then, we shall have the pleasure of having contributed to the victory. But if, by the wiles of our enemies or the treachery of some on our side, the evil ones win victory, then is it not cruel to condemn us to await in our homes a shameful death and all the horrors which will precede it? Or—an even worse misfortune—to survive the loss of what we hold most dear, our families and our liberty?

No, gentlemen, do not imagine it. If, for reasons we cannot guess, you refuse our just demands, these women you have raised to the ranks of *citoyennes* by granting that title to their husbands, these women who have sampled the promises of liberty, who have conceived the hope of placing free men in the world, and who have sworn to live free or die—such women, I say, will never consent to concede the day to slaves; they will die first. They will uphold their oath, and a dagger aimed at their breasts will deliver them from the misfortunes of slavery! They will die, regretting not life, but the use-

lessness of their death; regretting moreover, not having been able to drench their hands in the impure blood of the enemies of the fatherland and to avenge some of their own!

But, gentlemen, let us cast our eyes away from these cruel extremes. Whatever the rages and plots of aristocrats, they will not succeed in vanquishing a whole people of united brothers armed to defend their rights. We also demand only the honor of sharing their exhaustion and glorious labors and of making tyrants see that women also have blood to shed for the service of the fatherland in danger.

Gentlemen, here is what we hope to obtain from your justice and equity:

1. Permission to procure pikes, pistols, and sabers (even muskets for those who are strong enough to use them) within police regulations.

2. Permission to assemble on festival days and Sundays on the Champ de la Fédération, or in other suitable places, to practice maneuvers with these arms.

3. Permission to name the former French Guards to command us, always in conformity with the rulers which the mayor's wisdom prescribes for good order and public calm.

Signed,
Léon, *fille*, etc.

Pauline Léon, aged twenty-three in 1791, was a chocolatier in Paris. The National Guard refused her request for a weapon, but she continued her political campaigning, and in 1793 she founded the Society of Revolutionary Republican Women.

Alexander the Great at the Battle of Issus (detail), second century BC.

c. 1181: Hautefort

BERTRAN DE BORN SAVORS THE SWEETNESS OF WAR

I love the joyful time of Easter,
that makes the leaves and flowers come forth,
and it pleases me to hear the mirth
of the birds, who make their song
resound through the woods,
and it pleases me to see upon the meadows
tents and pavilions planted,
and I feel a great joy
when I see ranged along the field
knights and horses armed for war.

And it pleases me when the skirmishers
make the people and their baggage run away,
and it pleases me when I see behind them coming
a great mass of armed men together,
and I have pleasure in my heart
when I see strong castles besieged,
the broken ramparts caving in,
and I see the host on the water's edge,
closed in all around by ditches,
with palisades, strong stakes close together.

And I am as well pleased by a lord
when he is first in the attack,
armed, upon his horse, unafraid,
so he makes his men take heart
by his own brave lordliness.

And when the armies mix in battle,
each man should be poised
to follow him, smiling,
for no man is worth a thing
till he has given and gotten blow on blow.

Maces and swords and painted helms,
the useless shields cut through,
we shall see as the fighting starts,
and many vassals together striking,
and wandering wildly,
the unreined horses of the wounded and dead.
And once entered into battle
let every man proud of his birth
think only of breaking arms and heads,
for a man is worth more dead than alive and beaten.

I tell you there is not so much savor
in eating or drinking or sleeping,
as when I hear them scream, "There they are! Let's get them!"
on both sides, and I hear riderless
horses in the shadows, neighing,
and I hear them scream, "Help! Help!"
and I see them fall among the ditches,
little men and great men on the grass,
and I see fixed in the flanks of the corpses
stumps of lances with silken streamers.

Barons, pawn your castles,
and your villages, and your cities
before you stop making war on one another.

Papiols, gladly go
fast to my Lord Yes-and-No
and tell him he has lived in peace too long.

From the poem "I love the joyful time of Easter." The poet was a feudal viscount who provided the services of his sword and the lilt of his verse to several of the twelfth century's warring princes, among them England's Richard the Lionheart.

1865: Woolwich

JOHN RUSKIN OBSERVES THAT WAR GIVES BIRTH TO ART

All the pure and noble arts of peace are founded on war; no great art ever yet rose on Earth, but among a nation of soldiers. There is no art among a shepherd people if it remains at peace. There is no art among an agricultural people if it remains at peace. Commerce is barely consistent with fine art, but cannot produce it. Manufacture not only is unable to produce it, but invariably destroys whatever seeds of it exist. There is no great art possible to a nation but that which is based on battle.

Now, though I hope you love fighting for its own sake, you must, I imagine, be surprised at my assertion that there is any such good fruit of fighting. You supposed, probably, that your office was to defend the works of peace, but certainly not to found them; nay, the common course of war, you may have thought, was only to destroy

them. And truly I, who tell you this of the use of war, should have been the last of men to tell you so, had I trusted my own experience only.

Yet the conclusion is inevitable, from any careful comparison of the states of great historic races at different periods. The first dawn of it is in Egypt; and the power of it is founded on the perpetual contemplation of death, and of future judgment, by the mind of a nation of which the ruling caste were priests, and the second, soldiers. The greatest works produced by them are sculptures of their kings going out to battle or receiving the homage of conquered armies.

All the rudiments of art, then, and much more than the rudiments of all science, are laid first by this great warrior-nation, which held in contempt all mechanical trades, and in absolute hatred the peaceful life of shepherds. From Egypt art passes directly into Greece, where all poetry, and all painting, are nothing else than the description, praise, or dramatic representation of war, or of the exercises which prepare for it, in their connection with offices of religion. All Greek institutions had first respect to war, and their conception of it, as one necessary office of all human and divine life, is expressed simply by the images of their guiding gods. Apollo is the god of all wisdom of the intellect; he bears the arrow and the bow before he bears the lyre. Athena is the goddess of all wisdom in conduct. It is by the helmet and the shield, oftener than by the shuttle, that she is distinguished from other deities.

There were, however, two great differences in principle between the Greek and the Egyptian theories of policy. In Greece there was no soldier caste; every citizen was necessarily a soldier. And, again, while the Greeks rightly despised mechanical arts as much as the Egyptians, they did not make the fatal mistake of despising agricultural and pastoral life, but perfectly honored both. These two conditions of truer thought raise them quite into the highest rank of wise manhood that has yet been reached, for all our great arts, and nearly all our great thoughts, have been borrowed or derived from them. Take away from us what they have given, and I hardly can imagine how low the modern European would stand.

Now, you are to remember, in passing to the next phase of history, that though you *must* have war to produce art, you must also have much more than war—namely, an art-instinct or genius in the people; and that, though all the talent for painting in the world won't make painters of you, unless you have a gift for fighting as well, you may have the gift for fighting, and none for painting. Now, in the next great dynasty of soldiers, the art-instinct is wholly wanting. I have not yet investigated the Roman character enough to tell you the causes of this, but I believe, paradoxical as it may seem to you, that,

however truly the Roman might say of himself that he was born of Mars, and suckled by the wolf, he was nevertheless, at heart, more of a farmer than a soldier. The exercises of war were with him practical, not poetical; his poetry was

A young Liberian rebel sits in an abandoned classroom, 2003. Photograph by Tim A. Hetherington.

in domestic life only, and the object of battle, *pacis imponere morem.* And the arts are extinguished in his hands, and do not rise again, until, with Gothic chivalry, there comes back into the mind of Europe a passionate delight in war itself, for the sake of war. And then, with the romantic knighthood which can imagine no other noble employment—under the fighting kings of France, England, and Spain—and under the fighting dukeships and citizenships of Italy, art is born again, and rises to her height in the great valleys of Lombardy and Tuscany, through which there flows not a single stream, from all their Alps or Apennines, that did not once run dark red from battle, and it reaches its culminating glory in the city which gave to history the most intense type of soldiership yet seen among men—the city whose armies were led in their assault by their king, led through it to victory by their king, and so led, though that king of theirs was blind, and in the extremity of his age.

And from this time forward, as peace is established or extended in Europe, the arts decline. They reach an unparalleled pitch of costliness, but lose their life, enlist themselves at last on the side of luxury and various corruption, and, among wholly tranquil nations, wither utterly away, remaining only in partial practice among races who, like the French and

> I know not with what weapons World War III will be fought, but World War IV will be fought with sticks and stones.   —Albert Einstein

us, have still the minds, though we cannot all live the lives, of soldiers.

"It may be so," I can suppose that a philanthropist might exclaim. "Perish then the arts, if they can flourish only at such a cost. What worth is there in toys of canvas and stone, if compared to the joy and peace of artless domestic life?" And the answer is—truly, in themselves, none. But as expressions of the highest state of the human spirit, their worth is infinite. As results they may be worthless, but, as signs, they are above price. For it is an assured truth that, whenever the faculties of men are at their fullness, they *must* express themselves by art; and to say that a state is without such expression, is to say that it is sunk from its proper level of manly nature. So that, when I tell you that war is the foundation of all the arts, I mean also that it is the foundation of all the high virtues and faculties of men.

> *From a commencement speech, delivered by England's most renowned art critic to the cadets graduating from the Royal Military Academy at Woolwich in December 1865.*

1895: Allston

OLIVER WENDELL HOLMES JR. BRINGS THE SONG OF THE SWORD TO HARVARD'S GRADUATING CLASS

Any day in Washington Street, when the throng is greatest and busiest, you may see a blind man playing a flute. I suppose that someone hears him. Perhaps also my pipe may reach the heart of some passer in the crowd.

I once heard a man say, "Where Vanderbilt sits, there is the head of the table. I teach my son to be rich." He said what many think. For although the generation born about 1840, and now governing the world, has fought two at least of the greatest wars in history, and has witnessed others, war is out of fashion, and the man who commands attention of his fellows is the man of wealth. Commerce is the great power. The aspirations of the world are those of commerce. Moralists and philosophers, following its lead, declare that war is wicked, foolish, and soon to disappear.

The society for which many philanthropists, labor reformers, and men of fashion unite in longing is one in which they may be comfortable and may shine without much trouble or any danger. The unfortunately growing hatred of the poor for the rich seems to me to rest on the belief that money is the main thing (a belief in which the poor have been encouraged by the rich), more than on any other grievance. Most of my hearers would rather that their daughters or their sisters should marry a son of one of the great rich families than a regular army officer, were he as beautiful, brave, and gifted as Sir William Napier. I have heard the question asked whether our war was worth fighting, after all. There are many, poor and rich, who think that love of country is an old wives' tale, to be replaced by interest in a labor union, or, under the name of cosmopolitanism, by a rootless self-seeking search for a place where the most enjoyment may be had at the least cost.

Meantime we have learned the doctrine that evil means pain, and the revolt against pain in all its forms has grown more and more marked. From societies for the prevention of cruelty to animals up to socialism, we express in numberless ways the notion that suffering is a wrong which can be and ought to be prevented, and a whole literature of sympathy has sprung into being which points out in story and in verse how hard it is to be wounded in the battle of life, how terrible, how unjust it is that any one should fail.

Even science has had its part in the tendencies which we observe. It has shaken established religion in the minds of very many. It has pursued analysis until at last this thrilling world of colors and passions and sounds has seemed fatally to resolve itself into one vast network of vibrations endlessly weaving an aimless web, and the rainbow flush of cathedral windows, which once to enraptured eyes appeared the very smile of God, fades slowly out into the pale irony of the void.

And yet from vast orchestras still comes the music of mighty symphonies. Our painters even now are spreading along the walls of our library glowing symbols of mysteries still real, and the hardly silenced cannon of the East proclaim once more that combat and pain still are the portion of man. For my own part, I believe that the struggle for life is the order of the world, at which it is vain to repine. I can imagine the burden changed in the way it is to be borne, but I cannot imagine that it ever will be lifted from men's backs. I can imagine a future in which science shall have passed from the combative to the dogmatic stage, and shall have gained such catholic acceptance that it shall take control of life, and condemn at once with instant execution what now is left for nature to destroy. But we are far from such a future, and we cannot stop to amuse or to terrify ourselves with dreams. Now, at least, and perhaps as long as man dwells upon the globe, his destiny is battle, and he has to take the chances of war. If it is our business to fight, the book for the army is a war song, not a hospital sketch. It is not well for soldiers to think much about wounds. Sooner or later we shall fall; but meantime it is for us to fix our eyes upon the point to be stormed, and to get there if we can.

Behind every scheme to make the world over, lies the question: What kind of world do you want? The ideals of the past for men have been drawn from war, as those for women have been drawn from motherhood. For all our prophecies, I doubt if we are ready to give up our inheritance. Who is there who would not like to be thought a gentleman? Yet what has that name been built on but the soldier's choice of honor rather than life? To be a soldier or descended from soldiers, in time of peace to be ready to give one's life rather than suffer disgrace, that is what the word has meant; and if we try to claim it at less cost than a splendid carelessness for life, we are trying to steal the good will without the responsibilities of the place. We will not dispute about tastes. The man of the future may want

Col. Theodore Roosevelt and his Rough Riders at the top of San Juan Hill, Cuba, 1898.

something different. But who of us could endure a world, although cut up into five acre lots, and having no man upon it who was not well fed and well housed, without the divine folly of honor, without the senseless passion for knowledge outreaching the flaming bounds of the possible, without ideals the essence of which is that they can never be achieved? I do not know what is true. I do not know the meaning of the universe. But in the midst of doubt, in the collapse of creeds, there is one thing I do not doubt, that no man who lives in the same world with most of us can doubt, and that is that the faith is true and adorable which leads a soldier to throw away his life in obedience to a blindly accepted duty, in a cause which he little understands, in a plan of campaign of which he has little notion, under tactics of which he does not see the use.

1918: Petrograd

LENIN PRESERVES THE RUSSIAN REVOLUTION

Comrades! The revolt by the five kulak volosts must be suppressed without mercy. The interest of the entire revolution demands this because we have now before us our final decisive battle "with the kulaks." We need to set an example.

1) You need to hang (hang without fail, so that the public sees) at least one hundred notorious kulaks, the rich, and the bloodsuckers.
2) Publish their names.
3) Take away all of their grain.
4) Execute the hostages—in accordance with yesterday's telegram.

This needs to be accomplished in such a way that people for hundreds of miles around will see, tremble, know, and scream out: let's choke and strangle those blood-sucking kulaks.

Telegraph us acknowledging receipt and execution of this.

Yours,
Lenin

P.S. Use your toughest people for this.

Letter sent to Communist agents in the city of Penza on August 11, 1918. The kulaks, wealthy peasant farmers suspected of hoarding grain, were virtually eliminated by Stalin in an extensive liquidation campaign.

Most men who know battle know the cynic force with which the thoughts of common sense will assail them in times of stress; but they know that in their greatest moments faith has trampled those thoughts underfoot. If you wait in line, suppose on Tremont Street Mall, ordered simply to wait and do nothing, and have watched the enemy bring their guns to bear upon you down a gentle slope like that of Beacon Street, have seen the puff of the firing, have felt the burst of the spherical case-shot as it came toward you, have heard and seen the shrieking fragments go tearing through your company, and have known that the next or the next shot carries your fate; if you have advanced in line and have seen ahead of you the spot you must pass where the rifle bullets are striking; if you have ridden at night at a walk toward the blue line of fire at the dead angle of Spotsylvania, where for twenty-four hours the soldiers were fighting on the two sides of an earthwork, and in the morning the dead and dying lay piled in a row six deep, and as you rode you heard the bullets splashing in the mud and earth about you; if you have been in the picket line at night in a black and unknown wood, have heard the splat of the bullets upon the trees, and as you moved have felt your foot slip upon a dead man's body; if you have had a blind fierce gallop against the enemy, with your blood up and a pace that left no time for fear—if, in short, as some, I hope many, who hear me, have known, you have known the vicissitudes of terror and triumph in war; you know that there is such a thing as the faith I spoke of. You know your own weakness and are modest; but you know that man has in him that unspeakable somewhat which makes him capable of miracle, able to lift himself by the might of his own soul, unaided, able to face annihilation for a blind belief.

From the beginning, to us, children of the North, life has seemed a place hung about by dark mists, out of which comes the pale shine of dragon's scales and the cry of fighting men, and the sound of swords. Beowulf, Milton, Dürer, Rembrandt, Schopenhauer, Turner, Tennyson, from the first war song of the race to the stall-fed poetry of modern English drawing rooms, all have had the same vision, and all have had a glimpse of a light to be followed. "The end of worldly life awaits us all. Let him who may, gain honor ere death. That is best for a warrior when he is dead." So spoke Beowulf a thousand years ago.

When I went to the war I thought that soldiers were old men. I remembered a picture of the revolutionary soldier which some of you may have · seen, representing a white-haired man with his flintlock slung across his back. I remembered one or two examples of revolutionary soldiers whom I have met, and I took no account of the lapse of time. It was not long after, in winter quarters, as I was listening to some of the sentimental songs in vogue, such as:

Farewell, Mother, you may never
See your darling boy again,

that it came over me that the army was made up of what I should now call very young men. I dare say that my illusion has been shared by some of those now present, as they have looked at us upon whose heads the white shadows have begun to fall. But the truth is that war is the business of youth and early middle age. You who called this assemblage together, not we, would be the soldiers of another war, if we should have one, and it is for you to hear the bugles as once we heard them beneath the morning stars! For you it is that now is sung the Song of the Sword:

The War-Thing, the Comrade,
Father of Honor,
And Giver of kingship,
The fame-smith, the song master.
Priest (saith the Lord)
Of his marriage with victory

Clear singing, clean slicing;
Sweet spoken, soft finishing;
Making death beautiful
Life but a coin
To be staked in a pastime
Whose playing is more
Than the transfer of being;
Arch-anarch, chief builder,
Prince and evangelist,

I am the Will of God:
I am the Sword.

War, when you are at it, is horrible and dull. It is only when time has passed that you see that its message was divine. I hope it may be long before we are called again to sit at that master's feet. But some teacher of the kind we all need. In this snug, oversafe corner of the world we need it, that we may realize that our comfortable routine is no eternal necessity of things, but merely a little space of calm in the midst of the tempestuous untamed streaming of the world, and in order that we may be ready for danger. We need it in this time of individualist negations, with its literature of French and American humor, revolting at discipline, loving fleshpots, and denying that anything is worthy of reverence—in order that we may remember all that buffoons forget. We need it everywhere and at all times. For high and dangerous action teaches us to believe as right beyond dispute things for which our doubting

Bust of a Warrior, by Leonardo da Vinci.

minds are slow to find words of proof. Out of heroism grows faith in the worth of heroism. The proof comes later, and even may never come. Therefore I rejoice at every dangerous sport which I see pursued. The students at Heidelberg, with their sword-slashed faces, inspire me with sincere respect. I gaze with delight upon our polo players. If once in a while in our rough riding a neck is broken, I regard it, not as a waste, but as a price well paid for the breeding of a race fit for headship and command.

A samurai warrior, Japan, c. 1880.

As for us, our days of combat are over. Our swords are rust. Our guns will thunder no more. The vultures that once wheeled over our heads must be buried with their prey. Whatever of glory must be won in the council or the closet, never again in the field. I do not repine. We have shared the incommunicable experience of war; we have felt, we still feel, the passion of life to its top.

From a speech given at Soldiers Field on Memorial Day, 1895, in honor of Harvard University's Civil War dead. Theodore Roosevelt so admired the speech that soon after becoming President, he nominated Holmes to a seat on the Supreme Court.

1514: Istanbul

SULTAN SELIM I SENDS GREETINGS TO THE EMPEROR OF PERSIA

I, sovereign chief of the Ottomans, master of the heroes of the age; I, the exterminator of idolaters, destroyer of the enemies of the true faith, the terror of the tyrants and pharaohs of the age; I, before whom proud and unjust kings have humbled themselves, and whose hand breaks the strongest scepters; I address myself graciously to you, Emir Isma'il, chief of the troops of Persia, in order to make known to you that the works emanating from the Almighty are not the fragile products of caprice or folly, but make up an infinity of mysteries impenetrable to the human mind. The Lord Himself says in his holy book: "We have not created the heavens and the earth in order to play a game." Man, who is the noblest of the creatures and the summary of the marvels of God, is in consequence on earth the living image of the Creator. It is He who has set up caliphs on earth, because, joining faculties of soul with perfection of body, man is the only being who can comprehend the attributes of the divinity and adore its sublime beauties; but he possesses this rare intelligence, he attains this divine knowledge only in our religion and by observing the precepts of the prince of prophets, the Caliph of Caliphs, the right arm of the God of Mercy; it is then only by practicing the true religion that man will prosper in this world and merit eternal life in the other. As to you, Emir Isma'il, such a recompense will not be your lot; because you have denied the sanctity of the divine laws; because you have deserted the path of salvation and the sacred commandments; because you have impaired the purity of the dogmas of Islam; because you have dishonored, soiled, and destroyed the altars of the Lord, usurped the scepter of the East by unlawful and tyrannical means; because coming forth from the dust, you have raised yourself by odious devices to a place shining with splendor and magnificence; because you have opened to Muslims the gates of tyranny and oppression; because you have joined iniquity, perjury, and blasphemy to your sectarian impiety; because under the cloak of the hypocrite, you have sowed everywhere trouble and sedition; because you have raised the standard of irreligion and heresy; because yielding to the impulse of your evil passions, and giving yourself up without rein to the most infamous disorders, you have dared to throw off the control of Muslim laws and to permit lust and rape, the massacre of the most virtuous and respectable men, the destruction of pulpits and temples, the profanation of tombs, the ill treatment of the *ulema* [scholars], the doctors and Emirs descended from the Prophet, the repudiation of the Qur'an, the cursing of the legitimate caliphs. Now as the first duty of a Muslim and above all of a pious prince is to obey the commandment, "O, you faithful who believe, be the executors of the decrees of God!" The *ulema* and our doctors have pronounced sentence of death against you, perjurer and blasphemer, and have imposed on every Muslim the sacred obligation to arm in defense of religion and destroy heresy and impiety in your person and that of all your partisans.

Animated by the spirit of this fatwa, conforming to the Qur'an, the code of divine laws, and wishing on one side to strengthen Islam, on the other to liberate the lands and peoples who writhe under your yoke, we have resolved to lay aside our imperial robes in order to put on the shield and coat of mail, to raise our ever victorious banner, to assemble our invincible armies, to take up the gauntlet of the avenger. In pursuit of this noble resolution, we have entered upon the campaign, and guided by the hand of the Almighty, we hope soon to strike down your tyrannous arm, blow away the clouds of glory and grandeur which trouble your head and cause your fatal blindness, release from your despotism your trembling subjects, smother you in the end in the very mass of flames which your infernal *jinn* [spirit] raises everywhere along your passage, accomplishing in this way on you the maxim which says: "He who sows discord can only reap evils and afflictions."

However, anxious to conform to the spirit of the law of the Prophet, we come, before commencing war, to set out before you the words of the Qur'an, in place of the sword, and to exhort you to embrace the true faith; this is why we address this letter to you.

We all have a different nature, and the human race resembles mines of gold and silver. Among some, vice is deeply rooted; these are incorrigible, and one could no more draw them to virtue than one could whiten a Negro's skin; among others, vice has not become second nature; they retract their errors when they wish, by a serious return, to mortify their senses and repress their passions. The most efficacious means

It takes fifteen thousand casualties to train a major-general.   —*Ferdinand Foch*

of remedying evil is to search the conscience deeply, to open one's eyes to faults, and to ask pardon of the God of Mercy with true sorrow and repentance. We urge you to look into yourself, to renounce your errors, and to march toward the good with a firm and courageous step; we ask further that you give up possession of the territory violently seized from our state and to which you have only illegitimate pretensions, that you deliver it back into the hands of our lieutenants and officers; and if you value your safety and repose, this should be done without delay.

But if, to your misfortune, you persist in your past conduct; if, puffed up with the idea of your power and your foolish bravado, you wish to pursue the course of your iniquities, you will see in a few days your plains covered with our tents and inundated with our battalions. Then prodigies of valor will be done, and we shall see the decrees of the Almighty, Who is the God of Armies, and sovereign judge of the actions of men, accomplished. For the rest, victory to him who follows the path of salvation!

From a collection of Ottoman documents compiled in 1574 by a government official named Feridun Bey. The Sultan was a Sunni Muslim, the Emperor a Shiite Muslim. Refusing to renounce his errors, the Emperor lost his armies at the Battle of Chaldiran on what is now the border between Turkey and Iran.

c. 412: Hippo

SAINT AUGUSTINE CLASSIFIES WAR AS AN ACT OF BENEVOLENT SEVERITY

These precepts concerning patience ought to be always retained in the habitual discipline of the heart, and the benevolence which prevents the recompensing of evil for evil must be always fully cherished in the disposition. At the same time, many things must be done in correcting with a certain benevolent severity, even against their own wishes, men whose welfare rather than their wishes it is our duty to consult and the Christian Scriptures have most unambiguously commended this virtue in a magistrate. For in the correction of a son, even with some sternness, there is assuredly no diminution of a father's love; yet, in the correction, that is done which is received with reluctance and pain by one whom it seems necessary to heal by pain. And on this principle, if the commonwealth observe the precepts of the Christian religion, even its wars themselves will not be carried on without the benevolent design that, after the resisting nations have been conquered, provision may be more easily made for enjoying in peace the mutual bond of piety and justice. For the person from whom is taken away the freedom which he abuses in doing wrong is vanquished with benefit to himself; since nothing is more truly a misfortune than that good fortune of offenders, by which pernicious impunity is maintained, and the evil disposition, like an enemy within the man, is strengthened. But the perverse and froward hearts of men think human affairs are prosperous when men are concerned about magnificent mansions, and indifferent to the ruin of souls; when mighty theaters are built up, and the foundations of virtue are undermined; when the madness of extravagance is highly esteemed, and works of mercy are scorned; when, out of the wealth and affluence of rich men, luxurious provision is made for actors, and the poor are grudged the necessaries of life; when that God who, by the public declarations of His doctrine, protests against public vice, is blasphemed by impious communities, which demand gods of such character that even those theatrical representations which bring disgrace to both body and soul are fitly performed in honor of them. If God permit these things to prevail, He is in that permission showing more grievous displeasure: if He leave these crimes unpunished, such impunity is a more terrible judgment. When, on the other hand, He overthrows the props of vice, and reduces to poverty those lusts which were nursed by plenty, He afflicts in mercy. And in mercy, also, if such a thing were possible, even wars might be waged by the good, in order that, by bringing under the yoke the unbridled lusts of men, those vices might be abolished which ought, under a just government, to be either extirpated or suppressed.

For if the Christian religion condemned wars of every kind, the command given in the Gospel to soldiers asking counsel as to salvation would rather be to cast away their arms, and withdraw themselves wholly from military service; whereas the word spoken to such was, "Do violence to no man, neither accuse any falsely, and be content with your wages"—the command to be content with their wages manifestly implying no prohibition to continue in the service. Wherefore, let those who say that the doctrine of Christ is incompatible with the state's well-being, give us an army composed of soldiers such as the doctrine of Christ requires them to be; let them give us such subjects, such husbands and wives, such parents and children, such masters and servants, such kings, such judges—in fine, even such taxpayers and tax gatherers, as the Christian religion has taught that men should be, and then let them dare to say that it is adverse to the state's well-being; yea, rather, let them no longer hesitate to confess that this doctrine, if it were obeyed, would be the salvation of the commonwealth.

> From a letter written by the Bishop of Hippo to the Roman tribune Marcellinus, who had asked why and how acts of war could be reconciled with expressions of Christian piety.

1998: Afghanistan

OSAMA BIN LADEN ISSUES A FATWA

The Arabian Peninsula has never—since Allah made it flat, created its desert, and encircled it with seas—been stormed by any forces like the crusader armies spreading in it like locusts, eating its riches, and wiping out its plantations. All this is happening at a time in which nations are attacking Muslims like people fighting over a plate of food. In the light of the grave situation and the lack of support, we and you are obliged

Cornet Wilkin of the 11th Hussars at camp in the Crimean War, 1855. Photograph by Roger Fenton.

to discuss current events, and we should all agree on how to settle the matter.

No one argues today about three facts that are known to everyone; we will list them, in order to remind everyone:

First, for over seven years the United States has been occupying the lands of Islam in the holiest of places, the Arabian Peninsula, plundering its riches, dictating to its rulers, humiliating its people, terrorizing its neighbors, and turning its bases in the peninsula into a spearhead through which to fight the neighboring Muslim peoples.

If some people have in the past argued about the fact of the occupation, all the people of the peninsula have now acknowledged it. The best proof of this is the Americans' continuing aggression against the Iraqi people using the peninsula as a staging post, even though all its rulers are against their territories being used to that end, but they are helpless.

Second, despite the great devastation inflicted on the Iraqi people by the Crusader-Zionist alliance, and despite the huge number of those killed, which has exceeded one million—despite all this, the Americans are once again trying to repeat the horrific massacres, as though they are not content with the protracted blockade imposed after the ferocious war or the fragmentation and devastation.

So here they come to annihilate what is left of this people and to humiliate their Muslim neighbors.

Third, if the Americans' aims behind these wars are religious and economic, the aim is also to serve the Jews' petty state and divert attention from its occupation of Jerusalem and murder of Muslims there. The best proof of this is their eagerness to destroy Iraq, the strongest neighboring Arab state, and their endeavor to fragment all the states of the region, such as Iraq, Saudi Arabia, Egypt, and Sudan, into paper statelets and, through their disunion and weakness, to guarantee Israel's survival and the continuation of the brutal crusade occupation of the peninsula.

All these crimes and sins committed by the Americans are a clear declaration of war on Allah, His messenger, and Muslims. And *ulema* have throughout Islamic history unanimously agreed that the jihad is an individual duty if the enemy destroys the Muslim countries.

On that basis, and in compliance with Allah's order, we issue the following fatwa to all Muslims:

The ruling to kill the Americans and their allies—civilians and military—is an individual duty for every Muslim who can do it, in any country in which it is possible to do it, in order to liberate the al-Aqsa Mosque and the holy mosque from their grip, and in order for their armies to move out of all the lands of Islam, defeated and unable to threaten any Muslim. This is in accordance with the words of Almighty Allah, "And fight the pagans all together as they fight you all together," and, "Fight them until there is no more tumult or oppression, and there prevail justice and faith in Allah."

> Don't talk to me about naval tradition. It's nothing but rum, sodomy, and the lash.
> —Winston Churchill, 1939

This is in addition to the words of Almighty Allah: "And why should ye not fight in the cause of Allah and of those who, being weak, are ill-treated (and oppressed)—women and children, whose cry is: 'Our Lord, rescue us from this town, whose people are oppressors; and raise for us from the one who will help!'"

We—with Allah's help—call on every Muslim who believes in Allah and wishes to be rewarded to comply with Allah's order to kill the Americans and plunder their money wherever and whenever they find it. We also call on Muslim *ulema*, leaders, youths, and soldiers to launch the raid on Satan's U.S. troops and the devil's supporters allying with them, and to displace those who are behind them so that they may learn a lesson.

> *Fatwa issued on February 23, 1998, in the pages of* Al Quds al Arabi, *an Arabic newspaper published in London. Interviewed three months later in Afghanistan by a correspondent from ABC News who told him that the Americans intended to put a heavy price on his head, bin Laden said, "We do not care what the Americans believe. What we care for is to please Allah."*

1943: Berlin

JOSEPH GOEBBELS PROPOSES THE RESCUE OF WESTERN CIVILIZATION

The goal of Bolshevism is Jewish world revolution. They want to bring chaos to the Reich and Europe, using the resulting hopelessness and desperation to establish their international, Bolshevist-concealed capitalist tyranny.

I do not need to say what that would mean for the German people. A Bolshevization of the Reich would mean the liquidation of our entire intelligentsia and leadership and the descent of our workers into Bolshevist-Jewish slavery. In Moscow, they find workers for forced labor battalions in the Siberian tundra, as the Führer said in his proclamation on January 30. The revolt of the steppes is readying itself at the front, and the storm from the East that breaks against our lines daily in increasing strength is nothing other than a repetition of the historical devastation that has so often in the past endangered our part of the world.

That is a direct threat to the existence of every European power. No one should believe that Bolshevism would stop at the borders of the Reich, were it to be victorious. The goal of its aggressive policies and wars is the Bolshevization of every land and people in the world. In the face of such undeniable intentions, we are not impressed by paper declarations from the Kremlin or guarantees from London or Washington. We know that we are dealing in the East with an infernal political devilishness that does not recognize the norms governing relations between people and nations.

Only the German Reich and its allies are in the position to resist this danger. The European nations, including England, believe that they are strong enough to resist effectively the Bolshevization of Europe, should it come to that. This belief is childish and not even worth refuting. If the strongest military force in the world is not able to break the threat of Bolshevism, who else could do it? The neutral European nations have neither the potential nor the military means nor the spiritual strength to provide even the least resistance to Bolshevism. Bolshevism's robotic divisions would roll over them within a few days. In the capitals of the midsize and smaller European states, they console themselves with the idea that one must be spiritually armed against Bolshevism. That reminds us of the statements by bourgeois parties in 1932, who thought they could fight and win the battle against Communism with spiritual weapons. That was too stupid even then to be worth refuting. Eastern Bolshevism is not only a doctrine of terrorism, it is also the practice of terrorism. It strives for its goals with an infernal thoroughness, using every resource at its disposal, regardless of the welfare, prosperity, or peace of the peoples it ruthlessly oppresses. What would England and America do if, in the worst case, Europe fell into Bolshevism's arms? Will London perhaps persuade Bolshevism to stop at the English Channel?

No one in Germany thinks any longer of a cowardly compromise. The entire people thinks only of a hard war. As a spokesman for the leading nation of the continent, however, I claim the right to call a danger a danger if it threatens not only our own land, but our entire continent. We National Socialists have the duty to sound the alarm against International Jewry's attempt to plunge the European continent into chaos, and to warn that Jewry has in Bolshevism a terroristic military power whose danger cannot be overestimated.

The military challenges of the Reich in the East are at the center of everything. In resisting the grave and direct threat with its weapons, the German people and its Axis allies are fulfilling, in the truest sense of the word, a European mission. Our courageous and just battle against this worldwide plague will not be hindered by the worldwide outcry of International Jewry. It can and must end only with victory.

Total war is the demand of the hour. We must put an end to the bourgeois attitude that we have also seen in this war: Wash my back, but don't get me wet! The danger facing us is enormous. The efforts we take to meet it must be just as enormous. The time has come to remove the kid gloves and use our fists. We can no longer make only partial and careless use of the war potential at home and in the significant parts of Europe that we control. We must use our full resources as quickly and thoroughly as it is organizationally and practically possible. Unnecessary concern is wholly out of place. The future of Europe hangs on our success in the East. We are ready to defend it. The German people are shedding their most valuable national blood in this battle. The rest of Europe should at least work to support us. There are many serious voices in Europe that have already realized this. Others still resist. That cannot influence us. If danger faced them alone, we could view their reluctance as literary nonsense of no significance. But the danger faces us all, and we must all do our share. Those who today do not understand that will thank us tomorrow on bended knees that we courageously and firmly took on the task.

From a speech delivered by the Nazi minister, "Nation, Rise Up and Let the Storm Break Loose," on February 18, 1943, sixteen days after the German army's catastrophic defeat at the Battle of Stalingrad. Goebbels spoke to a cheering crowd, large but thoroughly vetted, in Berlin's Sportpalast.

Adolf Hitler practices a speech, 1925. Photographs by Heinrich Hoffman.

1914: St. Petersburg/Berlin

Tsar to Kaiser, July 29, 1:00 A.M.
Peter's Court Palais
Sa Majesté l'Empereur
Neues Palais

Am glad you are back. In this serious moment, I appeal to you to help me. An ignoble war has been declared to a weak country. The indignation in Russia shared fully by me is enormous. I foresee that very soon I shall be overwhelmed by the pressure forced upon me and be forced to take extreme measures which will lead to war. To try and avoid such a calamity as a European war, I beg you in the name of our old friendship to do what you can to stop your allies from going too far.

Nicky

Kaiser to Tsar, July 29, 1:15 A.M.
[This and the previous telegraph crossed.]
Berlin

It is with the gravest concern that I hear of the impression which the action of Austria against Serbia is creating in your country. The unscrupulous agitation that has been going on in Serbia for years has resulted in the outrageous crime, to which Archduke Francis Ferdinand fell a victim. The spirit that led Serbians to murder their own king and his wife still dominates the country. You will doubtless agree with me that we both, you and me, have a common interest, as well as all sovereigns, to insist that all the persons morally responsible for the dastardly murder should receive their deserved punishment. In this case, politics plays no part at all.

On the other hand, I fully understand how difficult it is for you and your government to face the drift of your public opinion. Therefore, with regard to the hearty and tender friendship which binds us both from long ago with firm ties, I am exerting my utmost influence to induce the Austrians to deal straightly to arrive to a satisfactory understanding with you. I confidently hope that you will help me in my efforts to smooth over difficulties that may still arise.

Your very sincere and
devoted friend and cousin,
Willy

Kaiser to Tsar, July 29, 6:30 P.M.

I received your telegram and share your wish that peace should be maintained. But as I told you in my first telegram, I cannot consider Austria's action against Serbia an "ignoble" war. Austria knows by experience that Serbian promises on paper are wholly unreliable. I understand its action must be judged as trending to get full guarantee that the Serbian promises shall become real facts. This, my reasoning, is borne out by the statement of the Austrian cabinet that Austria does not want to make any territorial conquests at the expense of Serbia. I therefore suggest that it would be quite possible for Russia to remain a spectator of the Austro-Serbian conflict without involving Europe in the most horrible war she ever witnessed. I think a direct understanding between your government and Vienna possible and desirable, and as I already telegraphed to you, my government is continuing its exercises to promote it. Of course, military measures on the part of Russia would be looked upon by Austria as a calamity we both

Notable Warrior Women

Artemisia I	(fifth century BC)
Cleopatra	(69–30 BC)
Boudicca	(d. 60)
Zenobia	(d. 274)
Empress Theodora	(c. 497–548)
Eleanor of Aquitaine	(c. 1122–1204)
Queen Isabella	(1451–1504)
Joan of Arc	(c. 1412–1431)
Queen Elizabeth I	(1533–1603)
Maria Theresa	(1717–1780)
Catherine the Great	(1729–1796)
Golda Meir	(1898–1978)
Margaret Thatcher	(b. 1925)

wish to avoid and jeopardize my position as mediator, which I readily accepted on your appeal to my friendship and my help.

Willy

Tsar to Kaiser, July 29, 8:20 P.M.
Peter's Court Palais

Thanks for your telegram conciliatory and friendly. Whereas official message presented today by your ambassador to my minister was conveyed in a very different tone. Beg you to explain this divergency! It would be right to give over the Austro-Serbian problem to the Hague conference. Trust in your wisdom and friendship.

Your loving Nicky

Tsar to Kaiser, July 30, 1:20 A.M.
Peter's Court Palais

Thank you heartily for your quick answer. Am sending Tatischev this evening with instructions. The military measures which have now come into force were decided five days ago for reasons of defense on account of Austria's preparations. I hope from all my heart that these measures won't in any way interfere with your part as mediator which I greatly value. We need your strong pressure on Austria to come to an understanding with us.

Nicky

Kaiser to Tsar, July 30, 1:20 A.M.
Berlin

Best thanks for telegram. It is quite out of the question that my ambassador's language could have been in contradiction with the tenor of my telegram. Count Pourtalès was instructed to draw the attention of your government to the danger & grave consequences involved by a mobilization; I said the same in my telegram to you. Austria has only mobilized against *Serbia* & only a *part* of her army. If, as it is now the case, according to the communication by you & your government, Russia mobilizes against Austria, my role as mediator you kindly entrusted me with & which I accepted at your express prayer, will be endangered if not ruined. The whole weight of the decision lies solely on your shoulders now, who have to bear the responsibility for Peace or War.

Willy

Kaiser to Tsar, July 31
Berlin

On your appeal to my friendship and your call for assistance, I began to mediate between your and the Austro-Hungarian government. While this action was proceeding, your troops were mobilized against Austro-Hungary, my ally. Thereby, as I have already pointed out to you, my mediation has been made almost illusory.

I have nevertheless continued my action. I now receive authentic news of serious preparations for war on my eastern frontier. Responsibility for the safety of my empire forces preventive measures of defense upon me. In my endeavors to maintain the peace of the world, I have gone to the utmost limit possible. The responsibility for the disaster which is now threatening the whole civilized world will not be laid at my door. In this moment it still lies in your power to avert it. Nobody is threatening the honor or power of Russia who can well afford to await the result of my mediation. My friendship for you and your empire, transmitted to me by my grandfather on his deathbed, has always been sacred to me, and I have honestly often backed up Russia when she was in serious trouble, especially in her last war.

The peace of Europe may still be maintained by you, if Russia will agree to stop the military measures which must threaten Germany and Austro-Hungary.

Willy

Tsar to Kaiser, July 31
[This and the previous telegram crossed.]
Petersburg, Palais
Sa Majesté l'Empereur,
Neues Palais

I thank you heartily for your mediation, which begins to give one hope that all may yet end peacefully. It is technically impossible to stop our military preparations, which were obligatory owing to Austria's mobilization. We are far from wishing war. As long as the negotiations with Austria on Serbia's account are taking place, my troops shall not make any *provocative* action. I give you my solemn word for this. I put all my trust in God's mercy and hope in your successful mediation in Vienna for the welfare of our countries and for the peace of Europe.

Your affectionate,
Nicky

Tsar to Kaiser, August 1
Peter's Court Palais
Sa Majesté l'Empereur
Berlin

I received your telegram. Understand you are obliged to mobilize but wish to have the same guarantee from you as I gave you, that these measures *do not* mean war and that we shall continue negotiating for the benefit of our countries and universal peace dear to all our hearts. Our long proved friendship must succeed, with God's help, in avoiding bloodshed. Anxiously, full of confidence, await your answer.

Nicky

Kaiser to Tsar, August 1
Berlin

Thanks for your telegram. I yesterday pointed out to your government the way by which alone war may be avoided. Although I requested an answer for noon today, no telegram from my ambassador conveying an answer from your government has reached me as yet. I therefore have been obliged to mobilize my army.

Immediate, affirmative, clear, and unmistakable answer from your government is the only way to avoid endless misery. Until I have received this answer, alas, I am unable to discuss the subject of your telegram. As a matter of fact, I must request you to immediately order your troops on no account to commit the slightest act of trespassing over our frontiers.

Willy

Exchange of telegrams between **Tsar Nicholas Alexandrovich Romanov** *of Russia and his cousin,* **Kaiser Friedrich Wilhelm Victor Albert** *of Germany, on the eve of World War I. The Russian army mobilized on July 29, the Germany army on July 31. The first shots were fired on August 20.*

1917: Washington

THE WORLD MUST BE MADE SAFE FOR DEMOCRACY

It is a war against all nations. American ships have been sunk, American lives taken, in ways which it has stirred us very deeply to learn of, but the ships and people of other neutral and friendly nations have been sunk and overwhelmed in the waters in the same way. There has been no discrimination. The challenge is to all mankind. Each nation must decide for itself how it will meet it. The choice we make for ourselves must be made with a moderation of counsel and a temperateness of judgment befitting our character and our motives as a nation. We must put excited feeling away. Our motive will not be revenge or the victorious assertion of the physical might of the nation, but only the vindication of right, of human right, of which we are only a single champion.

Armed neutrality, it now appears, is impracticable. In such circumstances and in the face of such pretensions, it is worse than ineffectual: it is likely only to produce what it was meant to prevent; it is practically certain to draw us into the war without either the rights or the effectiveness of belligerents. There is one choice we cannot make, we are incapable of making: we will not choose the path of submission and suffer the most sacred rights of our nation and our people to be ignored or violated. The wrongs against which we now array ourselves are no common wrongs; they cut to the very roots of human life.

With a profound sense of the solemn and even tragical character of the step I am taking and of the grave responsibilities which it involves, but in unhesitating obedience to what I deem my constitutional duty, I advise that the Congress declare the recent course of the Imperial German Government to be in fact nothing less than war against the government and people of the United States; that it formally accept the status of belligerent which has thus been thrust upon it; and that it take immedi-

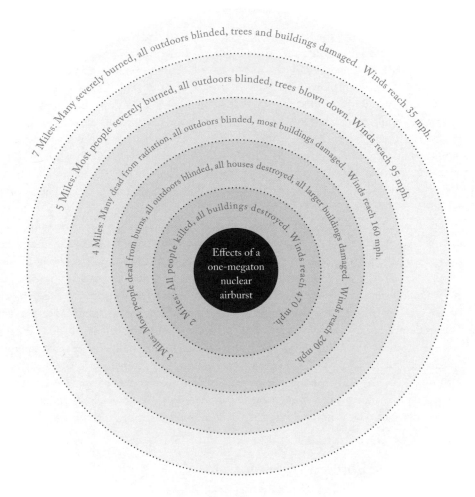

7 Miles: Many severely burned, all outdoors blinded, trees and buildings damaged. Winds reach 35 mph.

5 Miles: Most people severely burned, all outdoors blinded, trees blown down. Winds reach 95 mph.

4 Miles: Many dead from radiation, all outdoors blinded, most buildings damaged. Winds reach 160 mph.

3 Miles: Most people dead from burns, all outdoors blinded, all houses destroyed, all larger buildings damaged. Winds reach 290 mph.

2 Miles: All people killed, all buildings destroyed. Winds reach 470 mph.

Effects of a one-megaton nuclear airburst

ate steps not only to put the country in a more thorough state of defense, but also to exert all its power and employ all its resources to bring the government of the German Empire to terms and end the war.

While we do these things, these deeply momentous things, let us be very clear, and make very clear to all the world, what our motives and our objects are. My own thought has not been driven from its habitual and normal course by the unhappy events of the last two months, and I do not believe that the thought of the nation has been altered or clouded by them. I have exactly the same things in mind now that I had in mind when I addressed the Senate on the twenty-second of January last; the same that I had in mind when I addressed the Congress on the third of February and

on the twenty-sixth of February. Our object now, as then, is to vindicate the principles of peace and justice in the life of the world as against selfish and autocratic power and to set up amongst the really free and self-governed peoples of the world such a concert of purpose and of action as will henceforth ensure the observance of those principles. Neutrality is no longer feasible or desirable where the peace of the world is involved and the freedom of its peoples, and the menace to that peace and freedom lies in the existence of autocratic governments backed by organized force which is controlled wholly by their will, not by the will of their people. We have seen the last of neutrality in such circumstances. We are at the beginning of an age in which it will be insisted that the same standards of conduct and of responsibility for wrong done shall be observed among nations and their governments that are observed among the individual citizens of civilized states.

We have no quarrel with the German people. We have no feeling towards them but one of sympathy and friendship. It was not upon their impulse that their government acted in entering this war. It was not with their previous knowledge or approval. It was a war determined upon as wars used to be determined upon in the old, unhappy days when peoples were nowhere consulted by their rulers and wars were provoked and waged in the interest of dynasties or of little groups of ambitious men who were accustomed to use their fellow men as pawns and tools. Self-governed nations do not fill their neighbor states with spies or set the course of intrigue to bring about some critical posture of affairs which will give them an opportunity to strike and make conquest. Such designs can be successfully worked out only under cover and where no one has the right to ask questions. Cunningly contrived plans of deception or aggression, carried, it may be, from generation to generation, can be worked out and kept from the light only within the privacy of courts or behind the carefully guarded confidences of a narrow and privileged class. They are happily impossible where public opinion commands and insists upon full information concerning all the nation's affairs.

We are accepting this challenge of hostile purpose because we know that in such a government, following such methods, we can never have a friend; and that in the presence of its organized power, always lying in wait to accomplish we know not what purpose, there can be no assured security for the democratic governments of the world. We are now about to accept gauge of battle with this natural foe to liberty and shall, if necessary, spend the whole force of the nation to check and nullify its pretensions and its power. We are glad, now that we see the facts with no veil of false pretense about them, to fight thus for the ultimate

American Wars & Foreign Interventions

- The American Revolution, 1775–1783 vs. Great Britain
- The Indian Wars, 1775–1890 vs. American Indians
- Quasi-War with France, 1798–1800 vs. France
- The Barbary Wars, 1801–1805, 1815 vs. Barbary States (Tripoli, Algiers, & Morocco)
- The War of 1812, 1812–1815 vs. Great Britain
- Mexican-American War, 1846–1848 vs. Mexico
- United States Civil War, 1861–1865 vs. Confederate States of America
- U.S. Intervention in Hawaiian Revolution, 1893 vs. Hawaiian government
- The Spanish-American War, 1898 vs. Spain
- Intervention in Samoan Civil War, 1898–1899 vs. German-backed forces
- U.S.-Philippine War, 1899–1902 vs. Philippines
- Boxer Rebellion, 1900 vs. China
- The Moro Wars, 1901–1913 vs. Muslim Filipinos
- Intervention in Panamanian Revolution, 1903 vs. Colombia
- The Banana Wars, 1909–1933 vs. Central American rebels
- Occupation of Vera Cruz, 1914 vs. Mexico
- Pershing's Raid into Mexico, 1916–1917 vs. Mexico
- World War I, 1917–1918 vs. Germany et al.
- Intervention in Russian Civil War, 1919–1920 vs. Bolsheviks
- World War II, 1941–1945 vs. Germany, Japan, & Italy
- The Korean War, 1950–1953 vs. North Korea & China
- Intervention in Lebanon, 1958 vs. antigovernment rebels
- Vietnam War, 1964–1973 vs. North Vietnam & South Vietnamese rebels
- Intervention in Dominican Republic, 1965 vs. antigovernment rebels
- Bombing of Libya, 1981, 1986 vs. Colonel Gadhafi's regime
- Intervention in Lebanon, 1982–1984 vs. Syria & terrorist groups
- Invasion of Grenada, 1983 vs. Cubans & Grenadian communists
- The Tanker War, 1987–1988 vs. Iran
- Invasion of Panama, 1989 vs. General Manuel Noriega regime
- Persian Gulf War, 1991 vs. Iraq
- Intervention in Somalia, 1992–1994 vs. Somali militia
- Intervention in Bosnia, 1994–1995 vs. Bosnian Serbs
- Occupation of Haiti, 1994 vs. Haitian regime
- Bombing of Afghanistan and Sudan, 1998 vs. Al Qaeda
- Bombing of Iraq, 1998 vs. Iraq
- Kosovo War, 1999 vs. Serbia
- Afghanistan War, 2001–ongoing vs. Taliban & Al Qaeda
- Iraq War, 2003–ongoing vs. Iraq

A five-year-old Albanian boy at a military rally, Kosovo. Photograph by Chris Hondros.

peace of the world and for the liberation of its peoples, the German peoples included: for the rights of nations great and small and the privilege of men everywhere to choose their way of life and of obedience. The world must be made safe for democracy. Its peace must be planted upon the tested foundations of political liberty. We have no selfish ends to serve. We desire no conquest, no dominion. We seek no indemnities for ourselves, no material compensation for the sacrifices we shall freely make. We are but one of the champions of the rights of mankind. We shall be satisfied when those rights have been made as secure as the faith and the freedom of nations can make them.

Just because we fight without rancor and without selfish object, seeking nothing for ourselves but what we shall wish to share with all free peoples, we shall, I feel confident, conduct our operations as belligerents without passion and ourselves observe with proud punctilio the principles of right and of fair play we profess to be fighting for.

It is a distressing and oppressive duty, gentlemen of the Congress, which I have performed in thus addressing you. There are, it may be, many months of fiery trial and sacrifice ahead of us. It is a fearful thing to lead this great peaceful people into war, into the most terrible and disastrous of all wars, civilization itself seeming to be in the balance; but the right is more precious than peace, and we shall fight for the things which we have always carried nearest our hearts—for democracy, for the right of those who submit to authority to have a voice in their own governments, for the rights and liberties of small nations, for a universal dominion of right by such a concert of free peoples as shall bring peace and safety to all nations and make the world itself at last free. To such a task we can dedicate our lives and our fortunes, everything that we are and everything that we have, with the pride of those who know that the day has come when America is privileged to spend her blood and her might for the principles that gave her birth and happiness and the peace which she has treasured. God helping her, she can do no other.

President Woodrow Wilson, *message to a special session of Congress on April 2, 1917. Four days later, the United States declared war on Germany.*

KRISHNA OPENS THE DOORS OF HEAVEN

Sanjaya
Arjuna saw them standing there:
fathers, grandfathers, teachers,
uncles, brothers, sons,
grandsons, and friends.

He surveyed his elders
and companions in both armies,
all his kinsmen
assembled together.

Dejected, filled with strange pity,
he said this:

> "Krishna, I see my kinsmen
> gathered here, wanting war.
>
> My limbs sink,
> my mouth is parched,
> my body trembles,
> the hair bristles on my flesh.
>
> The magic bow slips
> from my hand, my skin burns,
> I cannot stand still,
> my mind reels.
>
> I see omens of chaos,
> Krishna; I see no good
> in killing my kinsmen
> in battle.
>
> Krishna, I seek no victory,
> or kingship or pleasures.
> What use to us are kingship,
> delights, or life itself?
>
> We sought kingship, delights,
> and pleasures for the sake of those
> assembled to abandon their lives
> and fortunes in battle.
>
> They are teachers, fathers, sons,
> and grandfathers, uncles, grandsons,
> fathers and brothers of wives,
> and other men of our family.
> What joy is there for us, Krishna,
> in killing Dhritarashtra's sons?

> Evil will haunt us if we kill them,
> though their bows are drawn to kill.
>
> Honor forbids us to kill
> our cousins, Dhritarashtra's sons;
> how can we know happiness
> if we kill our own kinsmen?
>
> The greed that distorts their reason
> blinds them to the sin they commit
> in ruining the family, blinds them
> to the crime of betraying friends.
>
> If Dhritarashtra's armed sons
> kill me in battle when I am unarmed
> and offer no resistance,
> it will be my reward."

Arjuna told this
to Krishna—then saying,
"I shall not fight,"
he fell silent.

Mocking him gently,
Krishna gave this counsel
as Arjuna sat dejected,
between the two armies.

Lord Krishna
You grieve for those beyond grief,
and you speak words of insight;
but learned men do not grieve
for the dead or the living.

Never have I not existed,
nor you, nor these kings;
and never in the future
shall we cease to exist.

Arjuna, when a man knows the self
to be indestructible, enduring, unborn,
unchanging, how does he kill
or cause anyone to kill?

Weapons do not cut it,
fire does not burn it,

waters do not wet it,
wind does not wither it.

If you think of its birth
and death as ever-recurring,
then too, Great Warrior,
you have no cause to grieve!

Look to your own duty;
do not tremble before it;
nothing is better for a warrior
than a battle of sacred duty.

The doors of heaven open
for warriors who rejoice
to have a battle like this
thrust on them by chance.

If you fail to wage this war
of sacred duty,
you will abandon your own duty
and fame only to gain evil.

People will tell
of your undying shame,
and for a man of honor
shame is worse than death.

The great chariot warriors will think
you deserted in fear of battle;
you will be despised
by those who held you in esteem.

Your enemies will slander you,
scorning your skill
in so many unspeakable ways—
could any suffering be worse?

If you are killed, you win heaven;
if you triumph, you enjoy the earth;
therefore, Arjuna, stand up
and resolve to fight the battle!

From the Bhagavad-Gita. *The divine
Lord Krishna instructs the hero Arjuna
in the sacred duty of a warrior.*

A young Confederate private, c. 1863.

1588: Tilbury

QUEEN ELIZABETH I TAKES UP ARMS
AGAINST KING PHILIP II OF SPAIN

My loving people,

We have been persuaded by some that are careful of our safety, to take heed how we commit our selves to armed multitudes, for fear of treachery; but I assure you I do not desire to live to distrust my faithful and loving people. Let tyrants fear. I have always so behaved myself that, under God, I have placed my chiefest strength and safeguard in the loyal hearts and goodwill of my subjects; and therefore I am come amongst you, as you see, at this time, not for my recreation and disport, but being resolved, in the midst and heat of the battle, to live or die amongst you all; to lay down for my God, and for my kingdom, and my people, my honour and my blood, even in the dust.

I know I have the body but of a weak and feeble woman; but I have the heart and stomach of a king, and of a king of England too, and think foul scorn that Parma or Spain, or any prince of Europe, should dare to invade the borders of my realm; to which, rather than any dishonour shall grow by me, I myself will take up arms, I myself will be your general, judge, and rewarder of every one of your virtues in the field.

I know already, for your forwardness you have deserved rewards and crowns; and We do assure you in the word of a prince, they shall be duly paid you. In the mean time, my lieutenant general shall be in my stead, than whom never prince commanded a more noble or worthy subject; not doubting but by your obedience to my general, by your concord in the camp, and your valour in the field, we shall shortly have a famous victory over those enemies of my God, of my kingdom, and of my people.

From a speech delivered to English soldiers at Tilbury. Confronted with the arrival of the Spanish Armada off the coast of England in July 1588, the Virgin Queen roused her subjects to a successful defense of the realm. Of the 130 ships that sailed in the Armada, fewer than seventy returned to Spain.

USS *Arizona* burns at Pearl Harbor, December 7, 1941.

1861: Boston

BATTLE HYMN OF THE REPUBLIC

Mine eyes have seen the glory of the coming of the Lord;
He is trampling out the vintage where the grapes of wrath are stored;
He hath loosed the fateful lightning of His terrible swift sword;
    His truth is marching on.

I have seen Him in the watchfires of a hundred circling camps;
They have builded Him an altar in the evening dews and damps;
I can read His righteous sentence by the dim and flaring lamps.
    His day is marching on.

I have read a fiery gospel writ in burnished rows of steel:
"As ye deal with My contemners, so with you My grace shall deal;
Let the Hero, born of woman, crush the serpent with His heel,
    Since God is marching on."

He has sounded forth the trumpet that shall never call retreat;
He is sifting out the hearts of men before His judgement seat;
O! be swift, my soul, to answer Him! be jubilant, my feet!
    Our God is marching on.

In the beauty of the lilies Christ was born across the sea,
With a glory in His bosom that transfigures you and me:
As He died to make men holy, let us die to make men free,
    While God is marching on.

> **Julia Ward Howe's** *text was first published on the cover of* The Atlantic Monthly. *The singing of the hymn in the Northern armies reinforced the spirit of the Union cause during the remaining three years of the American Civil War.*

1506: Tenochtitlán

WHY THE SUN MOVES

Moctezuma has conquered in Teuctepec.

Fire rages in the temples. The drums beat. One after another, prisoners mount the steps toward the round, sacrificial stone. The priest plunges the obsidian dagger into each breast, lifts up the heart, and shows it to the sun, which rises above the blue volcanoes.

To what god is the blood offered? The sun demands it, to be born each day and travel from one horizon to the other. But the ostentatious death ceremonies also serve another god who does not appear in the codices nor in the chants.

If that god did not reign over the world, there would be no slaves nor masters nor vassals nor colonies. The Aztec merchants could not wrest a diamond for a bean from the defeated peoples, nor an emerald for a grain of corn, nor gold for sweetmeats, nor cacao for stones. The carriers would not be crossing the immensity of the empire in long lines with tons of tribute on their backs. The common people would dare to put on cotton tunics and would drink chocolate and audaciously wear the forbidden quetzal feathers and gold bracelets and magnolias and orchids reserved for the nobility. Then the masks hiding the warrior chiefs' faces would fall, the eagle's beak, the tiger's jaws, the plumes that wave and sparkle in the air.

The steps of the great temple are stained with blood, and skulls accumulate in the center of the plaza. Not only so that the sun should move, no; also so that that secret god should decide instead of man. In homage to that god, across the sea inquisitors fry heretics on bonfires or twist them in the torture chambers. It is the God of Fear. The God of Fear, who has rat's teeth and vulture's wings.

> **Eduardo Galeano**, *from* Genesis, *volume I of the* Memory of Fire *trilogy, published in 1982. Among the gods of the Aztecs, the thirst for blood required a steady flow of prisoners (an estimated 20,000 annually) mounting the steps to the sacrificial stone.*

A mounted samurai cleans his sword, c. sixteenth–seventeenth centuries.

2002: Washington

MORAL IMPERATIVE

As we gather tonight, our nation is at war, our economy is in recession, and the civilized world faces unprecedented dangers. Yet the state of our Union has never been stronger.

The American flag flies again over our embassy in Kabul. Terrorists who once occupied Afghanistan now occupy cells at Guantánamo Bay. And terrorist leaders who urged followers to sacrifice their lives are running for their own.

Our progress is a tribute to the spirit of the Afghan people, to the resolve of our coalition, and to the might of the United States military. When I called our troops into action, I did so with complete confidence in their courage and skill. And tonight, thanks to them, we are winning the War on Terror. The men and women of our Armed Forces have delivered a message now clear to every enemy of the United States: Even seven thousand miles away, across oceans and continents, on mountaintops and in caves—you will not escape the justice of this nation.

Our cause is just, and it continues. Our discoveries in Afghanistan confirmed our worst fears, and showed us the true scope of the task ahead. We have seen the depth of our enemies' hatred in videos, where they laugh about the loss of innocent life. And the depth of their hatred is equaled by the madness of the destruction they design. We have found diagrams of American nuclear power plants and public water facilities, detailed instructions for making chemical weapons, surveillance maps of American cities, and thorough descriptions of landmarks in America and throughout the world.

What we have found in Afghanistan confirms that, far from ending there, our war against terror is only beginning. Most of the nineteen men who hijacked planes on September the eleventh were trained in Afghanistan's camps, and so were tens of thousands of others. Thousands of dangerous killers, schooled in the methods of murder, often supported by outlaw regimes, are now spread throughout the world like ticking time bombs, set to go off without warning.

Thanks to the work of our law enforcement officials and coalition partners, hundreds of terrorists have been arrested. Yet, tens of thousands of trained terrorists are still at large. These enemies view the entire world as a battlefield, and we must pursue them wherever they are. So long as training camps operate, so long as nations harbor terrorists, freedom is at risk. And America and our allies must not, and will not, allow it.

Our nation will continue to be steadfast and patient and persistent in the pursuit of two great objectives. First, we will shut down terrorist camps, disrupt terrorist plans, and bring terrorists to justice. And, second, we must prevent the terrorists and regimes who seek chemical, biological, or nuclear weapons from threatening the United States and the world.

Our military has put the terror training camps of Afghanistan out of business, yet camps still exist in at least a dozen countries. A terrorist underworld operates in remote jungles and deserts, and hides in the centers of large cities.

My hope is that all nations will heed our call, and eliminate the terrorist parasites who threaten their countries and our own. Many nations are acting forcefully. But some governments will be timid in the face of terror. And make no mistake about it: If they do not act, America will.

Our second goal is to prevent regimes that sponsor terror from threatening America or our friends and allies with weapons of mass destruction. Some of these regimes have been pretty quiet since September the eleventh. But we know their true nature. North Korea is a regime arming with missiles and weapons of mass destruction, while starving its citizens.

Iran aggressively pursues these weapons and exports terror, while an unelected few repress the Iranian people's hope for freedom.

Iraq continues to flaunt its hostility toward America and to support terror. The Iraqi regime has plotted to develop anthrax and nerve gas and nuclear weapons for over a decade. This is a regime that has already used poison gas to murder thousands of its own citizens—leaving the bodies of mothers huddled over their dead children. This is a regime that agreed to inter-national inspections—then kicked out the inspectors. This is a regime that has something to hide from the civilized world.

States like these, and their terrorist allies, constitute an axis of evil, arming to threaten the peace of the world. By seeking weapons of mass destruction, these regimes pose a grave and growing danger. They could provide these arms to terrorists, giving them the means to match their hatred. They could attack our allies or attempt to blackmail the United States. In any of these cases, the price of indifference would be catastrophic.

We will work closely with our coalition to deny terrorists and their state sponsors the materials, technology, and expertise to make and deliv-

There never was a good war or a bad peace.
—Benjamin Franklin, 1773

er weapons of mass destruction. We will develop and deploy effective missile defenses to protect America and our allies from sudden attack. And all nations should know: America will do what is necessary to ensure our nation's security.

We'll be deliberate, yet time is not on our side. I will not wait on events, while dangers gather. I will not stand by, as peril draws closer and closer. The United States of America will not permit the world's most dangerous regimes to threaten us with the world's most destructive weapons.

Our War on Terror is well begun, but it is only begun. This campaign may not be finished on our watch—yet it must be, and it will be waged on our watch.

Steadfast in our purpose, we now press on. We have known freedom's price. We have shown freedom's power. And in this great conflict, my fellow Americans, we will see freedom's victory.

President **George W. Bush**, *State of the Union address delivered to Congress on January 29, 2002. A year later, on March 19, 2003, the American invasion of Iraq made good the President's promise not to wait on events.*

c. 84: Caledonia

The Romans—pillagers of the world, they have exhausted the land by their indiscriminate plunder, and now they ransack the sea. A rich enemy excites their cupidity; a poor one, their lust for power. East and West alike have failed to satisfy them. They are the only people on earth to whose covetousness both riches and poverty are equally tempting. To robbery, butchery, and rapine, they give the lying name of "government"; they create a desolation and call it peace.

Nature has ordained that every man should love his children and his other relatives above all else. These are now being torn from us by conscription to slave in other lands. Our wives

> War is the statesman's game, the priest's delight,
> The lawyer's jest, the hired assassin's trade;
> And, to those royal murderers whose mean thrones
> Are bought by crimes of treachery and gore,
> The bread they eat, the staff on which they lean.
> —Percy Bysshe Shelley, 1813

and sisters, even if they are not raped by enemy soldiers, are seduced by men who are supposed to be our friends and guests. Our goods and money are consumed by taxation; our land is stripped of its harvest to fill their granaries; our hands and limbs are crippled by building roads through forests and swamps under the lash of our oppressors. Creatures born to be slaves are sold once for all, and, what is more, get their keep from their owners. We Britons are sold into slavery anew every day; we have to pay the purchase price ourselves and feed our masters into the bargain. In a private household, the latest arrival is made the butt even of his fellow slaves; so, in this establishment where all mankind have long been slaves, it is we, the cheap new acquisitions, who are marked out for destruction. For we have no fertile lands, no mines, no ports, which we might be spared to work in. Our courage, too, and our martial spirit are against us: masters do not like such qualities in their subjects. Even our remoteness and isolation, while they give us protection, are bound to make the Romans wonder what mischief we are up to. Since you cannot hope for mercy, therefore, take courage before it is too late to strive for what you hold most dear, whether it be life or honor. Let us then show, at the very first clash of arms, what manner of men Caledonia has kept in reserve.

All that can spur men on to victory is on our side. The enemy have no wives to fire their courage, no parents ready to taunt them if they run away. Most of them either have no fatherland they can remember, or belong to one other than Rome. See them, a scanty band, scared and bewildered, staring blankly at the unfamiliar sky, sea, and forests around them. The gods have given them, like so many prisoners bound hand and foot, into our hands. Be not afraid of the outward show that means nothing, the glitter of gold and silver that can neither avert nor inflict a wound. Even in the ranks of our enemies we shall find willing hands to help us. The Britons will recognize our cause as their own; the Gauls will remember their lost liberty; the rest of the Germans will desert them. And beyond this army that you see there is nothing to be frightened of—only forts without garrisons, colonies of graybeards, towns sick and distracted between rebel subjects and tyrant masters. Which will you choose—to follow your leader into battle, or to submit to taxation, labor in the mines, and all the other tribulations of slavery? Whether you are to endure these forever or take quick vengeance, this field must decide. On, then, into action; and as you go, think of those that went before you and of those that shall come after.

Tacitus, *from the* Agricola. *Agricola's legions were operating in Britain during the reign of Emperor Domitian. Tacitus at the time was a Roman magistrate; and in his history of the campaign, published in 98 after the death of Domitian, he arms the Caledonian leader, Calgacus, with his own bleak appraisal of Roman imperialism.*

Nineteenth century paintings of Iowa, Sauk and Fox, and Ojibwa warriors by George Catlin.

1811: Mississippi Territory

TECUMSEH BRINGS TO THE CHOCTAWS AND THE CHICKASAWS THE VOICE OF REBELLION

Have we not courage enough remaining to defend our country and maintain our ancient independence? Will we calmly suffer the white intruders and tyrants to enslave us? Shall it be said of our race that we knew not how to extricate ourselves from the three most dreadful calamities—folly, inactivity, and cowardice? But what need is there to speak of the past? It speaks for itself and asks: Where today is the Pequod? Where the Narragansetts, the Mohawks, Pocanokets, and many other once powerful tribes of our race? They have vanished before the avarice and oppression of the white men, as snow before a summer sun. In the vain hope of alone defending their ancient possessions, they have fallen in the wars with the white men. Look abroad over their once beautiful country, and what see you now? Naught but the ravages of the paleface destroyers meet our eyes. So it will be with you Choctaws and Chickasaws! Soon your mighty forest trees, under the shade of whose wide spreading branches you have played in infancy, sported in boyhood, and now rest your wearied limbs after the fatigue of the chase, will be cut down to fence in the land which the white intruders dare to call their own. Soon their broad roads will pass over the grave of your fathers, and the place of their rest will be blotted out forever.

The annihilation of our race is at hand unless we unite in one common cause against the common foe. Think not, brave Choctaws and Chickasaws, that you can remain passive and indifferent to the common danger, and thus escape the common fate. Your people, too, will soon be as falling leaves and scattering clouds before their blighting breath. You, too, will be driven away from your native land and ancient domains as leaves are driven before the wintry storms.

Sleep not longer, O Choctaws and Chickasaws, in false security and delusive hopes. Our broad domains are fast escaping from our grasp. Every year our white intruders become more greedy, exacting, oppressive, and overbearing. Every year contentions spring up between them and our people and when blood is shed we have to make atonement whether right or wrong, at the cost of the lives of our greatest chiefs, and the yielding up of large tracts of our lands. Before the palefaces came among us, we enjoyed the happiness of unbounded freedom, and were acquainted with neither riches, wants, nor oppression. How is it now? Wants and oppression are our lot; for are we not controlled in everything, and dare we move without asking, by your leave? Are we not being stripped day by day of the little that remains of our ancient liberty? Do they not even kick and strike us as they do their blackfaces? How long will it be before they will tie us to a post and whip us, and make us work for them in their cornfields as they do them? Shall we wait for that moment, or shall we die fighting before submitting to such ignominy?

Have we not for years had before our eyes a sample of their designs, and are they not sufficient harbingers of their future determinations? Will we not soon be driven from our respective countries and the graves of our ancestors? Will not the bones of our dead be plowed up, and their graves be turned into fields? Shall we calmly wait until they become so numerous that we will no longer be able to resist oppression? Will we wait to be destroyed in our turn, without making an effort worthy of our race? Shall we give up our homes, our country, bequeathed to us by the Great Spirit, the graves of our dead, and everything that is dear and sacred to us, without a struggle? I know you will cry with me: Never! Never! Then let us by unity of action destroy them all, which we now can do, or drive them back whence they came. War or extermination is now our only choice. Which do you

A man's greatest pleasure is to defeat his enemies, to drive them before him, to take from them that which they possessed, to see those whom they cherished in tears, to ride their horses, and to hold their wives and daughters in his arms.
—Genghis Khan

choose? I know your answer. Therefore, I now call on you, brave Choctaws and Chickasaws, to assist in the just cause of liberating our race from the grasp of our faithless invaders and heartless oppressors. The white usurpation in our common country must be stopped, or we, its rightful owners, be forever destroyed and wiped out as a race of people. I am now at the head of many warriors backed by the strong arm of English soldiers. Choctaws and Chickasaws, you have too long borne with grievous usurpation inflicted by the arrogant Americans. Be no longer their dupes. If there be one here tonight who believes that his rights will not sooner or later be taken from him by the avaricious American palefaces, his ignorance ought to excite pity, for he knows little of the character of our common foe.

And if there be one among you mad enough to undervalue the growing power of the white race among us, let him tremble in considering the fearful woes he will bring down upon our entire race, if by his criminal indifference he assists the designs of our common enemy against our common country. Then listen to the voice of duty, of honor, of nature, and of your endangered country. Let us form one body, one heart, and defend to the last warrior our country, our homes, our liberty, and the graves of our fathers.

Choctaws and Chickasaws, you are among the few of our race who sit indolently at ease. You have indeed enjoyed the reputation of being brave, but will you be indebted for it more from report than fact? Let no one in this council imagine that I speak more from malice against the paleface Americans than just grounds of complaint. Complaint is just toward friends who have failed in their duty; accusation is against enemies guilty of injustice. And surely, if any people ever had, we have good and just reasons to believe we have ample grounds to accuse the Americans of injustice; especially when such great acts of injustice have been committed by them upon our race, of which they seem to have no manner of regard, or even to reflect. They are a people fond of innovations, quick to contrive, and quick to put their schemes into effectual execution no matter how great the wrong and injury to us; while we are content to preserve what we already have. Their designs are to enlarge their possessions by taking yours in turn.

Do you imagine that that people will not continue longest in the enjoyment of peace who timely prepare to vindicate themselves, and manifest a determined resolution to do themselves right whenever they are wronged? Far otherwise. Then haste to the relief of our common cause, as by consanguinity of blood you are bound; lest the day be not far distant when you will be left single-handed and alone to the cruel mercy of our most inveterate foe.

A speech delivered to a tribal gathering in the spring of 1811. A Shawnee chief, Tecumseh objected to the sale of Indian lands to the U. S. government without the consent of all the tribes. The tribes didn't answer his call to arms, and he died a British brigadier general fighting the Americans in the War of 1812.

1415: Harfleur

Once more unto the breach, dear friends, once more,
Or close the wall up with our English dead!
In peace there's nothing so becomes a man
As modest stillness and humility,
But when the blast of war blows in our ears,
Then imitate the action of the tiger:
Stiffen the sinews, summon up the blood,
Disguise fair nature with hard-favored rage;
Then lend the eye a terrible aspect:
Let it pry through the portage of the head
Like the brass cannon; let the brow o'erwhelm it
As fearfully as doth a gallèd rock
O'erhang and jutty his confounded base,
Swilled with the wild and wasteful ocean.
Now set the teeth and stretch the nostril wide,
Hold hard the breath and bend up every spirit
To his full height! On, on, you noble English!
Whose blood is fet from fathers of war-proof,
Fathers that like so many Alexanders
Have in these parts from morn till even fought
And sheathed their swords for lack of argument.
Dishonor not your mothers; now attest
That those whom you called fathers did beget you!
Be copy now to men of grosser blood
And teach them how to war! And you, good yeomen,
Whose limbs were made in England, show us here
The mettle of your pasture. Let us swear
That you are worth your breeding; which I doubt not;
For there is none of you so mean and base
That hath not noble lustre in your eyes.
I see you stand like greyhounds in the slips,
Straining upon the start. The game's afoot!
Follow your spirit; and upon this charge
Cry "God for Harry! England and Saint George!"

William Shakespeare, *from* Henry V, *Act III, Scene i. The heroic sentiment mustered into the ranks of poetry roused some twenty subsequent generations of noble English to unsheathe the sword of empire.*

Uniforms of the Austrian Imperial Cavalry after the Reform of 1767.

RULES OF ENGAGEMENT

2005: Haditha

BY THE BOOK

A white Opel sedan came driving up the street. It was an unmarked taxi carrying five young men, four of them college students bound for school in Baghdad, the fifth their driver. Through their windshield—dirty, bug-splattered, against the sun—they would have seen one of the most dangerous sights in Iraq: smoke rising from a shattered Humvee, a stopped convoy, and American soldiers in full fighting mettle coming at them down the street. The Marines halted the car from a distance. When soldiers do this in Iraq, they are supposed to follow a progressive escalation of force, with hand signals first, followed by raised weapons, then warning shots with tracers visible, then shots to the engine block, and finally, if the car keeps coming, shots directly into the driver. Because of the risk of car bombs, however, the procedure is typically shortened: weapons go up, and if the car doesn't stop, the driver and other occupants are liberally sprayed with fire. Those are the rules of the road, and so be it; given the circumstances, they are well enough understood to seem fair.

This time the driver stopped, as most drivers do. Some witnesses in the nearby houses later said that he tried to back away but then desisted. The Marines came running up, shouting and cursing. Presumably they told the occupants to get out of the car and to kneel on the street with their hands on their heads. What the Marines thought of them is not clear. But the truth is that the Marines neither knew nor needed to know why they stopped the car. The stop was legitimate. It was a necessary act to limit the risks to the squad, and to keep the confusion from growing.

The problem is what happened next, after a quick search revealed that the car contained no weapons or explosives, or any other evidence that linked the men to the insurgency. The Iraqis perhaps should have been held for a while or, better yet, allowed to take their car and leave. Instead, all five of them were shot dead by the Marines. Later, the Marines reported that they killed them because they had started to run away. War is fog, civilians die, and these fools should not have tried to escape.

It was now perhaps 7:30 in the morning. Fire seemed to come from a house on the south side of the street. In hindsight, we know that no insurgents were discovered there, but chances are they were present nonetheless, if not in that house, then in others nearby. The evidence remains uncertain, but commanding officer Sergeant Frank Wuterich, for one, insists that his men believed the house contained aggressors, and that they proceeded with a by-the-book operation to clear them out, exactly as the rules of engagement allowed.

The power was out in the house, and the light inside was dim, all the more so for the Marines, who were piling in from the sunshine of the street. Inside a hostile house, survival requires fast reactions. The Marines fired on a figure down the hall who turned out too late to be an old woman. There could have been a message there, but guerrilla wars are tricky, and the Marines were not about to slow down. She screamed when she was hit, apparently in the back, and then she died. The Marines were shouting excitedly to one another. They worked down the hallway until, busting open a door, they came upon a room full of people. Later some of the squad said they had heard AK-47s being racked, though whatever they heard turned out not to be that. The room was dim, and the people were glimpsed rather than clearly seen. The Marines rolled in a grenade, hugged the hallway for the blast, and then charged into the dust and smoke to mop up with their rifles as they had been trained to do. *This is my weapon, this is my gun.* Nine people had sheltered in that room, three generations of the same family, from an ancient man paralyzed by a stroke to an infant girl just three months old. When the grenade exploded, it blew some of them apart, wounded others with penetrating shrapnel, and littered the room with evil-smelling body parts. In the urgency of the moment, the old man forgot that he was paralyzed and tried to stand up. He took rounds to the chest, vomited blood as he fell, and then lay on the floor twitching as he died. In that room, four residents survived. A young woman left her husband behind, grabbed the infant girl, and managed to run away; a ten year old girl and her younger brother lay wounded beside their dead mother and remained conscious enough to be terrified.

The Marines went on to the neighboring house, still seeking insurgents, as they believed. What happened there was a repeat of what had just happened next door, only this time the Americans knocked before they shot the man at the gate, and a grenade tossed into an empty bathroom ignited a washing machine, and a grenade tossed into the room where the family was sheltering failed to go off, and perhaps only one American came in and sprayed the room with automatic fire. This time there was just a single survivor, a girl of about thirteen, who later was able to provide some details of her

family's death. There was a lot of smoke, but:

Daddy was shot through the heart. He was forty-three.

Mommy was shot in the head and chest. She was forty-one.

Aunt Huda was shot in the chest. She was twenty-seven.

My sister Nour was shot in the right side of her head. She was fifteen.

My sister Saba was shot through the ear. She was eleven.

My brother Muhammad was shot in the hand and I don't know where else. He was ten.

My sister Zainab was shot in the hand and the head. She was five.

My sister Aysha was shot in the leg and I don't know where else. She was three.

Wuterich's men pursued the search to the north side of Route Chestnut, where they put the women and children under guard and killed four men of another family. There on the north side they found the only AK-47 that was discovered that day—apparently a household defensive weapon of the type that is legal and common in Iraq. No one has claimed that the rifle had been fired.

On the afternoon of November 19, when the reports of civilian casualties reached Captain Lucas McConnell, it did not cross his mind that anything unusual had occurred: The killing by American forces of noncombatants in Iraq is simply so commonplace. Sergeant Wuterich reported on the fight as he defined it. An intelligence sergeant who surveyed the carnage said much the same thing. Captain McConnell scarcely reacted, because this slaughter seemed to lie within the rules of engagement, and in that sense was little different from any other.

William Langewiesche, *from the November 2006 issue of* Vanity Fair. *Reports from witnesses who saw the Haditha killings on November 19, 2005, prompted an investigation by American military authorities. As of September 20, 2007, charges were dropped against two of the four enlisted Marines accused of murder. Charges of dereliction of duty were dropped against two of the four officers in the chain of command.*

c. 1600: Rhineland

BOOTS ON THE GROUND

Each and every officer, captain of horse, or other captain, knows well that no doctors, magisters, or any other God-fearing people follow in his train, but only a heap of ill-disposed lads, out of all kinds of nations; strange folks who leave wives and children, abandon their duties, and follow the army; all that will not follow the pursuits of their fathers and mothers must follow the calf-skin which is spread over the drum, till they come to a battle or assault where thousands lie on the field of battle, shot or cut to pieces; for a *Landsknecht's* life hangs by a hair, and his soul flutters on his cap or his sleeve.

Soldiers must be hardy and enduring people, like unto steel and iron, and like the wild beasts that can eat all kinds of food. The *Landsknecht* must be able to digest the points of their wheel-nails; nothing must come amiss to them, even if necessity require that they should eat dogs' or cats' flesh, and the flesh of horses from the meadow must be like good venison to them, with herbs, unseasoned by salt or butter. A *Landsknecht* must make three campaigns before he can become an honorable man. After the first campaign, he must return home wearing torn clothes; after the second, he should return with a scar on one cheek and be able to tell much of alarms, battles, skirmishes, and storming parties, and to show by his scars that he has got the marks of a *Landsknecht*; after the third, he should return well appointed on a fine charger, bringing with him a purse full of gold, so that he may be able to distribute whole dollars as he would booty-pence.

A *Landsknecht* has neither house nor farm, cows nor calves, and no one to bring him food; therefore, he must procure it himself wherever it is to be found, and buy without money whether the peasants look sweet or sour. Sometimes they must suffer hunger and evil days; at others, they have abundance, and indeed such superfluity that they might clean their shoes with wine or beer. Then the dogs eat roast; the women and children get good appointments; they become stewards and cellarers of other people's property. When the householder is driven away with his wife and children, the fowls, geese, fat cows, oxen, pigs, and sheep have a bad time of it. The money is portioned out in their caps, velvet and silk stuffs and cloth are measured out by long spears, a cow is slaughtered for the sake of the hide, chests and trunks are broken open, and when all has been plundered and nothing more remains, the house is set on fire. That is the true *Landsknecht's* fire, when fifty villages and country towns are in flames. Then they go to other quarters and do the like again; this makes soldiers jolly and is a desirable life for those who do not pay for it. This entices to the field many a mother's child who does not return home and forgets his friends. For the proverb says, "The *Landsknecht* have crooked fingers and maimed hands for work, but for pilfering and plundering, all the maimed hands become sound." That has been so before our days and will remain so truly after us. The longer the *Landsknecht* learn this handiwork, the better they do it. Wherever the soldiers come, they bring with them the keys of all the rooms, their axes and hatchets, and if there are not enough stalls in a place for their horses, it does not signify, they stall them in the churches, monasteries, chapels, and best rooms. If there is no dry wood for fire, it matters not; they burn chairs, benches, plows, and everything that is in the house. If they want green wood, no one need go far; they cut down the fruit trees in the nearest orchard, for they say, whilst we live here, we keep house. Tomorrow we go off again into the country; therefore, Mr. Host, be comforted; you have a few guests you would gladly be free from; therefore, give freely and write it on the slate. When the house is burnt the account is burnt also. This is the *Landsknecht's* custom: to make a reckoning and ride off, and pay when we return.

Adam Junghans, *a seventeenth-century correspondent known only for his contribution to* Pictures of German Life, *collected in the nineteenth century by Gustav Freytag. The term* Landsknecht *translates as "servant of the country," in this instance referring to mercenary soldiers recruited for service in the Thirty Years' War from among the peasantry in Alsace, Baden, Württemberg, and the Austrian Tyrol.*

209 BC: New Carthage

SCIPIO DIVIDES THE SPOILS

When Scipio thought that a sufficient number of troops had entered, he sent most of them, as is the Roman custom, against the inhabitants of the city with orders to kill all they encountered, sparing none, and not to start pillaging until the signal was given. They do this, I think, to inspire terror, so that when towns are taken

A young Greek straps on his sword, shield, and helmet, fifth century BC.

by the Romans, one may often see not only the corpses of human beings, but dogs cut in half, and the dismembered limbs of other animals, and on this occasion such scenes were very many owing to the numbers of those in the place.

Upon the signal being given, the massacre ceased, and they began pillaging. At nightfall, such of the Romans as had received orders to that effect remained in the camp while Scipio, with his thousand men, bivouacked in the cita-

del, and recalling the rest from the houses, ordered them, through the tribunes, to collect the booty in the market, each maniple separately, and sleep there, keeping guard over it.

Next day, the booty, both the baggage of the troops in the Carthaginian service and the household stuff of the townsmen and working classes having been collected in the market, was divided by the tribunes among the legions on the usual system.

According to the size of the town, sometimes a certain number of men from each maniple, at other times certain whole maniples, are told off to collect booty, but they never thus employ more than half their total force, the rest remaining in their ranks at times outside and at times inside the city, ready for the occasion. All those who are told off to spoil bring the booty back, each man to his own legion, and, after it has been sold, the tribunes distribute the profits equally among all, including not only those who were left behind in the protecting force but also the men who are guarding the tents, the sick, and those absent on any special service. I have already stated at some length in my chapters on the Roman state how it is that no one appropriates any part of the loot, but that all keep the oath they make when first assembled in camp on setting out for a campaign. So that when half of the army disperse to pillage and the other half keep their ranks and afford them protection, both the spoilers and those who remain to safeguard them have equal confidence that they will get their share of the booty.

Polybius, *from his history of the Punic Wars. The historian served as mentor to Scipio Africanus' adopted grandson, also a Roman general named Scipio, who destroyed what remained of the Carthaginian Empire in 146 BC.*

1994: Rwanda

VOICES OF DOOM

Pancrace: During that killing season, we rose earlier than usual to eat lots of meat, and we went up to the soccer field at around nine or ten o'clock. The leaders would grumble about latecomers, and we would go off on the attack. Rule number one was to kill. There was no rule number two. It was an organization without complications.

Ignace: Suddenly Hutus of every kind were patriotic brothers without any partisan discord. We were through playing around with the political words. We were no longer in our each-to-his-own mood. We were doing a job to order. We were lining up behind everyone's enthusiasm. We gathered into teams on the soccer field and went out hunting as kindred spirits.

Fulgence: First I cracked an old mama's skull with a club. But she was already lying almost dead on the ground, so I did not feel death at the end of my arm. I went home that evening without even thinking about it.

Alphonse: It was before the decision about vast total killings. A group of Tutsis had retreated into the forest of Kintwi to resist. We spotted them behind clumps of trees—they were standing with stones and branches or tools. Grenades from some of our leaders showered onto them. Then came a big to-do. The Tutsis scattered, and we followed them. In the stampede an old man, not so sturdy anymore, was knocked down as he ran. He fell in front of me. I hacked him across his back with my *inkota*, a sharp blade for slaughtering cattle—I had snatched it up that morning.

A youth next to me helped out silently with his machete, as if the victim were his. When we heard the old man finish, my young colleague indicated to me that he had known him for a long time. His own house was just up the hill from the old man's. He said he was well rid of him this way—you could see he was pleased. Me, I knew this old man by name, but I had heard nothing unpleasant about him.

That evening, I told my wife everything. She knew only routine details about him; we did not discuss it, and I went to sleep.

Adalbert: We were roaming around, looking to rout out Tutsis who might be hidden on plots of land in Rugazi. I came upon two children sitting in the corner of a house. They were keeping quiet as mice. I asked them to come out; they stood up, they wanted to show they were being good. I had them walk at the head of our group, to bring them back to the village

> *If one analyzes human glory, it is composed of nine-tenths twaddle, perhaps ninety-nine-hundredths twaddle.*
> —*Major-General Charles Gordon, 1884*

square in Nyarunazi. It was time to go home, so my men and I set out, talking about our day.

As leader, I had recently been given a gun, besides the grenades. Walking along, without thinking, I decided to try it out. I put the two children side by side twenty meters away. I stood still; I shot twice at their backs. It was the first time in my life I had used a gun, because hunting is no longer customary in the Bugesera since the wild animals disappeared. For me, it was strange to see the children drop without a sound. It was almost pleasantly easy.

Alphonse: At first you cut timidly, then time helps you grow into it. Some colleagues learned the exact way to strike—on the side of the neck or the back of the head—to hasten the end. But other colleagues were all thumbs right up to the finish. Their moves were slow, they did not dare—they hit the arm instead of the neck, for example, then ran away yelling, "That's it, I killed this one dead!" But everyone knew it wasn't true. A specialist had to intervene, catch up with the target, and dispatch it.

Ignace: Some hunted like grazing goats, others like wild beasts. Some hunted slowly because they were afraid, some because they were lazy. Some struck slowly from wickedness, some struck quickly so as to finish up and go home early to do something else. It was not important; it was each to his own technique and personality.

Me, because I was older, I was excused from trudging around the marshes. My duty was to patrol in stealth through the surrounding fields. I chose the ancestral method, with bow and arrows, to skewer a few Tutsis passing through. As an old-timer, I had known such watchful hunting since my childhood.

Alphonse: Man can get used to killing if he kills on and on. He can even become a beast without noticing it. Some threatened one another when they had no more Tutsis under the machete. In their faces, you could see the need to kill.

But for others, on the contrary, killing a person drove a share of fear into their hearts.

Knights fight an insurrection of peasants in northeastern France, 1358. From the *Chronicle of Saint Denis*, 1375.

They did not feel it at first, but later it tormented them. They felt frightened or sickened. Some felt cowardly for not killing enough, some felt cowardly for being forced to kill, so some drank overmuch to stop thinking about their cowardice. Later on they got used to the drink and the cowardice.

Pancrace: When you receive a new order, you hesitate but you obey, or else you're taking a risk. When you have been prepared the right way by the radios and the official advice, you obey more easily, even if the order is to kill your neighbors. The mission of a good organizer is to stifle your hesitations when he gives you instructions.

For example, when he shows you that the act will be total and have no grave consequences for anyone left alive, you obey more easily; you don't worry about anything. You forget your misgivings and fears of punishment. You obey freely.

Léopord: We began the day by killing; we ended the day by looting. It was the rule to kill going out and to loot coming back. We killed in teams, but we looted every man for himself or in small groups of friends. Except for drinks and cows, which we enjoyed sharing. And the plots of land, of course, they were discussed with the organizers. As district leader, I had gotten a huge fertile plot, which I counted on planting when it was all over.

Those who killed a lot had less time to pillage, but since they were feared, they would catch up because of their power. No one wound up ahead, no one wound up robbed.

Anyone who couldn't loot because he had to be absent, or because he felt tired from all he had done, could send his wife. You would see wives rummaging through houses. They ventured even into the marshes to get the belongings of the unfortunate women who had just been killed. People would steal anything—bowls, pieces of cloth, jugs, religious images, wedding pictures—from anywhere, from the houses, from the schools, from the dead.

They stole blood-soaked clothing that they were not afraid to wash. They stole stashes of money from underwear.

Jean-Baptiste: It is a country custom that women do not concern themselves with any bothersome task of cutting. The machete is for a man's work. This was as true for the farming as for the killing.

So during the killings, the women continued to prepare the meals in the morning, and during the rest of day they went looting. They were storing up goods instead of crops, so they were not unhappy. They didn't complain because they knew that, in any case, the operation was intended to succeed completely. They dared not show any sign of disagreement with the men's brutality, not even the simple gesture of a mama's kindness.

In Ntarama, I do not know of a single Hutu woman who hid away a little Tutsi child to save it from the massacre of its family. Not even a toddler wrapped in a cloth or a nursling unrecognizable to her neighbors because of its tender age. Not one woman on the whole hill cheated in the way of a rescue, not even for a short moment of trying.

Ignace: I did not hear many women protesting against Tutsis being raped. They knew this work of killing fiercely heated up the men in the marshes. They agreed on this, except of course if the men did their dirty sex work near the houses.

Any wife who wished to tag along on the hunting raids got sent back by her husband, who asked her to mind the house and see to the looting.

Léopord: I saw colleagues linger over their catch to make the agony last. But often they left before polishing someone off because they were too eager to go looting. For example, they gave the first machete blow and then spotted a bike, and—hop, they'd rather jump on the bike than finish the job. Same for a roof with good sheets of corrugated metal. It was greed more than wickedness. I trusted that there was time for each of those occupations. I struck fast and true; I struck just to get it done.

Alphonse: Some offenders claim that we changed into wild animals, that we were blinded by ferocity, that we buried our civilization under branches, and that's why we are unable to find the right words to talk properly about it.

That is a trick to sidetrack the truth. I can say this: outside the marshes, our lives seemed quite ordinary. We sang on the paths, we downed Primus beer or *urwagwa* [banana beer], we had our choice amid abundance. We chatted about our good fortune, we soaped off our bloodstains in the basin, and our noses enjoyed the aromas of full cooking pots. We rejoiced in the new life about to begin by feasting on leg of veal. We were hot at night atop our wives, and we scolded our rowdy children. Although no longer willing to feel pity, we were still greedy for good feelings.

The days all seemed much alike, as I told you. We put on our field clothes. We swapped gossip at the *cabaret* [social club], we made bets on our victims, spoke mockingly of cut girls, squabbled foolishly over looted grain. We sharpened our tools on whetting stones. We traded stories about desperate Tutsi tricks, we made fun of every "Mercy!" cried by someone who'd been hunted down, we counted up and stashed away our goods.

We went about all sorts of human business without a care in the world—provided we concentrated on killing during the day, naturally.

At the end of the season in the marshes, we were so disappointed we had failed. We were disheartened by what we were going to lose and truly frightened by the misfortune and vengeance reaching out for us. But deep down, we were not tired of anything.

From Machete Season, *edited by Jean Hatzfeld. The interviewees took part in the mass murdering of an estimated 800,000 Rwandans in the spring and summer of 1994.*

1063: Thérouanne

DISARMAMENT TREATY

Dearest brothers in the Lord, these are the conditions which you must observe during the time of the peace which is commonly called the Truce of God, and which begins with sunset on Wednesday and lasts until sunrise on Monday.

1. During those four days and five nights, no man or woman shall assault, wound, or slay another, or attack, seize, or destroy a castle, burg, or villa, by craft or by violence.

2. If anyone violates this peace and disobeys these commands of ours, he shall be exiled for thirty years as a penance, and, before he leaves the bishopric, he shall make compensation for the injury which he committed. Otherwise, he shall be excommunicated by the Lord God and excluded from all Christian fellowship.

3. All who associate with him in any way, who give him advice or aid, or hold converse with him, unless it be to advise him to do penance and to leave the bishopric, shall be under excommunication until they have made satisfaction.

4. If any violator of the peace shall fall sick and die before he completes his penance, no Christian shall visit him or move his body from the place where it lay, or receive any of his possessions.

5. In addition, brethren, you should observe the peace in regard to lands and animals and all things that can be possessed. If anyone takes from another an animal, a coin, or a garment during the days of the truce, he shall be excommunicated unless he makes satisfaction. If he desires to make satisfaction for his crime, he shall first restore the thing which he stole or its value in money and shall do penance for seven years within the bishopric. If he should die before he makes satisfaction and completes his penance, his body shall not be buried or removed from the place where it lay, unless his family shall make satisfaction for him to the person whom he injured.

6. During the days of the peace, no one shall make a hostile expedition on horseback except when summoned by the count; and all who go with the count shall take for their support only as much as is necessary for themselves and their horses.

7. All merchants and other men who pass through your territory from other lands shall have peace from you.

8. You shall also keep this peace every day of the week from the beginning of Advent to the octave of Epiphany and from the beginning of Lent to the octave of Easter, and from the feast of Rogations to the octave of Pentecost.

9. We command all priests on feast days and Sundays to pray for all who keep the peace and to curse all who violate it or support its violators.

10. If anyone has been accused of violating the peace and denies the charge, he shall take the communion and undergo the ordeal of hot iron. If he is found guilty, he shall do penance within the bishopric for seven years.

> *From a Church edict. The terms of the ceasefire were issued by the clergy in Flanders negotiating for peace in God's time among the local feudal lords and barons.*

1972: Washington

RICHARD NIXON THINKS BIG

Nixon: See, the attack in the North that we have in mind… power plants, whatever's left—POL (petroleum), the docks…. And I still think we ought to take the dikes out now. Will that drown people?
Kissinger: About two hundred thousand people.
Nixon: No, no, no… I'd rather use the nuclear bomb. Have you got that, Henry?
Kissinger: That, I think, would just be too much.
Nixon: The nuclear bomb, does that bother you? I just want you to think big, Henry, for chrissakes. The only place where you and I disagree is with regard to the bombing. You're so goddamned concerned about civilians, and I don't give a damn. I don't care.
Kissinger: I'm concerned about the civilians because I don't want the world to be mobilized against you as a butcher.

> *From the Nixon White House tapes, recorded on April 25, 1972, made public by the National Archives on February 28, 2002.*

1356: Poitiers

EXCHANGE OF COURTESIES

Among the battles, recounterings, chases, and pursuits that were made that day in the field, it fortuned so to Sir Oudart of Renty that when he departed from the field because he saw the field was lost without recovery, he thought not to abide the danger of the Englishmen; wherefore he fled all alone and was gone out of the field a league, and an English knight pursued him and ever cried to him and said, "Return again, sir knight; it is a shame to fly away thus." Then the knight turned, and the English knight thought to have stricken him with his spear in the targe, but he failed, for Sir Oudart swerved aside from the stroke; but he failed not the English knight, for he struck him such a stroke on the helm with his sword that he was astonied and fell from his horse to the earth and lay still. Then Sir Oudart alighted and came to him and said, "Yield you, rescue or no rescue, or else I shall slay you." The Englishman yielded and went with him, and afterward was ransomed.

Also it fortuned that another squire of Picardy called John de Hellenes was fled from the battle and met with his page, who delivered him a new fresh horse, whereon he rode away alone. The same season there was in the field the Lord Berkeley of England, a young lusty knight, who the same day had reared his banner; and he all alone pursued the said John of Hellenes. And when he had followed the space of a league, the said John turned again and laid his sword in the rest instead of a spear, and so came running toward the Lord Berkeley, who lift up his sword to have stricken the squire; but when he saw the stroke come, he turned from it, so that the Englishman lost his stroke, and John struck him as he passed on the arm, that the Lord Berkeley's sword fell into the field. When he saw his sword down, he alighted suddenly off his horse and came to the place where his sword lay, and as he stooped down to take up his sword, the French squire did pike his sword at him and by hap, struck him through both the thighs, so that

the knight fell to the earth and could not help himself. And John alighted off his horse and took the knight's sword that lay on the ground, and came to him and demanded if he would yield him or not. The knight then demanded his name. "Sir," said he, "I hight John of Hellenes, but what is your name?" "Certainly," said the knight. "My name is Thomas and am Lord of Berkeley, a fair castle on the river of Severn in the marches of Wales." "Well sir," quoth the squire,

> War is an ugly thing, but not the ugliest of things: the decayed and degraded state of moral and patriotic feeling which thinks nothing worth war, is worse. A man who has nothing which he is willing to fight for, nothing which he cares more about than he does about his personal safety, is a miserable creature who has no chance of being free unless made and kept so by the exertions of better men than himself.
> —John Stuart Mill, 1862

"then ye shall be my prisoner, and I shall bring you in safeguard, and I shall see that you shall be healed of your hurt." "Well," said the knight, "I am content to be your prisoner, for ye have by law of arms won me." There he sware to be his prisoner, rescue or no rescue. Then the squire drew forth the sword out of the knight's thighs and the wound was open. Then he wrapped and bound the wound and set him on his horse and so brought him fair and easily to Châtellerault, and there tarried more than fifteen days for his sake, and did get him remedy for his hurt. And when he was somewhat amended, then he got him a litter and so brought him at his ease to his house in Picardy. There he was more than a year till he was perfectly whole. And when he departed, he paid for his ransom six thousand nobles, and so this squire was made a knight by reason of the profit that he had of the Lord Berkeley.

Jean Froissart, Chronicles. *Similar incidents of medieval chivalry appear throughout the author's reporting from the front lines of the Hundred Years' War.*

1517: Cairo

When Emir Kurtbay was captured by the Ottomans, he was brought before Selim. Selim asked him, "Are you Kurtbay?" He answered, "I am." The Sultan said, "Where is your *furusiya* [horsemanship], and where is your bravery?" He answered, "They are the same as before." The Sultan asked, "Do you remember what you have done to my army?" He answered, "I know, and I have not forgotten anything of it." The Sultan asked, "What have you done to Ali, the son of

1945: Japan

FAIR WARNING

TO THE JAPANESE PEOPLE:
America asks that you take immediate heed of what we say on this leaflet.

We are in possession of the most destructive explosive ever devised by man. A single one of our newly developed atomic bombs is actually the equivalent in explosive power to what two thousand of our giant B-29s can carry on a single mission. This awful fact is one for you to ponder, and we solemnly assure you it is grimly accurate.

We have just begun to use this weapon against your homeland. If you still have any doubt, make inquiry as to what happened to Hiroshima when just one atomic bomb fell on that city.

Before using this bomb to destroy every resource of the military by which they are prolonging this useless war, we ask that you now petition the emperor to end the war. Our president has outlined for you the thirteen consequences of an honorable surrender. We urge that you accept these consequences and begin the work of building a new, better, and peace-loving Japan.

You should take steps now to cease military resistance. Otherwise, we shall resolutely employ this bomb and all our other superior weapons to promptly and forcefully end the war.

EVACUATE YOUR CITIES

On August 6, 1945, the day the atomic bomb fell on Hiroshima, the U.S. Army Air Forces dropped thousands of these leaflets on Japan.

Shahsiwar?" He answered, "I killed him along with the others of your army whom I killed."

Then, when Kurtbay saw treachery in the eyes of Sultan Selim and realized that the latter would kill him anyway, he threw politeness and good manners to the wind and spoke the words of a man who despaired of life. He fixed his eyes on the Sultan's eyes and raised his right hand in the Sultan's face and said to him, "Hear my words and listen to them, so that you and others will know that amongst us are the horsemen of destiny and red death. A single one of us can defeat your whole army. If you do not believe it, you may try, *only please order your army to stop shooting with firearms.*

"You have here with you 200,000 soldiers of all races. Remain in your place and array your army in battle order. Only three of us will come out against you: I, the servant of God; the charging horseman, Sultan Tumanbay; and Emir Allan, and you will see with your own eyes the feats performed by these three. Moreover, you will then know your own self, and you will learn whether you are a king or deserve to be a king, because kingship befits only him who is an experienced, gallant man, for such were our upright predecessors. Study the books of history, and there you will learn of the bravery of the caliphs. As for you who are totally different from them, you have patched up an army from all parts of the world—Christians, Greeks, and others—and you have brought with you this contrivance artfully devised by the Christians of Europe when they were incapable of meeting the Muslim armies on the battlefield. The contrivance is that *bunduq* [arquebus] which, even if a woman were to fire it, would hold up such and such a number of men. Had we chosen to employ this weapon, you would not have preceded us in its use. But we are the people who do not discard the *sunna* [traditions] of our prophet Muhammad, which is the jihad for the sake of Allah, with sword and lance. And woe to thee! How darest thou shoot with firearms at Muslims!

"A Maghribi brought this arquebus to Sultan al-Malik al-Ashraf Qansuh al-Ghawri and informed him that this arquebus had emanated from Venice and that all the armies of the Ottomans and the West have already made use of it. The Mamluk Sultan ordered the Maghribi to train some of his Mamluks in the use of the arquebus, and that is what he did. Then these Mamluks were brought before the Sultan, and they fired their arquebuses in his presence. The Sultan was displeased with their firing and said to the Maghribi, 'We shall not abandon the *sunna* of our Prophet and follow the *sunna* of the Christians, for Allah has already said that if Allah helps you, nobody will defeat you.' So the Maghribi went back to his country saying, 'Those now living will live to see the conquest of this kingdom by this arquebus,' and that is what really happened."

Then Sultan Selim asked Kurtbay, "If bravery and brave men and horsemen had been amongst you, and you had followed the Qur'an and the *sunna*, then why have we defeated you and expelled you from your country and enslaved your children and annihilated most of you, and why are you yourself my prisoner?"

Kurtbay answered, "By Allah, you have not conquered my country by your power and by your *furusiya*. This was ordained and predestined by Allah from eternity, for God has made a beginning and an end to everything, and he has allotted a fixed period of existence to every kingdom…. You yourself will die, and your kingdom will come to an end."

> **Ibn Zunbul**, The Conquest of Cairo. *The Mamluks ruled in Egypt for nearly three centuries by virtue of their unmatched skill as archers and horsemen. Disdaining the use of firearms, they refused to enter the fifteenth-century weapons race for the means of mass destruction. Their dynasty collapsed in 1517 at the Battle of Ridanieh, when an army of Ottoman Turks equipped with gunpowder shot down their cavalry.*

The Sabine Women Halting the Battle Between Romans and Sabines, by Jacques Louis David, 1799.

1944: London

WINSTON CHURCHILL QUESTIONS THE WISDOM OF PLAYING THE GENTLEMAN

1. I want you to think very seriously over this question of poison gas. I would not use it unless it could be shown either that (a) it was life or death for us, or (b) that it would shorten the war by a year.

2. It is absurd to consider morality on this topic when everybody used it in the last war without a word of complaint from the moralists or the Church. On the other hand, in the last war, the bombing of open cities was regarded

> *I have seen war. I have seen war on land and sea. I have seen blood running from the wounded. I have seen men coughing out their gassed lungs. I have seen the dead in the mud. I have seen cities destroyed. I have seen two hundred limping, exhausted men come out of the line—the survivors of a regiment of one thousand that went forward forty-eight hours before. I have seen children starving. I have seen the agony of mothers and wives. I hate war.* —Franklin D. Roosevelt, 1936

as forbidden. Now everybody does it as a matter of course. It is simply a question of fashion changing, as she does between long and short skirts for women.

3. I want a cold-blooded calculation made as to how it would pay us to use poison gas, by which I mean principally mustard. We will want to gain more ground in Normandy so as not to be cooped up in a small area. We could probably deliver twenty tons to their one, and for the sake of the one, they would bring their bomber aircraft into the area against our superiority, thus paying a heavy toll.

4. Why have the Germans not used it? Not certainly out of moral scruples or affection for us. They have not used it because it does not pay them. The greatest temptation ever offered to them was the beaches of Normandy. This

they could have drenched with gas greatly to the hindrance of our troops. That they thought about it is certain, and that they prepared against our use of gas is also certain. But the only reason they have not used it against us is that they fear the retaliation. What is to their detriment is to our advantage.

5. Although one sees how unpleasant it is to receive poison gas attacks, from which nearly everyone recovers, it is useless to protest that an equal amount of high explosives will not inflict greater casualties and suffering on troops or civilians. One really must not be bound within silly conventions of the mind, whether they be those that ruled in the last war or those in reverse which rule in this.

6. If the bombardment of London really became a serious nuisance, and great rockets with far-reaching and devastating effect fell on many centers of government and labor, I should be prepared to do *anything* that would hit the enemy in a murderous place. I may certainly have to ask you to support me in using poison gas. We could drench the cities of the Ruhr and many other cities in Germany in such a way that most of the population would be requiring constant medical attention. We could stop all work at the flying bomb starting points. I do not see why we should always have all the disadvantages of being the gentleman while they have all the advantages of being the cad. There are times when this may be so, but not now.

7. I quite agree that it may be several weeks or even months before I shall ask you to drench Germany with poison gas, and if we do it, let us do it 100 percent. In the meanwhile, I want the matter studied in cold blood by sensible people, and not by that particular set of psalm-singing, uniformed defeatists which one runs across now here, now there. Pray address yourself to this. It is a big thing and can only be discarded for a big reason. I shall, of course, have to square Uncle Joe and the President; but you need not bring this into your calculations at the present time. Just try to find out what it is like on its merits.

Prime Minister's personal minutes, July 6, 1944.

1864: Atlanta

TWO GENERALS CONTEST THE DEFINITION OF CRUELTY

Headquarters Army of Tennessee,
Office Chief of Staff, September 9.

Major General W. T. Sherman, Commanding United States Forces in Georgia.

GENERAL: Your letter of yesterday's date, borne by James M. Ball and James R. Crew, citizens of Atlanta, is received. You say therein, "I deem it to be to the interest of the United States that the citizens now residing in Atlanta should remove," etc. I do not consider that I have any alternative in this matter. I therefore accept your proposition to declare a truce of two days, or such time as may be necessary to accomplish the purpose mentioned, and shall render all assistance in my power to expedite the transportation of citizens in this direction. I suggest that a staff officer be appointed by you to superintend the removal from the city to Rough and Ready, while I appoint a like officer to control their removal farther south; that a guard of one hundred men be sent by either party as you propose, to maintain order at that place, and that the removal begin on Monday next.

And now, sir, permit me to say that the unprecedented measure you propose transcends, in studied and ingenious cruelty, all acts ever before brought to my attention in the dark history of war.

In the name of God and humanity, I protest, believing that you will find that you are expelling from their homes and firesides the wives and children of a brave people.

I am, general, very respectfully,
Your obedient servant,
J. B. Hood,
General

Headquarters Military Division of the Mississippi,
in the Field, Atlanta, Georgia, September 10.

General J. B. Hood, Commanding Army of Tennessee, Confederate Army.

GENERAL: I have the honor to acknowledge the receipt of your letter of this date, at the hands of Messrs. Ball and Crew, consenting to the arrangements I had proposed to facilitate the removal south of the people of Atlanta who prefer to go in that direction. I inclose you a copy of my orders, which will, I am satisfied, accomplish my purpose perfectly.

You style the measure proposed "unprecedented," and appeal to the dark history of war for a parallel as an act of "studied and ingenious cruelty." I say that it is kindness to these families of Atlanta to remove them now, at once, from scenes that women and children should not be exposed to, and the "brave people" should scorn to commit their wives and children to the rude barbarians who thus, as you say, violate the laws of war, as illustrated in the pages of its dark history. In the name of common sense, I ask you not to appeal to a just God in such a sacrilegious

Use of Greek Fire, c. thirteenth–fourteenth centuries. From a Byzantine manuscript.

manner. You, who in the midst of peace and prosperity, have plunged a nation into war—dark and cruel war—who dared and badgered us to battle, insulted our flag, seized our arsenals and forts that were left in the honorable custody of peaceful ordnance-sergeants, seized and made "prisoners of war" the very garrisons sent to protect your people against Negroes and Indians, long before any overt act was committed by the (to you) hated Lincoln Government. If we must be enemies, let us be men and fight it out as we propose to do, and not deal in such hypocritical appeals to God and humanity. God will judge us in due time, and He will pronounce whether it be more humane to fight with a town full of women and the families of "a brave people" at our back, or to remove them in time to places of safety among their own friends and people.

I am, very respectfully,
Your obedient servant,
W. T. Sherman,
Major General, commanding

Headquarters Army of Tennessee,
September 12.

Major General W. T. Sherman, Commanding Military Division of the Mississippi.

GENERAL: I have the honor to acknowledge the receipt of your letter of the ninth inst., with its inclosure in reference to the women, children, and others, whom you have thought proper to expel from their homes in the city of Atlanta. Had you seen proper to let the matter rest there, I would gladly have allowed your letter to close this correspondence, and without your expressing it in words, would have been willing to believe that, while "the interests of the United States," in your opinion, compelled you to an act of barbarous cruelty, you regretted the necessity, and we would have dropped the subject; but you have chosen to indulge in statements which I feel compelled to notice, at least so far as to signify my dissent, and not allow silence in regard to them to be construed as acquiescence.

Normans load their boats before crossing the English Channel, 1066. Detail from the Bayeux tapestry, c. fifteenth century.

I see nothing in your communication which induces me to modify the language of condemnation with which I characterized your order. It but strengthens me in the opinion that it stands "preeminent in the dark history of war for studied and ingenious cruelty." Your original order was stripped of all pretenses; you announced the edict for the sole reason that it was "to the interest of the United States." This alone you offered to us and the civilized world as an all-sufficient reason for disregarding the laws of God and man.

You order into exile the whole population of a city; drive men, women, and children from their homes at the point of the bayonet, under the plea that it is to the interest of your government and on the claim that it is an act of "kindness to these families of Atlanta." You issue a sweeping edict covering all the inhabitants of a city, and add insult to the injury heaped upon the defenseless by assuming that you have done them a kindness. And, because I characterize what you call a kindness as being real cruelty, you presume to sit in judgment between me and my God, and you decide that my earnest prayer to the Almighty Father to save our women and children from what you call kindness is a "sacrilegious, hypocritical appeal."

You came into our country with your army, avowedly for the purpose of subjugating free white men, women, and children, and not only intend to rule over them, but you make Negroes your allies and desire to place over us an inferior race, which we have raised from barbarism to its present position, which is the highest ever attained by that race, in any country, in all time. I must, therefore, decline to accept your statements in reference to your kindness toward the people of Atlanta and your willingness to sacrifice everything for the peace and honor of the South, and refuse to be governed by your decision in regard to matters between myself, my country, and my God.

You say, "Let us fight it out like men." To this my reply is—for myself, and I believe for all the true men, ay, and women and children, in my country—we will fight you to the death! Better die a thousand deaths than submit to

live under you or your government and your Negro allies!

Having answered the points forced upon me by your letter of the ninth of September, I close this correspondence with you and, notwithstanding your comments upon my appeal to God in the cause of humanity, I again humbly and reverently invoke His almighty aid in defense of justice and right.

> Respectfully,
> Your obedient servant,
> J. B. Hood,
> General

Headquarters Military Division of the Mississippi, in the Field, Atlanta, Georgia, September 14.

General J. B. Hood, Commanding Army of Tennessee, Confederate Army.

GENERAL: Yours of September 12 is received and has been carefully perused. I agree with you that this discussion by two soldiers is out of place and profitless; but you must admit that you began the controversy by characterizing an official act of mine in unfair and improper terms. I reiterate my former answer, and to the only new matter contained in your rejoinder add: we have no "Negro allies" in this army; not a single Negro soldier left Chattanooga with this army or is with it now.

I was not bound by the laws of war to give notice of the shelling of Atlanta, a "fortified town with magazines, arsenals, foundries, and public stores;" you were bound to take notice. See the books.

This is the conclusion of our correspondence, which I did not begin, and terminate with satisfaction.

> I am, with respect,
> Your obedient servant,
> W. T. Sherman,
> Major-General, commanding

> *Two months after the exchange of letters, Sherman, having burned Atlanta to the ground, marched his scorched-earth policy eastward through Georgia to the sea.*

512 BC: China

SUN TZU RECONNOITERS THE TERRAIN

The art of war recognizes nine varieties of ground: dispersive ground; facile ground; contentious ground; open ground; ground of intersecting highways; serious ground; difficult ground; hemmed-in ground; desperate ground.

When a chieftain is fighting in his own territory, it is dispersive ground.

When he has penetrated into hostile territory, but to no great distance, it is facile ground.

Ground, the possession of which imports great advantage to either side, is contentious ground.

Ground on which each side has liberty of movement is open ground.

Ground which forms the key to three contiguous states, so that he who occupies it first has most of the empire at his command, is a ground of intersecting highways.

When an army has penetrated into the heart of a hostile country, leaving a number of fortified cities in its rear, it is serious ground.

Mountain forests, rugged steeps, marshes and fens—all country that is hard to traverse: this is difficult ground.

Ground which is reached through narrow gorges, and from which we can only retire by tortuous paths, so that a small number of the enemy would suffice to crush a large body of our men: this is hemmed-in ground.

Ground on which we can only be saved from destruction by fighting without delay, is desperate ground.

On dispersive ground, therefore, fight not. On facile ground, halt not. On contentious ground, attack not.

On open ground, do not try to block the enemy's way. On ground of intersecting highways, join hands with your allies.

On serious ground, gather in plunder. In difficult ground, keep steadily on the march.

On hemmed-in ground, resort to stratagem. On desperate ground, fight.

The different measures suited to the nine

varieties of ground; the expediency of aggressive or defensive tactics; and the fundamental laws of human nature: these are things that must most certainly be studied.

When invading hostile territory, the general principle is that penetrating deeply brings cohesion; penetrating but a short way means dispersion.

When you leave your own country behind and take your army across neighboring territory, you find yourself on critical ground. When there are means of communication on all four sides, the ground is one of intersecting highways.

When you penetrate deeply into a country, it is serious ground. When you penetrate but a little way, it is facile ground.

When you have the enemy's strongholds on your rear and narrow passes in front, it is hemmed-in ground. When there is no place of refuge at all, it is desperate ground.

Therefore, on dispersive ground, I would inspire my men with unity of purpose. On facile ground, I would see that there is close connection between all parts of my army.

On contentious ground, I would hurry up my rear.

On open ground, I would keep a vigilant eye on my defenses. On ground of intersecting highways, I would consolidate my alliances.

On serious ground, I would try to ensure a continuous stream of supplies. On difficult ground, I would keep pushing on along the road.

On hemmed-in ground, I would block any way of retreat. On desperate ground, I would proclaim to my soldiers the hopelessness of saving their lives.

> *From* The Art of War, *a Chinese text dating from the fifth century* BC. *The treatise so pleased the ruler of the Kingdom of Wu that he appointed Sun Tzu to the post of Military Adviser.*

2004: Rafah

THE ISRAELI ARMY SETS UP THE GOAL POSTS

Sentry: We spotted an Arab female about a hundred meters below our emplacement, near the light armored vehicle gate.
Headquarters: Observation Post "Spain," do you see it?
Observation Post: Affirmative; it's a young girl. She's now running east.
HQ: What is her position?
OP: She's currently north of the authorized zone.
Sentry: Very inappropriate location.
[Gunfire]
OP: She's now behind an embankment, 250 meters from the barracks. She keeps running east. The hits are right on her.
HQ: Are you talking about a girl under ten?
OP: Approximately a ten-year-old girl.
HQ: Roger.
OP: OP to HQ.
HQ: Receiving, over.
OP: She's behind the embankment, dying of fear; the hits are right on her, a centimeter from her.
Sentry: Our troops are storming toward her now. They are around seventy meters from her.
HQ: I understand that the company commander and his squad are out?
Sentry: Affirmative, with a few more soldiers.
OP: Receive. Looks like one of the positions dropped her.
HQ: What, did you see the hit? Is she down?
OP: She's down. Right now she isn't moving.
Company Commander: [to HQ] Me and another solider are going in. [To the squad] Forward, to confirm the kill.
CC: [to HQ] We fired and killed her. She has… wearing pants… jeans and a vest, shirt. Also, she had a kaffiyeh on her head. I also confirmed the kill. Over.
HQ: Roger.
CC: [on general communications band] Any motion, anyone who moves in the zone, even if it's a three year old, should be killed. Over.

From a transcript of radio communications among Israeli soldiers on the border between Egypt and the Gaza Strip in October 2004. The Palestinian schoolgirl in the forbidden zone was hit by seventeen bullets.

1716: Japan

YAMAMOTO TSUNETOMO ON THE REASON FOR WEARING A MUSTACHE

Even if it seems certain that you will lose, retaliate. Neither wisdom nor technique has a place in this. A real man does not think of victory or defeat. He plunges recklessly toward an irrational death. By doing this, you will awaken from your dreams.

A warrior should be careful in all things and should dislike to be the least bit worsted. Above all, if he is not careful in his choice of words, he may say things like, "I'm a coward," or, "At that time I'd probably run," or, "How

> I detest war. It spoils armies.
> —Grand Duke Constantine of Russia, c. 1820

frightening," or, "How painful." These are words that should not be said even in jest, on a whim, or when talking in one's sleep. If a person with understanding hears such things, he will see to the bottom of the speaker's heart. This is something that should be carefully thought about beforehand.

In the words of the ancients, one should make his decisions within the space of seven breaths. Lord Takanobu said, "If discrimination is long, it will spoil." Lord Naoshige said, "When matters are done leisurely, seven out of ten will turn out badly. A warrior is a person who does things quickly." When your mind is going hither and thither, discrimination will never be brought to a conclusion. With an intense, fresh, and undelaying spirit, one will make his judgments within the space of seven breaths. It is a matter of being determined and having the spirit to break right through to the other side.

Even if one's head were to be suddenly cut off, he should be able to do one more action with certainty. With martial valor, if one becomes like a revengeful ghost and shows great determination, though his head is cut off, he should not die.

According to what one of the elders said, taking an enemy on the battlefield is like a hawk taking a bird. Even though it enters into the midst of a thousand of them, it gives no attention to any bird other than the one that it has first marked.

A certain general said, "For soldiers other than officers, if they would test their armor, they should test only the front. Furthermore, while ornamentation on armor is unnecessary, one should be very careful about the appearance of his helmet. It is something that accompanies his head to the enemy's camp."

Nakano Jin'emon said, "Learning such things as military tactics is useless. If one does not strike out by simply closing his eyes and rushing into the enemy, even if it is only one step, he will be of no use."

Meditation on inevitable death should be performed daily. Everyday when one's body and mind are at peace, one should meditate upon being ripped apart by arrows, rifles, spears, and swords, being carried away by surging waves, being thrown into the midst of a great fire, being struck by lightning, being shaken to death by a great earthquake, falling from thousand-foot cliffs, dying of disease, or committing *seppuku* [ritual suicide] at the death of one's master. And every day without fail, one should consider himself as dead.

The warriors of old cultivated mustaches, for as proof that a man had been slain in battle, his ears and nose would be cut off and brought to the enemy's camp. So that there would be no mistake as to whether the person was man or woman, the mustache was also cut off with the nose. At such a time the head was thrown away if it had no mustache, for it might be mistaken for that of a woman. Therefore, growing a mustache was one of the disciplines of a samurai so that his head would not be thrown away upon his death.

> From the Hagakure, *the collected wisdoms of a revered samurai. The book was intended to teach a younger generation of warriors how to live as if one were already dead.*

1954: Guatemala City

THE CIA SENDS ADVICE AND CONSENT

DEFINITION

"Assassination" is a term thought to be derived from "hashish," a drug similar to marijuana that is said to have been used by the eleventh-century Islamic leader Hasan ibn al Sabbah to induce motivation in those of his followers who would carry out political and other murders, usually at the cost of their lives.

EMPLOYMENT

Assassination is an extreme measure, and it should be assumed that it will never be ordered or authorized by any U.S. headquarters, though officials may in rare instances agree to its execution by members of an associated foreign service.

No assassination instructions should ever be written or recorded. Ideally, only one person will be involved. No report may be made, though the act will usually be properly covered by news services.

JUSTIFICATION

Murder is not morally justifiable. Assassination can seldom be employed with a clear conscience. Persons who are morally squeamish should not attempt it.

CLASSIFICATIONS

The techniques employed will vary depending on whether or not the assassin himself is to be killed with the subject. If the assassin is to die with the subject, the act will be called "lost." If the assassin is to escape, the act will be called "safe." It should be noted that no compromise should exist here. The assassin must not fall alive into enemy hands.

Assassination techniques will also be affected by the subject's vulnerability. Assassinations in which the subject is unaware of his danger will be termed "simple"; those in which the subject is aware but unguarded will be termed "chase;" those in which the victim is aware but guarded will be termed "guarded."

A further division concerns whether or not it is necessary to conceal the fact that the subject was actually the victim of assassination. If such concealment is desirable, the act will be called "secret;" if concealment is immaterial, the act will be called "open." If the assassination requires publicity to be effective, it will be termed "terroristic."

Assyrian warriors after conquering the Jewish fortress of Lachish, 701 BC.

Following these definitions, the assassination of Julius Caesar was safe, simple, and terroristic, while that of Huey Long was lost, guarded, and open. Obviously, successful secret assassinations are not recorded as assassinations at all.

THE ASSASSIN

Except in terroristic assassinations, it is desirable that the assassin be transient. In a lost assassination, the assassin must be a fanatic of some sort. Politics, religion, and revenge are about the only feasible motives. Since a fanatic is unstable psychologically, he must be handled with extreme care.

TECHNIQUES

A human being may be killed in many ways, but the assassin should always be cognizant of one point: death must be absolutely certain. The attempt on Hitler's life failed because those planning the conspiracy did not give this matter proper attention.

Techniques may be considered as follows:

Manual

It is possible to kill a man with bare hands, but very few are skillful enough to do it well. Even a highly trained judo expert will hesitate to risk killing by hand unless he has absolutely no alternative. The simplest local tools are often the most efficient means of assassination—a hammer, ax, wrench, screwdriver, fire poker, kitchen knife, lamp stand, or anything hard, heavy, and handy. A length of rope or wire or a belt will do if the assassin is strong and agile. All such improvised weapons have the important advantage of availability and apparent innocence. The obviously lethal machine-gun failed to kill Trotsky where an item of sporting goods succeeded.

Accidents

For a secret assassination, the contrived accident is the most effective technique. When successfully executed, it causes little excitement and is only casually investigated.

The most efficient accident is a fall of seventy-five feet or more onto a hard surface. Elevator shafts, stairwells, unscreened windows, and bridges will serve. Bridge falls into water are not reliable.

British Guardsmen in full kit complete an obstacle course, 1941.

A private meeting with the subject may be arranged at a properly cased location. The act may be executed by a sudden, vigorous tripping at the ankles, tipping the subject over the edge. If the assassin immediately sets up an outcry, playing the "horrified witness," no alibi or surreptitious withdrawal is necessary.

Falls in front of trains or subway cars are usually effective, but these require exact timing and can seldom be free from unexpected observation.

Automobile accidents are less satisfactory. If the subject is to be deliberately run down, exact timing is necessary and investigation is likely to be thorough. The subject may be stunned or drugged and then placed in a car, but this is reliable only when the car can be run off a high cliff or into deep water without observation.

Edge and Blunt Weapons

Any locally obtained sharp-edged device may be successfully employed, though a minimum amount of anatomical knowledge is needed for reliability. The most reliable methods are severing the spinal cord in the cervical region (with the point of a knife or a light blow with an ax or hatchet) and severing the jugular and carotid blood vessels on both sides of the windpipe.

As for blunt weapons, their main advantage is their universal availability. A hammer may be picked up almost anywhere in the world. Baseball bats are widely distributed. Even a rock or a heavy stick will do, and no weapon need be disposed of.

Blows should be directed to the temple, the area just below and behind the ear, and the lower, rear portion of the skull. Of course, if the blow is very heavy, any portion of the upper skull will do. The lower frontal portion of the head, from the eyes to the throat, can withstand enormous blows without fatal consequences.

Explosives

A small or moderate explosive charge is highly unreliable as a cause of death, and time-delay or booby-trap devices are extremely prone to kill the wrong man.

Bombs or grenades should never be thrown at a subject. While this will always cause a commotion and may even result in the subject's death, it is sloppy, unreliable, and bad propaganda.

EXAMPLES

[Agents] may be presented brief outlines, with critical evaluations of the following assassinations and attempts: Archduke Francis Ferdinand, Gandhi, Harding, Hitler, Lincoln, Huey Long, Marat, Mussolini, Rasputin, Roosevelt, Trotsky, and Truman.

> *From "A Study of Assassination," unsigned and undated by its authors in Washington before its transmission to Guatemala, there to be studied by operatives wondering how best to approach the problem of Jacobo Arbenz Guzmán, the newly elected Guatemalan president advocating democratic land reform.*

Rates of fire through the ages:

Weapon	Date	r.p.m*
Arquebus/matchlock musket	15th century	2
Wheel-lock musket	16th century	2 to 3
Flintlock musket	17th century	3
Gatling gun	1860s	200
Maxim gun	1880s	600
Lee-Enfield rifle	1900s	8
Thompson submachine-gun	1920s	725
Bren gun	1930s	500
M-1 Garand Rifle	1940s	24
Kalashnikov AK-47	1940s	600
M-16 assault rifle	1950s	800
General purpose machine-gun	1950s	1,000
M-134 minigun	1960s	6,000
SA-80 assault rifle	1980s	770
Metal Storm (fired by electronic ignition)	1990s	1 million

*r.p.m. = rounds per minute

1962: Washington

Operation FREE RIDE:

a. *Objective*: The objective is to create unrest and dissension amongst the Cuban people.

b. *Concept*: This to be accomplished by air dropping valid Pan American or KLM one-way airline tickets good for passage to Mexico City, Caracas, etc. (none to the U.S.). Tickets could be intermixed with other leaflets planned to be dropped. The number of tickets dropped could be increased. The validity of the tickets would have to be restricted to a time period.

Operation GOOD TIMES:

a. *Objective*: To disillusion the Cuban population with Castro image by distribution of fake photographic material.

b. *Concept*: Prepare a desired photograph, such as an obese Castro with two beauties in any situation desired, ostensibly within a room in the Castro residence, lavishly furnished, and a table brimming over with the most delectable Cuban food with an underlying caption (appropriately Cuban) such as, "My ration is different." Make as many prints as desired on sterile paper and then distribute over the countryside by air drops or agents. This should put even a Commie dictator in the proper perspective with the underprivileged masses.

Operation TRUE BLUE:

1. *Objective*: To degrade Castro and his government in the eyes of the Cuban people by communications intrusion.

Concept of Operations:

2. By utilizing high-powered transmitters in the vicinity of Cuba (Florida, Inagwa, Jamaica, aboard Naval ship), which have the capability of overriding commercial Cuban radio and TV stations, periodically degrade Castro and other government figures in the minds of the Cuban people.

3. The technique of communications intrusion could be exploited by pretaping or live broadcasts of anticommunist and anti-Castro propaganda at station breaks, Castro speeches, etc. This idea envisions the use of a Cuban refugee to make such broadcasts and naturally would require close monitoring of stations to be worked. Any number of thoughts could be injected such as:

    a. "Cuba Sí, Russia No."

    b. Communism exploits the masses.

    c. Communism is ruthless totalitarianism.

    d. Castro and henchmen feast off the land while we are rationed.

    e. Castro and his reign of terror.

    f. Castro is a lunatic and should be put away.

    g. Castro is the cause of all our troubles.

    h. Rise up against the pig Castro, etc., etc.

4. If approved, this operation could become a continuous project, perhaps under control of USLA.

Operation "NO LOVE LOST":

a. *Objective*: To confuse and harass Castro Cuban pilots by use of radio conversations.

b. *Concept*: Fly Cuban refugee pilot in sterile aircraft in proximity of Cuba at periodic intervals while communication monitoring Cuban air/ground frequencies utilized for airdrome control. Cuban refugee pilot in sterile aircraft would personally know many of the pilots still flying for Castro. Refugee pilot would get into argument with Castro pilots over radio thus distracting, confusing, etc. Would be real trouble for Castro pilots in actual weather conditions. Argument could go, "I'll get you, you Red son of a gun," and call by name if appropriate.

Memorandum, "Justification for U.S. Military Intervention in Cuba," submitted by the Joint Chiefs of Staff to then Secretary of Defense Robert McNamara on March 13, 1962, seven months prior to the Cuban Missile Crisis. Other elements of the proposal, codenamed Operation Northwoods and designed to justify an American invasion of Cuba, foresaw the assassination of Cuban residents in the United States, the faking of a Cuban Air Force attack on an American airliner, and the blowing up of an American ship in Cuban waters.

1969: Tegucigalpa

THE NEWS MEDIA LOOK
FOR A HEADLINE

I awoke in my hotel the next morning and found that the city was preparing for a siege. People had been digging trenches and putting up barricades for hours. Women were laying in supplies and crisscrossing their windows with masking tape. People scurried aimlessly through the streets; an atmosphere of panic reigned. Student brigades were painting outsized slogans on walls and fences. A bubble full of poetry had burst over Tegucigalpa, and within hours thousands of verses covered the walls:

Only an imbecile worries:
Nobody *beats Honduras*

Pick up your guns and let's go guys
Cut those Salvadorans down to size

Porfirio Ramos should be ashamed of himself for living with a Salvadoran woman

Anyone seeing Raimundo Grandos call the police
He's a Salvadoran spy

Latins generally have an obsession with spies, conspiracies, and plots. Now, in wartime conditions, they regarded everyone as a fifth-column diversionist. My own situation did not look good. Official propaganda on both sides had featured wild campaigns blaming Communists for every misfortune, and in the whole region I was the only correspondent from a socialist country. They could expel me.

I went to the post office and invited the telex operator for a beer. He was in terror, because although he had a Honduran father, his mother was a citizen of El Salvador. As a mixed national, he found himself among the suspected. He did not know what would happen next. All morning the police had been herding Salvadorans into provisional camps, most often in stadiums. Throughout Latin America, stadiums play a double role: in peacetime they are sports venues, and in times of war they turn into prisons.

In the afternoon forty correspondents, my colleagues, arrived from Mexico. Because the airport in Tegucigalpa was closed, they flew into Guatemala and hired a bus there. They all wanted to drive to the front. We went to the presidential palace to try to arrange permission. It was an ugly turn-of-the-century building, painted bright blue, in the very center of the town. There were machine-gun nests, covered with sandbags, set up around the palace. Anti-aircraft guns stood in the courtyard. Inside, in the corridors, soldiers were dozing or lolling around in full battle dress. It was quite a mess.

Every war is a horrible mess and a great waste of life and property. People have been making war for thousands of years, but it looks each time as if they were starting from scratch, as if the first war in the world were being held.

A captain appeared and said he was the army press spokesman. He told us that they

390: Rome

IMPERIAL BAND MUSIC

The music of the legion consists of trumpets, cornets, and buccinae. The trumpet sounds the charge and the retreat. The cornets are used only to regulate the motions of the colors; the trumpets serve when the soldiers are ordered out to any work without the colors; but in time of action, the trumpets and cornets sound together. The classicum, which is a particular sound of the buccina or horn, is appropriated to the commander-in-chief and is used in the presence of the general, or at the execution of a soldier, as a mark of its being done by his authority. The ordinary guards and outposts are always mounted and relieved by the sound of trumpet, which also directs the motions of the soldiers on working parties and on field days. The cornets sound whenever the colors are to be struck or planted. These rules must be punctually observed in all exercises and reviews so that the soldiers may be ready to obey them in action without hesitation according to the general's orders either to charge or halt, to pursue the enemy, or to retire. For reason will convince us that what is necessary to be performed in the heat of action should constantly be practiced in the leisure of peace.

Vegetius, Epitoma Rei Militaris, *a treatise on Roman military strategy written in the fourth century that remained popular among European tacticians throughout the Middle Ages.*

were winning all along the front and that the enemy was suffering heavy losses.

"Okay," said the man from AP. "And we want to see."

We always sent the Americans first because this was their sphere of influence—they commanded obedience and could arrange all sorts of things. The captain said we could go to the front the next day.

We drove to a place where two artillery pieces stood under some trees. Cannons were firing, and stacks of ordnance were lying around.

I have loved war too well. —Louis XIV, 1715

Ahead of us we could see the road that led to El Salvador. Swamp stretched along both sides of the road, and dense green bush began past the belt of swamp.

The sweaty, unshaven major charged with holding the road said we could go no farther. Beyond this point both armies were in action, and it was hard to tell who was who or what belonged to which side. The bush was too thick to see anything. Two opposing units often noticed each other only at the last moment, when, wandering through the overgrowth, they met face to face. In addition, since both armies wore the same uniforms, carried the same equipment, and spoke the same language, it was difficult to distinguish friend from foe.

The major advised us to return to Tegucigalpa because advancing might mean getting killed without even knowing who had done it. (As if that mattered, I thought.) But the television cameramen said they had to push forward, to the front line, to film soldiers in action, firing, dying. Gregor Straub of NBC said he had to have a close-up of a soldier's face dripping sweat. Rodolfo Carillo of CBS said he had to catch a despondent commander sitting under a bush and weeping because he had lost his whole unit. A French cameraman wanted a panorama shot with a Salvadoran unit charging a Honduran unit from one side, or vice versa. Somebody else wanted to capture the image of a soldier carrying his dead comrade. The radio reporters sided with the cameramen. One wanted to record the cries of a casualty summoning help, growing weaker and weaker, until he breathed his last breath. Charles Meadows of Radio Canada wanted the voice of a soldier cursing war amid a hellish racket of gunfire. Naotake Mochida of Radio Japan wanted the bark of an officer shouting to his commander over the roar of artillery—using a Japanese field telephone.

Many others also decided to go forward. Competition is a powerful incentive. Since American television was going, the American wire services had to go as well. Since the Americans were going, Reuters had to go. Excited by patriotic ambition, I decided, as the only Pole on the scene, to attach myself to the group that intended the desperate march. Those who said they had bad hearts, or professed to be uninterested in particulars since they were writing general commentaries, we left behind, under a tree.

There might have been twenty of us who set out along an empty road bathed in intense sunlight. The risk, or even the madness, of the march lay in the fact that the road ran along the top of an embankment: we were perfectly visible to both of the armies hiding in the bush that began about a hundred yards away. One good burst of machine-gun fire in our direction would be enough.

At the beginning, everything went well. We heard intense gunfire and the detonation of artillery shells, but it was a mile or so away. To keep our spirits up, we were all talking (nervously and without necessarily making sense). But soon fear began to take its toll. It is, indeed, a rather unpleasant feeling to walk with the awareness that at any moment a bullet can find you. No one, however, acknowledged fear openly. First, somebody simply proposed we take a rest. So we sat down and caught our breath. Then, when we started again, two began lagging behind—apparently immersed in conversation. Then somebody spotted an especially interesting group of trees that deserved long, careful inspection. Then two others announced that they had to go back because they had forgotten the filters they needed for their cameras. We took another rest. We rested more and more often, and the pauses grew longer. There were ten of us left.

In the meantime, nothing was happening in our vicinity. We were walking along an empty road in the direction of El Salvador. The air was wonderful. The sun was setting. That very sun helped us extricate ourselves. The television men suddenly pulled out their light meters and stated that it was already too dark to film. Nothing could be done—not long shots, nor close-ups, nor action shots, nor stills. And it was a long way to the front line yet. By the time we got there, it would be night.

The whole group started back. The ones who had heart trouble, who were going to write general commentaries, who had turned back earlier because they had forgotten their filters, were waiting for us under the tree, beside the two artillery pieces.

> **Ryszyard Kapuściński**, *from* The Soccer War. *Fighting erupted between Honduras and El Salvador during the soccer matches being played to decide which of the two countries would qualify to compete in the 1970 FIFA World Cup. The war went on for four days in July 1969, with the result that about two thousand people died on both sides of the ball.*

c. 1944: Ukraine

CURZIO MALAPARTE GOES TO SCHOOL WITH THE WEHRMACHT

Then began the first "lessons in the open," the first reading exercises in the yards of the *kolkhoz*—the collective farm. Only once, in a *kolkhoz* of a village near Nemirovskoye, I chanced to be present at one of those lessons. After that I always refused to assist with these reading exercises. "*Warum nicht?*—Why not?" the German officers of General von Schobert asked me. "Why don't you want to watch the lessons in the open? It is a very interesting experiment, *sehr interessant.*"

The prisoners were lined up in the yard of the *kolkhoz*. Along the walls of the yard and under the large sheds were piled haphazardly, hundreds of agricultural machines—reapers, cultivators, mechanical plows, threshing machines. It rained, and the prisoners were soaked to their skins. They had been standing there, in silence, leaning against each other; they were big, fair boys, with close-cropped heads and light eyes in their broad faces. Their hands were flat and thick, with squat, arched, calloused thumbs.

Cavalry Combat, by Théodore Géricault.

Almost all were peasants. The workmen, mostly engineers and mechanics from the *kolkhoz*, could be distinguished among them by their height and their hands; they were taller, leaner, and lighter-skinned; their hands were bony, with long fingers and smooth fingertips glazed from gripping hammers, planes, wrenches, screwdrivers, and controls. They could be distinguished by their stern faces and glazed eyes.

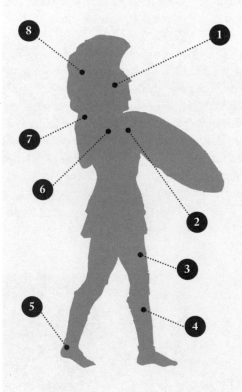

Eight wounds sustained by Alexander the Great

1. Cleaver slash to the head
2. Catapult missile to the chest
3. Sword blow in the thigh
4. Arrow through the leg
5. Arrow in the ankle
6. Arrow through the lung
7. Dart through the shoulder
8. Stone strike to the head and neck

Finally, a German NCO, a *Feldwebel* [sergeant major], came into the yard followed by an interpreter. The *Feldwebel* was short and fat, the type I playfully called "Fettwebel." Standing with his legs wide apart, he faced the prisoners and began talking to them in the good-natured way of a head of a family. He said that a reading test was to be held, and each would have to read aloud a passage from a newspaper. Those who passed the examination well would be drafted as clerks into the offices of the prisoners' camps; the others, those who failed, would be sent to work on the land or be employed as laborers and dockworkers.

The interpreter was a *Sonderführer* [civilian technician with the army], short and thin, not more than thirty years old, his face covered with little red pimples. He had been born in Russia in the *Deutschvolk* colony of Melitopol and spoke Russian with an odd German accent. The first time I met him, I said jokingly that Melitopol means the city of honey. "Yes," he replied in a harsh voice and with a sullen look, "there is a lot of honey in that district, but I am not concerned with bees; I am a schoolmaster." The *Sonderführer* translated the brief and good-natured speech of the *Fettwebel* word for word, and he added, in a tone of a schoolmaster upbraiding his pupils, that they had to be careful with the pronunciation and read with attention and ease because, if they failed to pass the examination, they would have reasons to regret it. Later, when I recalled his words, I felt a shiver creeping down my spine.

The prisoners listened in silence, and when the *Sonderführer* stopped they all began talking among themselves and laughing. Many of them seemed to feel humiliated. They gazed around like whipped dogs and glanced from time to time at their horny peasant hands, but many others laughed contentedly; they felt certain of passing, and of being sent into some office as clerks. "*Eh, Pyotr! Eh, Ivanushka!*" they shouted to their companions, and slapped each other roughly on the backs with the simpleminded gaiety of the Russian peasant. The workmen among them were silent, turning their stern faces toward the administration building of the *kolkhoz*, where the German headquarters were. From time to time they looked at the *Feldwebel*, but they never deigned to glance at the *Sonderführer*. Their eyes were deep and glazed.

"*Ruhe!*—Silence!" suddenly shouted the *Feldwebel*.

A group of officers was already approaching, led by an old colonel, tall and thin, a little stooped, with gray mustaches clipped short; he walked slightly dragging one of his legs. The colonel glanced absentmindedly at the prisoners and began speaking rapidly in a monotonous voice, swallowing half of his words, as if he were in a hurry to finish his sentences. At the end of each sentence, he made a long pause, but his eyes remained fixed on the ground. He said that those who would pass the examination and so on, and so on…. The *Sonderführer* translated the colonel's brief speech word for word. Then, on his own account, he added that

the Moscow government had spent millions on Soviet schools, that he knew this because he had been a schoolmaster among the *Deutschvolk* of Melitopol before the war, and that all those who failed in the examination were to be set to work as laborers and dockworkers; it was their fault if they had learned nothing in school. The *Sonderführer* seemed very anxious that all of them should read fluently and with a good pronunciation.

"How many are there?" the colonel asked the *Feldwebel* as he scratched his chin with a gloved hand.

"One hundred and eighteen," replied the *Feldwebel*.

The colonel gave a sign to one of the officers who was clutching a bundle of newspapers under his arm, and the examination began.

Five prisoners took a step forward. Each of them stretched out a hand, took a paper that the officer held out to him—they were old issues of

Japanese kamikaze plane destroyed by its target near the Marshall Islands, 1943.

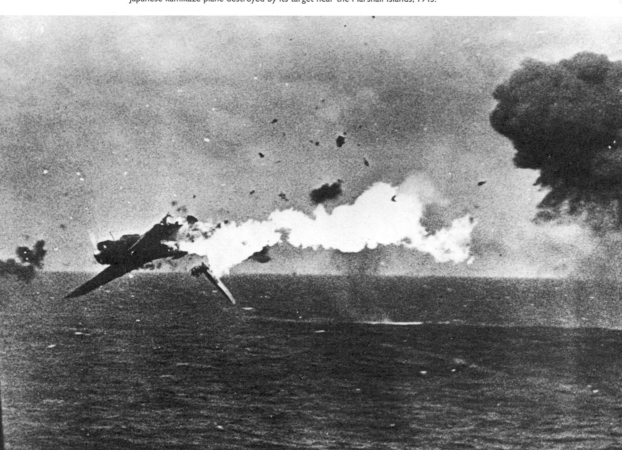

Izvestia and *Pravda* found in the office of the *kolkhoz*—and began reading aloud. The colonel raised his left arm to look at his wristwatch. He kept his arm breast-high and his eyes fixed on the watch. It was raining, and the newspapers were soaked; they drooped in the hands of the five prisoners whose faces were either red or extremely pale and sweating as they stumbled over the words, halted, stammered, blundered the accents, and skipped lines. They could all read

In Italy for thirty years under the Borgias they had warfare, terror, murder, bloodshed—they produced Michelangelo, Leonardo da Vinci, and the Renaissance. In Switzerland, they had brotherly love, five hundred years of democracy, and what did they produce? The cuckoo clock!
—Orson Welles, 1949

with difficulty, except one very young man who read with assurance, from time to time raising his eyes from the paper. The *Sonderführer* listened to the reading with an ironical smile in which I seemed to sense a vengefulness—as interpreter, he was the sole judge. He stared at the readers, shifting his eyes from one to the other with a deliberate and nasty slowness. "Stop!" said the colonel.

The five prisoners raised their eyes from the papers and waited. At a nod from the judge, the *Feldwebel* shouted, "Those who have failed will go and stand on the left; those who have been promoted, over there, to the right." The first four failures, at a sign from the judge, went dejectedly to cluster on the left, and a youthful ripple of laughter ran along the ranks of the prisoners, a gay, mischievous, peasant laughter. The *Sonderführer* also laughed. "*O, bednii*—O poor fellows!" the prisoners called to those who had failed. "You will be sent to work on the roads, *O bednii*, you'll carry stones on your backs," and they laughed. The one who had passed, all alone on the other side, laughed more than the others, chaffing his unlucky comrades. They all laughed except the prisoners who

looked like workmen; they stared at the colonel's face and were silent.

Then came the turn of the next five. They also struggled to read well, without stumbling over the words, without placing the wrong accents, but only two could read fluently; the other three, red with shame or pale with anxiety, clutched the papers tightly in their hands, and from time to time licked their parched lips. "Stop!" said the colonel. The five prisoners raised their faces, wiping the sweat with the papers. "You three, over there, to the left; you two, to the right!" shouted the *Feldwebel* at a nod from the *Sonderführer*. The prisoners continued chaffing the ones who had failed, saying, "*O, bednii Ivan!*" or, "*O, bednii Pyotr!*" and patted their shoulders as if to say, "You will be hauling stones!" They all laughed.

Again, one of the five prisoners in the third batch read excellently, fluently, pronouncing each syllable, and from time to time he raised his eyes to look at the colonel. The newspaper he was reading was an old issue of *Pravda*, dated June 24, 1941, and the page read: "The Germans have invaded Russia! Comrade soldiers, the Soviet people will win the war and will crush the invaders!" The words rang out under the rain, and the colonel laughed, the *Sonderführer*, the *Feldwebel*, the officers laughed, everybody laughed; and the prisoners also laughed, looking with envy and admiration at their companion who could read like a schoolmaster. "Well done!" said the *Sonderführer*, and his face shone. He seemed proud of the prisoner who could read so well; he was happy and proud as if the prisoner had been his pupil. "You, to the right, over there," said the *Feldwebel* in a good-natured voice, giving him a kindly push with his hand. The colonel glanced at the *Feldwebel*, started to say something, but checked himself, and I noticed that he was blushing.

The group assembled on the right laughed contentedly; those who had passed looked at their less fortunate companions with a bantering air; they pointed their fingers at their own breasts saying, "Clerks!" Making grimaces, they pointed at those who had failed and said,

"Stones on the back!" Only the prisoners who looked like workmen and who, one by one, went to swell the ranks of those sent to the left, kept silent and gazed at the colonel who, chancing to meet their eyes, blushed and shouted with a gesture of impatience, "*Schnell!*—Quick!"

The examination lasted for about an hour. When the last batch of three prisoners completed the two minutes of reading, the colonel turned to the *Feldwebel* and said, "Count them!" The *Feldwebel* began counting from a distance, pointing at each man with his finger, "*Ein, zwei, drei…*" On the left were eighty-seven, on the right were thirty-one who had passed successfully. Then, at the colonel's bidding, the *Sonderführer* began to speak. He seemed like a schoolmaster dissatisfied with his pupils. He said that he was disappointed, that he was sorry to have flunked so many, that he would have preferred to pass them all. At any rate, he added, those who had not succeeded in getting through the examination would have no reason to complain, provided they worked and displayed a greater skill than they had displayed at school. While he spoke, the group of the successful prisoners gazed at their less fortunate comrades with a compassionate air, and the younger ones dug their elbows into each other's ribs and giggled. When the *Sonderführer* had finished speaking, the colonel turned to the *Feldwebel* and said: "*Alles in Ordnung. Weg!*—Everything in order. Away!" and he walked off toward his headquarters followed by the other officers who looked back occasionally and exchanged whispers.

"You'll stay here until tomorrow, and tomorrow you will start for the labor camp," said the *Feldwebel* to the group on the left. Then he turned toward the group on the right who had passed and harshly ordered them to fall in line. As soon as the prisoners formed a close line touching one another's elbows—they looked pleased, and laughed, glancing at their companions as if making fun of them—he counted them again quickly, said, "Thirty-one," and made a sign with his hand to a squad of SS men waiting at the end of the courtyard. He ordered, "Right about, turn!" The prisoners turned right about, marched

Developments in Weapons Technology

c. 3500 BC	___ chariot (Sumer)
c. 3000 BC	___ bronze (Assyria)
c. 1500 BC	___ wrought iron (Hittite)
c. 650 BC	___ trireme (Greece)
c. 300 BC	___ steel (India)
c. 200	___ chain-mail armor (Rome)
c. 300	___ stirrup (China)
672	___ Greek fire (Byzantium)
1100	___ crossbow (France)
1160	___ longbow (England)
c. 1200	___ gunpowder (China)
c. 1250	___ rockets (China)
c. 1350	___ firearms (France)
1451	___ mortar (Ottoman Empire)
1592	___ armored warship (Korea)
1718	___ machine-gun (Great Britain)
1776	___ submarine (American colonies)
1776	___ sea mine (American colonies)
1797	___ parachute (France)
1866	___ torpedo (United Kingdom)
1903	___ airplane (United States)
1915	___ poison gas (Germany)
1916	___ tank (United Kingdom)
1918	___ aircraft carrier (United Kingdom)
1918	___ sonar (France)
1933	___ radar (United Kingdom)
1937	___ helicopter (Germany)
1939	___ jet aircraft (United Kingdom)
1942	___ napalm (United States)
1943	___ guided missile (Germany)
1945	___ atomic bomb (United States)
1953	___ hydrogen bomb (United States)
1955	___ nuclear submarine (United States)
1968	___ antiballistic missile (Soviet Union)
1977	___ neutron bomb (United States)

forward, stamping their feet hard in the mud and, when they came face to face with the wall surrounding the yard, the *Feldwebel* commanded, "Halt!" Then turning to the SS men who had lined up behind the prisoners and had already raised their tommy guns, he cleared his throat, spat on the ground, and shouted, "Fire!"

When he heard the rattle of the guns, the colonel, who was within a few steps of the office, stopped, turned abruptly; the other officers

War, my lord,
Is of eternal use to human kind,
For, ever and anon, when you have passed
A few dull years in peace and propagation,
The world is overstocked with fools and wants
A pestilence at least, if not a hero.

—G. Jeffreys

stopped and also turned. The colonel passed his hand over his face as if wiping away sweat and, followed by his officers, entered the building.

"*Ach, so,*" said the Melitopol *Sonderführer* walking past me. "Russia must be cleared of all this learned rabble. The peasants and workers who can read and write too well are dangerous. They are all Communists."

"*Natürlich,*" I replied, "but in Germany everyone, whether they are peasants or workers, can read and write well."

"The German people are a people of high *Kultur.*"

"Naturally," I replied. "The German people have a high *Kultur.*"

"*Nicht wahr?*—You think so?" said the *Sonderführer*, laughing, and walked toward headquarters.

I was left alone in the center of the yard facing the prisoners who could not read well, and my whole body was shaking.

> *A correspondent for* Corriere della Sera *during World War II, Curzio Malaparte had also fought in the Italian army. His reports from the German side of the war in Poland and the Ukraine he subsequently transformed into the novel,* Kaputt.

1945: Potsdam

THE PRICE PAID FOR DEFEAT

1. We—the President of the United States, the President of the National Government of the Republic of China, and the Prime Minister of Great Britain, representing the hundreds of millions of our countrymen, have conferred and agree that Japan shall be given an opportunity to end this war.

2. The prodigious land, sea, and air forces of the United States, the British Empire, and of China, many times reinforced by their armies and air fleets from the west, are poised to strike the final blows upon Japan. This military power is sustained and inspired by the determination of all the Allied Nations to prosecute the war against Japan until she ceases to resist.

3. The result of the futile and senseless German resistance to the might of the aroused free peoples of the world stands forth in awful clarity as an example to the people of Japan. The might that now converges on Japan is immeasurably greater than that which, when applied to the resisting Nazis, necessarily laid waste to the lands, the industry, and the method of life of the whole German people. The full application of our military power, backed by our resolve, will mean the inevitable and complete destruction of the Japanese armed forces and, just as inevitably, the utter devastation of the Japanese homeland.

4. The time has come for Japan to decide whether she will continue to be controlled by those self-willed militaristic advisers whose unintelligent calculations have brought the Empire of Japan to the threshold of annihilation, or whether she will follow the path of reason.

5. Following are our terms. We will not deviate from them. There are no alternatives. We shall brook no delay.

6. There must be eliminated for all time the authority and influence of those who have deceived and misled the people of Japan into embarking on world conquest, for we insist that a new order of peace, security, and justice will be impossible until irresponsible militarism is driven from the world.

7. Until such a new order is established, and until there is convincing proof that Japan's war-making power is destroyed, points in Japanese territory to be designated by the Allies shall be occupied to secure the achievement of the basic objectives we are here setting forth.

8. The terms of the Cairo Declaration shall be carried out, and Japanese sovereignty shall be limited to the islands of Honshu, Hokkaido, Kyushu, Shikoku, and such minor islands as we determine.

9. The Japanese military forces, after being completely disarmed, shall be permitted to return to their homes with the opportunity to lead peaceful and productive lives.

10. We do not intend that the Japanese shall be enslaved as a race or destroyed as a nation, but stern justice shall be meted out to all war criminals, including those who have visited cruelties upon our prisoners. The Japanese government shall remove all obstacles to the revival and strengthening of democratic tendencies among the Japanese people. Freedom of speech, of religion, and of thought, as well as respect for the fundamental human rights shall be established.

11. Japan shall be permitted to maintain such industries as will sustain her economy and permit the exaction of just reparations in kind, but not those which would enable her to rearm for war. To this end, access to, as distinguished from control of, raw materials shall be permitted. Eventual Japanese participation in world trade relations shall be permitted.

12. The occupying forces of the Allies shall be withdrawn from Japan as soon as these objectives have been accomplished and there has been established, in accordance with the freely expressed will of the Japanese people, a peacefully inclined and responsible government.

13. We call upon the government of Japan to proclaim now the unconditional surrender of all Japanese armed forces and to provide proper and adequate assurances of their good faith in such action. The alternative for Japan is prompt and utter destruction.

The Potsdam Declaration was issued on July 26, 1945, by the governments of Britain, China, and the United States. Within two weeks, the U.S. Army Air Forces had dropped atomic bombs on Hiroshima and Nagasaki, obliging the Japanese to accede to the terms of surrender.

The things they carried
from Tim O'Brien's *The Things They Carried*:

mosquito repellent, cigarettes, **PACKETS OF KOOL-AID**, matches, sewing kits, C rations, two or three canteens of water, M-18 colored smoke grenade, ghosts, USO stationary, pencils, pens, Sterno, trip flares, chewing tobacco, **STATUETTES OF THE SMILING BUDDHA**, The Stars and Stripes, fingernail clippers, **PSY-OPS LEAFLETS**, memory, what others could no longer bear, each other, the wounded, the weak, chess sets, basketballs, Vietnamese-English dictionaries, insignia of rank, Bronze Stars, **PURPLE HEARTS**, Code of Conduct cards, malaria, dysentery, lice, ringworm, leeches, various rots and molds, the land itself, the sky, poise, pride, a kind of dignity, **WISTFUL RESIGNATION**, stiff soldierly discipline, good humor, macho zeal, grief, terror, love, longing, shameful memories, cowardice barely restrained, **THE INSTINCT TO RUN OR FREEZE OR HIDE**, reputations

Some also carried:

canned peaches in heavy syrup, several hotel-sized bars of soap, tranquilizers, Dr. Scholl's foot powder, **SIX OR SEVEN OUNCES OF PREMIUM DOPE**, condoms, comic books, distrust of the white man, responsibility, M&M's, **TOILET PAPER**, black market Uzis, .38 caliber Smith & Wesson's, bayonets, C-4, slingshots, **BRASS KNUCKLES**, silent awe, a good-luck pebble, night-sight vitamins, brandy, a girlfriend's pantyhose, earplugs, rabbit's foot, a VC thumb

1862: Tennessee

Q & A

Headquarters, Fort Donelson
February 16.

To Brigadier-General U. S. Grant, Com'ding U.S. Forces Near Fort Donelson.

SIR: In consideration of all the circumstances governing the present situation of affairs at this station, I propose to the commanding officer of the Federal forces the appointment of commissioners to agree upon terms of capitulation of the forces and fort under my command and in that view suggest an armistice until twelve o'clock today.

> I am, sir, very respectfully,
> Your ob't se'v't,
> S. B. Buckner,
> Brig. Gen., C. S. A.

Headquarters, Army in the Field Camp near Donelson
February 16.

To General S. B. Buckner, Confederate Army.

SIR: Yours of this date, proposing armistice and appointment of commissioners to settle terms of capitulation, is just received. No terms except an unconditional and immediate surrender can be accepted. I propose to move immediately upon your works.

> I am, sir, very respectfully,
> Your ob't se'v't,
> U. S. Grant,
> Brig. Gen.

Headquarters, Dover
February 16.

To Brig. Gen'l U. S. Grant, U.S. Army.

SIR: The distribution of the forces under my command, incident to an unexpected change of commanders, and the overwhelming force under your command, compel me, notwithstanding the brilliant success of the Confederate arms yesterday, to accept the ungenerous and unchivalrous terms which you propose.

> I am, sir,
> Your very ob't se'v't,
> S. B. Buckner,
> Brig. Gen., C. S. A.

Generals Grant and Buckner were friends who had known one another since they were fellow students at West Point. The ultimatum earned Grant the nickname "Unconditional Surrender."

Achilles and Memnon. Greek bowl, c. 490 BC.

c. 1943: Pianosa

JOSEPH HELLER GETS THE CATCH

"You're wasting your time," Doc Daneeka was forced to tell him.

"Can't you ground someone who's crazy?"

"Oh, sure. I have to. There's a rule saying I have to ground anyone who's crazy."

"Then why don't you ground me? I'm crazy. Ask Clevinger."

"Clevinger? Where *is* Clevinger? You find Clevinger and I'll ask him."

"Then ask any of the others. They'll tell you how crazy I am."

"They're crazy."

"Then why don't you ground them?"

"Why don't they ask me to ground them?"

"Because they're crazy, that's why."

"Of course they're crazy," Doc Daneeka replied. "I just told you they're crazy, didn't I? And you can't let crazy people decide whether you're crazy or not, can you?"

Yossarian looked at him soberly and tried another approach. "Is Orr crazy?"

"He sure is," Doc Daneeka said.

"Can you ground him?"

"I sure can. But first he has to ask me to. That's part of the rule."

"Then why doesn't he ask you to?"

"Because he's crazy," Doc Daneeka said. "He has to be crazy to keep flying combat missions after all the close calls he's had. Sure, I can

ground Orr. But first he has to ask me to."

"That's all he has to do to be grounded?"

"That's all. Let him ask me."

"And then you can ground him?" Yossarian asked.

"No. Then I can't ground him."

"You mean there's a catch?"

"Sure there's a catch," Doc Daneeka replied. "Catch-22. Anyone who wants to get out of combat duty isn't really crazy."

There was only one catch and that was Catch-22, which specified that a concern for one's own safety in the face of dangers that were real and immediate was the process of a rational mind. Orr was crazy and could be grounded. All he had to do was ask; and as soon as he did, he would no longer be crazy and would have to fly more missions. Orr would be crazy to fly more missions and sane if he didn't, but if he was sane he had to fly them. If he flew them he was crazy and didn't have to; but if he didn't want to he was sane and had to. Yossarian was moved very deeply by the absolute simplicity of this clause of Catch-22 and let out a respectful whistle.

"That's some catch, that Catch-22," he observed.

"It's the best there is," Doc Daneeka agreed.

From Catch-22, *his novel published in 1961. Heller flew sixty missions as a B-25 bombardier in World War II.*

416 BC: Melos

THE STRONG DO WHAT THEY CAN, AND THE WEAK SUBMIT

Athenians

If you have met us in order to make surmises about the future, or for any other purpose than to look existing facts in the face and to discuss the safety of your city on this basis, we will break off the conversations; otherwise, we are ready to speak.

Melians

In our position it is natural and excusable to explore many ideas and arguments. But the problem that has brought us here is our security, so, if you think fit, let the discussion follow the line you propose.

Athenians

Then we will not make a long and unconvincing speech, full of fine phrases, to prove that our victory over Persia justifies our empire, or that we are now attacking you because you have wronged us. Let each of us say what we really think and reach a practical agreement. You know and we know, as practical men, that the question of justice arises only between parties equal in strength, and that the strong do what they can, and the weak submit.

Melians

As you ignore justice and have made self-interest the basis of discussion, we must take the same ground, and we say that in our opinion it is in your interest to maintain a principle which is for the good of all—that anyone in danger should have just and equitable treatment and any advantage, even if not strictly his due, which he can secure by persuasion. This is your interest as much as ours, for your fall would involve you in a crushing punishment that would be a lesson to the world.

Athenians

Leave that danger to us to face. At the moment we shall prove that we have come in the interest of our empire and that in what we shall say we are seeking the safety of your state; for we wish you to become our subjects with least trouble to ourselves, and we would like you to survive in our interests as well as your own.

Melians

It may be your interest to be our masters; how can it be ours to be your slaves?

Athenians

By submitting you would avoid a terrible fate, and we should gain by not destroying you.

Melians

Would you not agree to an arrangement under which we should keep out of the war, and be your friends instead of your enemies, but neutral?

Athenians

No. Your hostility injures us less than your friendship. That, to our subjects, is an illustration of our weakness, while your hatred exhibits our power.

Melians

But do you see no safety in our neutrality? Will you not make enemies of all neutral powers when they see your conduct and reflect that someday you will attack them? Will not your action strengthen your existing opponents, and induce those who would otherwise never be your enemies to become so against their will?

Athenians

No. The mainland states, secure in their freedom, will be slow to take defensive measures against us, and we do not consider them so formidable as independent island powers like yourselves, or subjects already smarting under our yoke. These are most likely to take a thoughtless step and bring themselves and us into obvious danger.

Melians

Surely then, if you are ready to risk so much to maintain your empire, and the enslaved peoples so much to escape from it, it would be criminal cowardice in us, who are still free, not to take any and every measure before submitting to slavery.

Athenians

No, if you reflect calmly, for this is not a competition in heroism between equals where your honor is at stake, but a question of self-preservation, to save you from a struggle with a far stronger power.

Melians

Still, we know that in war fortune is more impartial than the disproportion in numbers might lead one to expect. If we submit at once, our position is desperate; if we fight, there is still a hope that we shall stand secure.

Athenians

Hope encourages men to take risks; men in a strong position may follow her without ruin, if not without loss. But when they stake all that they have to the last coin (for she is a spendthrift), she reveals her real self in the hour of failure, and when her nature is known, she leaves them without means of self-protection. You are weak, your future hangs on a turn of the scales; avoid the mistake most men make, who might save themselves by human means, and then, when visible hopes desert them, in their extremity turn to the invisible—prophecies and oracles and all those things which delude men with hopes, to their destruction.

Melians

Still, we trust that heaven will not allow us to be worsted by fortune, for in this quarrel we are right and you are wrong. Besides, we expect the support of Sparta to supply the deficiencies in our strength, for she is bound to help us as her kinsmen, if for no other reason, and from a sense of honor. So our confidence is not entirely unreasonable.

Athenians

You said that you proposed to discuss the safety of your city, but we observe that in all your speeches you have never said a word on which any reasonable expectation of it could be founded. Your strength lies in deferred hopes; in comparison with the forces now arrayed against you, your resources are too small for any hope of success. You will show a great want of judgment if you do not come to a more reasonable decision after we have withdrawn. Surely you will not fall back on the idea of honor, which has been the ruin of so many when danger and disgrace were staring them in the face. How often, when men have seen the fate to which they were tending, have they been enslaved by a phrase and drawn by the power of this seductive word to fall of their own free will into irreparable disaster, bringing on themselves by their folly a greater dishonor than fortune could inflict! If you are wise, you will avoid that fate. The greatest of cities makes you a fair offer: to keep your own land and become her tributary ally; there is no dishonor in that. The choice between war and safety is given you; do not obstinately take the worse alternative. The most successful people are those who stand up to their equals, behave properly to their superiors, and treat their inferiors fairly. Think it over, and reflect once and again that you have only one country, and that its prosperity or ruin depends on one decision.

Melians

Our resolution, Athenians, is unaltered. We will not in a moment deprive of freedom a city that has existed for seven hundred years; we put our trust in the fortune by which the gods have preserved it until now, and in the help of men, that is, of the Spartans; and so we will try and save ourselves. Meanwhile, we invite you to allow us to be friends to you and foes to neither party, and to retire from our country after making such a treaty as shall seem fit to us both.

Athenians

To judge from your decision, you are unique in regarding the future as more certain than the present and in allowing your wishes to convert the unseen into reality; and as you have staked most on, and trusted most in, the Spartans, your fortune, and your hopes, so will you be most completely deceived.

Thucydides, *from* History of the Peloponnesian War. *The Athenian army that came ashore on the island of Melos in the summer of 416 BC offered the Melians a discussion. Thucydides records the last exchange of views before every Melian man of military age was executed and the women and children sold for slaves.*

The 2nd of May, 1808: The Charge of the Mamelukes, by Francisco de Goya y Lucientes, 1814.

FIELD REPORTS

c. 1970: Vietnam

FIRST BLOOD

His jaw was in his throat, his upper lip and teeth were gone, his one eye was shut, his other eye was a star-shaped hole, his eyebrows were thin and arched like a woman's, his nose was undamaged, there was a slight tear at the lobe of one ear, his clean black hair was swept upward into a cowlick at the rear of the skull, his forehead was lightly freckled, his fingernails were clean, the skin at his left cheek was peeled back in three ragged strips, his right cheek was smooth and hairless, there was a butterfly on his chin, his neck was open to the spinal cord and the blood there was thick and shiny and it was this wound that had killed him. He lay face-up in the center of the trail, a slim, dead, almost dainty young man. He had bony legs, a narrow waist, long shapely fingers. His chest was sunken and poorly muscled—a scholar, maybe. His wrists were the wrists of a child. He wore a black shirt, black pajama pants, a gray ammunition belt, a gold ring on the third finger of his right hand. His rubber sandals had been blown off. One lay beside him, the other a few meters up the trail. He had been born, maybe, in 1946 in the village of My Khe near the central coastline of Quang Ngai Province, where his parents farmed, and where his family had lived for several centuries, and where, during the time of the French, his father and two uncles and many neighbors had joined in the struggle for independence. He was not a Communist. He was a citizen and a soldier. In the village of My Khe, as in all of Quang Ngai,

patriotic resistance had the force of tradition, which was partly the force of legend, and from his earliest boyhood the man I killed would have listened to stories about the heroic Trung sisters and Tran Hung Dao's famous rout of the Mongols and Le Loi's final victory against the Chinese at Tot Dong. He would have been taught that to defend the land was a man's highest duty and highest privilege. He had accepted this. It was never open to question. Secretly, though, it also frightened him. He was not a fighter. His health was poor, his body small and frail. He liked books. He wanted someday to be a teacher of mathematics. At night, lying on his mat, he could not picture himself doing the brave things his father had done, or his uncles, or the heroes of the stories. He hoped in his heart that he would never be tested. He hoped the Americans would go away. Soon, he hoped. He kept hoping and hoping, always, even when he was asleep.

"Oh, man, you fuckin' trashed the fucker," Azar said. "You scrambled his sorry self, look at that, you *did*, you laid him out like Shredded fuckin' Wheat."

"Go away," Kiowa said.

"I'm just saying the truth. Like oatmeal."

"Go," Kiowa said.

"Okay, then, I take it back," Azar said. He started to move away, then stopped and said, "Rice Krispies, you know? On the dead test, this particular individual gets A-plus."

Smiling at this, he shrugged and walked

up the trail toward the village behind the trees.

Kiowa kneeled down.

"Just forget that crud," he said. He opened up his canteen and held it out for a while and then sighed and pulled it away. "No sweat, man. What else could you do?"

Later, Kiowa said, "I'm serious. Nothing *anybody* could do. Come on, stop staring."

The trail junction was shaded by a row of trees and tall brush. The slim young man lay with his legs in the shade. His jaw was in his

I went [to war] because I couldn't help it. I didn't want the glory or the pay; I wanted the right thing done. —Louisa May Alcott, 1863

throat. His one eye was shut and the other was a star-shaped hole.

Kiowa glanced at the body.

"All right, let me ask a question," he said. "You want to trade places with him? Turn it all upside down—you *want* that? I mean, be honest."

The star-shaped hole was red and yellow. The yellow part seemed to be getting wider, spreading out at the center of the star. The upper lip and gum and teeth were gone. The man's head was cocked at a wrong angle, as if loose at the neck, and the neck was wet with blood.

"Think it over," Kiowa said.

Then later he said, "Tim, it's a *war*. The guy wasn't Heidi—he had a weapon, right? It's a tough thing, for sure, but you got to cut out that staring. "

Then he said, "Maybe you better lie down a minute."

Then after a long empty time he said, "Take it slow. Just go wherever the spirit takes you."

The butterfly was making its way along the young man's forehead, which was spotted with small dark freckles. The nose was undamaged. The skin on the right cheek was smooth and fine-grained and hairless. Frail-looking, delicately boned, the young man would not have wanted to be a soldier and in his heart would have feared performing badly in battle. Even as a

boy growing up in the village of My Khe, he had often worried about this. He imagined covering his head and lying in a deep hole and closing his eyes and not moving until the war was over. He had no stomach for violence. He loved mathematics. His eyebrows were thin and arched like a woman's, and at school the boys sometimes teased him about how pretty he was, the arched eyebrows and long shapely fingers, and on the playground they mimicked a woman's walk and made fun of his smooth skin and his love for mathematics. The young man could not make himself fight them. He often wanted to, but he was afraid, and this increased his shame. If he could not fight little boys, he thought, how could he ever become a soldier and fight the Americans with their airplanes and helicopters and bombs? It did not seem possible. In the presence of his father and uncles, he pretended to look forward to doing his patriotic duty, which was also a privilege, but at night he prayed with his mother that the war might end soon. Beyond anything else, he was afraid of disgracing himself, and therefore his family and village. But all he could do, he thought, was wait and pray and try not to grow up too fast.

"Listen to me," Kiowa said. "You feel terrible, I know that."

Then he said, "Okay, maybe I *don't* know."

Along the trail there were small blue flowers shaped like bells. The young man's head was wrenched sideways, not quite facing the flowers, and even in the shade a single blade of sunlight sparkled against the buckle of his ammunition belt. The left cheek was peeled back in three ragged strips. The wounds at his neck had not yet clotted, which made him seem animate even in death, the blood still spreading out across his shirt.

Kiowa shook his head.

There was some silence before he said, "Stop *staring*."

The young man's fingernails were clean. There was a slight tear at the lobe of one ear, a sprinkling of blood on the forearm. He wore a gold ring on the third finger of his right hand. His chest was sunken and poorly muscled—a scholar, maybe. His life was now a constellation of possibilities. So, yes, maybe a scholar. And for years, despite his family's poverty, the man I killed would have been determined to continue his education in mathematics. The means for this were arranged, perhaps, through the village liberation cadres, and in 1964 the young man began attending classes at the university in Saigon, where he avoided politics and paid attention to the problems of calculus. He devoted himself to his studies. He spent his nights alone, wrote romantic poems in his journal, took pleasure in the grace and beauty of differential equations. The war, he knew, would finally take him, but for the time being he would not let himself think about it. He had stopped praying; instead, now, he waited. And as he waited, in his final year at the university, he fell in love with a classmate, a girl of seventeen, who one day told him that his wrists were like the wrists of a child, so small and delicate, and who admired his narrow waist and the cowlick that rose up like a bird's tail at the back of his head. She liked his quiet manner; she laughed at his freckles and bony legs. One evening, perhaps, they exchanged gold rings.

Now one eye was a star.

"You okay?" Kiowa said.

The body lay almost entirely in shade. There were gnats at the mouth, little flecks of pollen drifting above the nose. The butterfly was gone. The bleeding had stopped except for the neck wounds.

Kiowa picked up the rubber sandals, clapping off the dirt, then bent down to search the body. He found a pouch of rice, a comb, a fingernail clipper, a few soiled piasters, a snapshot of a young woman standing in front of a parked motorcycle. Kiowa placed these items in his rucksack along with the gray ammunition belt and rubber sandals.

Then he squatted down.

"I'll tell you the straight truth," he said. "The guy was dead the second he stepped on the trail. Understand me? We all had him zeroed. A good kill—weapon, ammunition, everything." Tiny beads of sweat glistened at Kiowa's forehead. His eyes moved from the sky to the dead man's body to the knuckles of his own hands. "So listen, you best pull your shit together. Can't just sit here all day."

Later he said, "Understand?"

Then he said, "Five minutes, Tim. Five more minutes and we're moving out."

The one eye did a funny twinkling trick, red to yellow. His head was wrenched sideways, as if loose at the neck, and the dead young man seemed to be staring at some distant object beyond the bell-shaped flowers along the trail. The blood at the neck had gone to a deep purplish black. Clean fingernails, clean hair—he had been a soldier for only a single day. After his years at the university, the man I killed returned with his new wife to the village of My Khe, where he enlisted as a common rifleman with the 48th Vietcong Battalion. He knew he would die quickly. He knew he would see a flash of light. He knew he would fall dead and wake up in the stories of his village and people.

A civil war is like the heat of a fever, but a foreign war is like the heat of exercise and serveth to keep the body in health.
                              —Francis Bacon, 1625

Kiowa covered the body with a poncho.

"Hey, you're looking better," he said. "No doubt about it. All you needed was time—some mental R&R."

Then he said, "Man, I'm sorry."

Then later he said, "Why not talk about it?"

Then he said, "Come on, man, talk."

He was a slim, dead, almost dainty young man of about twenty. He lay with one leg bent beneath him, his jaw in his throat, his face neither expressive nor inexpressive. One eye was shut. The other was a star-shaped hole.

"Talk," Kiowa said.

Tim O'Brien, The Things They Carried, *a collection of short stories published in 1990. The stories derived from the author's year as an infantry footsoldier with the Americal Division in Vietnam.*

1453: Constantinople

REGIME CHANGE

Several days were employed by the sultan in the preparations of the assault, and a respite was granted by his favourite science of astrology, which had fixed on the twenty-ninth of May as the fortunate and fatal hour. On the evening of the twenty-seventh, he issued his final orders, assembled in his presence the military chiefs, and dispersed his heralds through the camp to proclaim the duty and the motives of the perilous enterprise. Fear is the first principle of a despotic government, and his menaces were expressed in the Oriental style that the fugitives and deserters, had they the wings of a bird, should not escape from his inexorable justice. In this holy warfare, the Moslems were exhorted to purify their minds with prayer, their bodies with seven ablutions, and to abstain from food till the close of the ensuing day. A crowd of dervishes visited the tents to instil the desire of martyrdom and the assurance of spending an immortal youth amidst the rivers and gardens of paradise, and in the embraces of the black-eyed virgins. Yet Mahomet principally trusted to the efficacy of temporal and visible rewards. A double pay was promised to the victorious troops; "The city and the buildings," said Mahomet, "are mine, but I resign to your valour the captives and the spoil, the treasures of gold and beauty: be rich and be happy. Many are the provinces of my empire: The intrepid soldier who first ascends the walls of Constantinople shall be rewarded with the government of the fairest and most wealthy, and my gratitude shall accumulate his honours and fortunes above the measure of his own hopes." Such various and potent motives diffused among the Turks a general ardour, regardless of life and impatient for action: the camp re-echoed with the Moslem shouts of "God is Good: there is but one God, and Mahomet is the Apostle of God."

At daybreak, without the customary signal of the morning gun, the Turks assaulted the city

Bloody footprints in the snow, Kosovo, 1999. Photograph by Andrew Testa.

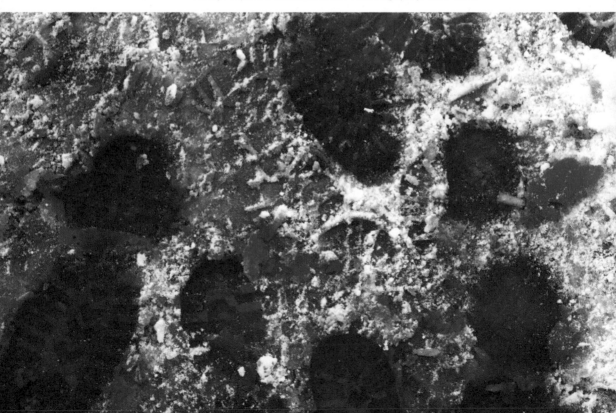

by sea and land, and the similitude of a twined or twisted thread had been applied to the closeness and continuity of their line of attack. The foremost ranks consisted, of the refuse of the host, a voluntary crowd who fought without order or command, of the feebleness of age or childhood, of peasants and vagrants, and of all who had joined the camp in the blind hope of plunder and martyrdom. The common impulse drove them onwards to the wall; the most audacious to climb were instantly precipitated; and not a dart, not a bullet of the Christians was idly wasted on the accumulated throng. But their strength and ammunition were exhausted in this laborious defence: The ditch was filled with the bodies of the slain; they supported the footsteps of their companions, and of this devoted vanguard, the death was more serviceable than the life. Under their respective *bashaws* [officers] and *sanjaks* [banners], the troops of Anatolia and Romania were successively led to the charge; their progress was various and doubtful, but after a conflict of two hours, the Greeks still maintained, and improved, their advantage; and the voice of the emperor was heard, encouraging his soldiers to achieve, by a last effort, the deliverance of their country. In that fatal moment, the Janizaries arose, fresh, vigorous, and invincible. The sultan himself on horseback, with an iron mace in his hand, was the spectator and judge of their valour; he was surrounded by ten thousand of his domestic troops, whom he reserved for the decisive occasions, and the tide of battle was directed and impelled by his voice and eye. His numerous ministers of justice were posted behind the line, to urge, to restrain, and to punish; and if danger was in the front, shame and inevitable death were in the rear of the fugitives. The cries of fear and of pain were drowned in the martial music of drums, trumpets, and attaballs; and experience has proved that the mechanical operation of sounds, by quickening the circulation of the blood and spirits, will act on the human machine more forcibly than the eloquence of reason and honour. From the lines, the gallies, and the bridge, the Ottoman artillery thun-

dered on all sides; and the camp and city, the Greeks and the Turks, were involved in a cloud of smoke which could only be dispelled by the final deliverance or destruction of the Roman Empire. The single combats of the heroes of history or fable amuse our fancy and engage

You furnish the pictures, and I'll furnish the war. —William Randolph Hearst, 1898

our affections; the skilful evolutions of war may inform the mind and improve a necessary, though pernicious, science. But in the uniform and odious pictures of a general assault, all is blood, and horror, and confusion; nor shall I strive, at the distance of three centuries and a thousand miles, to delineate a scene, of which there could be no spectators, and of which the actors themselves were incapable of forming any just or adequate idea.

The victorious Turks rushed through the breaches of the inner wall, and as they advanced into the streets, they were soon joined by their brethren, who had forced the gate Phenar on the side of the harbour. In the first heat of the pursuit, about two thousand Christians were put to the sword, but avarice soon prevailed over cruelty, and the victors acknowledged that they should immediately have given quarter if the valour of the emperor and his chosen bands had not prepared them for a similar opposition in every part of the capital. It was thus, after a siege of fifty-three days, that Constantinople, which had defied the power of Chosroes, the Chagan, and the caliphs, was irretrievably subdued by the arms of Mahomet the Second. Her empire only had been subverted by the Latins; her religion was trampled in the dust by the Moslem conquerors.

The tidings of misfortune fly with a rapid wing, yet such was the extent of Constantinople, that the more distant quarters might prolong some moments the happy ignorance of their ruin. But in the general consternation, in the feelings of selfish or social anxiety, in the tumult and thunder of the assault, a *sleepless* night and morning must have elapsed; nor can I believe that many Grecian ladies were awakened by the Janizaries from a sound and tranquil slumber. On the assurance of the public calamity, the houses and convents were instantly deserted, and the trembling inhabitants flocked together in the streets like a herd of timid animals, as if accumulated weakness could be productive of strength, or in the vain hope that amid the crowd, each individual might be safe and invisible. From every part of the capital, they flowed into the church of Saint Sophia; in the space of an hour, the sanctuary, the choir, the nave, the upper and lower galleries were filled with the multitudes of fathers and husbands, of women and children, of priests, monks, and religious virgins; the doors were barred on the inside, and they sought protection from the sacred dome, which they had so lately abhorred as a profane and polluted edifice. Their confidence was founded on the prophecy of an enthusiast or impostor, that one day the Turks would enter Constantinople and pursue the Romans as far as the column of Constantine in the square before Saint Sophia, but that this would be the term of their calamities: that an angel would descend from heaven, with a sword in his hand, and would deliver the empire, with that celestial weapon, to a poor man seated at the foot of the column. "Take this sword," would he say, "and avenge the people of the Lord." At these animating words, the Turks would instantly fly, and the victorious Romans would drive them from the West, and from all Anatolia, as far as the frontiers of Persia.

While they expected the descent of the tardy angel, the doors were broken with axes, and as the Turks encountered no resistance, their bloodless hands were employed in selecting and securing the multitude of their prisoners. Youth, beauty, and the appearance of wealth attracted

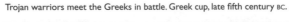
Trojan warriors meet the Greeks in battle. Greek cup, late fifth century BC.

their choice, and the right of property was decided among themselves by a prior seizure, by personal strength, and by the authority of command. In the space of an hour, the male captives were bound with cords, the females with their veils and girdles. The senators were linked with their slaves, the prelates with the porters of the church, and young men of a plebeian class, with noble maids, whose faces had been invisible to the sun and their nearest kindred. In this common captivity, the ranks of society were confounded; the ties of nature were cut asunder; and the inexorable soldier was careless of the father's groans, the tears of the mother, and the lamentations of the children. The loudest in their wailings were the nuns, who were torn from the altar with naked bosoms, outstretched hands, and dishevelled hair; and we should piously believe that few could be tempted to prefer the vigils of the harem to those of the monastery. Of these unfortunate Greeks, of these domestic animals, whole strings were rudely driven through the streets, and as the conquerors were eager to return for more prey, their trembling pace was quickened with menaces and blows. At the same hour, a similar rapine was exercised in all the churches and monasteries, in all the palaces and habitations of the capital; nor could any place, however sacred or sequestered, protect the persons or the property of the Greeks. Above sixty thousand of this devoted people were transported from the city to the camp and fleet, exchanged or sold according to the caprice or interest of their masters, and dispersed in remote servitude through the provinces of the Ottoman Empire.

The wealth of Constantinople had been granted by the sultan to his victorious troops, and the rapine of an hour is more productive than the industry of years. But as no regular division was attempted of the spoil, the rewards of valour were stolen away by the followers of the camp who had declined the toil and danger of the battle. The narrative of their depredations could not afford either amusement or instruction: the total amount, in the last poverty of the empire, has been valued at four millions of ducats; and of this sum, a small part was the property of the Venetians, the Genoese, the Florentines, and the merchants of Ancona. Of these foreigners, the stock was improved in quick and perpetual circulation: But the riches of the Greeks were displayed in the idle ostentation of palaces and wardrobes, or deeply buried in treasures of ingots and old coin, lest

> *The free man is a warrior. He tramples ruthlessly upon that contemptible kind of comfort that grocers, Christians, cows, women, Englishmen, and other democrats worship.*   —*Friedrich Nietzsche, 1889*

it should be demanded at their hands for the defence of their country. The profanation and plunder of the monasteries and churches excited the most tragic complaints. The dome of Saint Sophia itself, the earthly heaven, the second firmament, the vehicle of the cherubim, the throne of the glory of God, was despoiled of the oblations of ages; and the gold and silver, the pearls and jewels, the vases and sacerdotal ornaments were most wickedly converted to the service of mankind. After the divine images had been stripped of all that could be valuable to a profane eye, the canvases, or the wood, was torn, or broken, or burnt, or trod under foot, or applied, in the stables or the kitchen, to the vilest uses. The example of sacrilege was imitated, however, from the Latin conquerors of Constantinople, and the treatment which Christ, the Virgin, and the saints had sustained from the guilty Catholic might be inflicted by the zealous Musulman on the monuments of idolatry. Perhaps, instead of joining the public clamour, a philosopher will observe, that in the decline of the arts, the workmanship could not be more valuable than the work, and that a fresh supply of visions and miracles would speedily be renewed by the craft of the priest and the credulity of the people.

Edward Gibbon, *from his* History of the Decline and Fall of the Roman Empire.

c. 1250 bc: Troy

VIRGIL BESTOWS ON THE KING OF TROY
THE CONSOLATION OF AN IMMORTAL DEATH

There at the very edge of the front gates
springs Pyrrhus, son of Achilles, prancing in arms,
aflash in his shimmering brazen sheath like a snake
buried the whole winter long under frozen turf,
swollen to bursting, fed full on poisonous weeds
and now it springs into light, sloughing its old skin
to glisten sleek in its newfound youth, its back slithering,
coiling, its proud chest rearing high to the sun,
its triple tongue flickering through its fangs.
Backing him now comes Periphas, giant fighter,
Automedon too, Achilles' henchman, charioteer
who bore the great man's armor—backing Pyrrhus,
the young fighters from Scyros raid the palace,
hurling firebrands at the roofs. Out in the lead,
Pyrrhus seizes a double-axe and batters the rocky sill
and ripping the bronze posts out of their sockets,
hacking the rugged oaken planks of the doors,
makes a breach, a gaping maw, and there, exposed,
the heart of the house, the sweep of the colonnades,
the palace depths of the old kings and Priam lie exposed
and they see the armed sentries bracing at the portals.

But all in the house is turmoil, misery, groans,
the echoing chambers ring with cries of women,
wails of mourning hit the golden stars.
Mothers scatter in panic down the palace halls
and embrace the pillars, cling to them, kiss them hard.
But on he comes, Pyrrhus with all his father's force,
no bolts, not even the guards can hold him back—
under the ram's repeated blows the doors cave in,
the doorposts, prised from their sockets, crash flat.
Force makes a breach and the Greeks come storming through,
butcher the sentries, flood the entire place with men-at-arms.
No river so wild, so frothing in spate, bursting its banks
to overpower the dikes, anything in its way, its cresting
tides stampeding in fury down on the fields to sweep
the flocks and stalls across the open plain.
I saw him myself, Pyrrhus crazed with carnage
and Atreus' two sons just at the threshold—

I saw
Hecuba with her hundred daughters and daughters-in-law,
saw Priam fouling with blood the altar fires
he himself had blessed.

Those fifty bridal-chambers
filled with the hope of children's children still to come,
the pillars proud with trophies, gilded with Eastern gold,
they all come tumbling down—
and the Greeks hold what the raging fire spares.

Perhaps you wonder how Priam met his end.
When he saw his city stormed and seized, his gates
wrenched apart, the enemy camped in his palace depths,
the old man dons his armor long unused, he clamps it
round his shoulders shaking with age and, all for nothing,
straps his useless sword to his hip, then makes
for the thick of battle, out to meet his death.
At the heart of the house an ample altar stood,
naked under the skies,
an ancient laurel bending over the shrine,
embracing our household gods within its shade.
Here, flocking the altar, Hecuba and her daughters
huddled, blown headlong down like doves by a black storm—
clutching, all for nothing, the figures of their gods.
Seeing Priam decked in the arms he'd worn as a young man,
"Are you insane?" she cries, "poor husband, what impels you
to strap that sword on now? Where are you rushing?
Too late for such defense, such help. Not even
my own Hector, if *he* came to the rescue now…
Come to me, Priam. This altar will shield us all
or else you'll die with us."

With those words,
drawing him toward her there, she made a place
for the old man beside the holy shrine.

Suddenly,

Detail from *Sketches of War Machines*, by Leonardo da Vinci.

look, a son of Priam, Polites, just escaped
from slaughter at Pyrrhus' hands, comes racing in
through spears, through enemy fighters, fleeing down
the long arcades and deserted hallways—badly wounded,
Pyrrhus hot on his heels, a weapon poised for the kill,
about to seize him, about to run him through and pressing
home as Polites reaches his parents and collapses,
vomiting out his lifeblood before their eyes.
At that, Priam, trapped in the grip of death,
not holding back, not checking his words, his rage:
"You!" he cries, "you and your vicious crimes!
If any power on high recoils at such an outrage,
let the gods repay you for all your reckless work,
grant you the thanks, the rich reward you've earned.
You've made me see my son's death with my own eyes,
defiled a father's sight with a son's lifeblood.
You say you're Achilles' son? You lie! Achilles
never treated his enemy Priam so. No, he honored
a suppliant's rights, he blushed to betray my trust,
he restored my Hector's bloodless corpse for burial,
sent me safely home to the land I rule!"

                                    With that
and with all his might the old man flings his spear—
but too impotent now to pierce, it merely grazes
Pyrrhus' brazen shield that blocks its way
and clings there, dangling limp from the boss,
all for nothing. Pyrrhus shouts back: "Well then,
down you go, a messenger to my father, Peleus' son!
Tell him about my vicious work, how Neoptolemus
degrades his father's name—don't you forget.
Now—die!"

          That said, he drags the old man
straight to the altar, quaking, slithering on through
slicks of his son's blood, and twisting Priam's hair
in his left hand, his right hand sweeping forth his sword—
a flash of steel—he buries it hilt-deep in the king's flank.

          Such was the fate of Priam, his death, his lot on earth,
with Troy blazing before his eyes, her ramparts down,
the monarch who once had ruled in all his glory
the many lands of Asia, Asia's many tribes.
A powerful trunk is lying on the shore.
The head wrenched from the shoulders.
A corpse without a name.

> *From the* Aeneid, *Book II*

The Rambo Movies Body Count*	First Blood	Rambo: First Blood, Part II	Rambo III
Number of bad guys killed by Rambo with his shirt on	1	12	33
Number of bad guys killed by Rambo with his shirt off	0	46	45
Total number of bad guys killed by Rambo regardless of attire	1	58	78
Number of bad guys killed by accomplices of Rambo acting on their own	0	10	17
Number of good guys killed by bad guys	0	1	37
Total number of people killed	1	69	132
Number of people killed per minute	0.01	0.72	1.30
Time at which the first person is killed	0:29:31	0:33:34	0:41:09
Number of people killed per minute from that point until the end of the film (not including ending credits)	0.02	1.18	2.39
Sequences in which Rambo is shot at without significant result	12	24	38
Number of sequences in which good guys are tortured by bad guys	2	5	7
Number of sex scenes	0	0	0

*The body count includes only those who visibly fall inert after being bombed, garroted, blasted, stabbed, or strangled; blown up by mines, artillery, grenades, or other explosives; shot by bullets, artillery, or arrows; incinerated by fires or flame throwers; bludgeoned or beaten; pushed or tossed off precipices or aircraft; or having their necks snapped. In addition, there are many instances in which Rambo blows up tanks, helicopters, cars, trucks, guard towers, and other buildings that are occupied. These presumed fatalities are not included in the body count unless the people inside are clearly shown to die by, for example, bolting into the open from their erstwhile place of refuge, clutching various body parts, grimacing meaningfully, and collapsing to the ground.

1937: Catalonia

GEORGE ORWELL REFLECTS ON THE
BLOOD BUBBLING OUT OF HIS MOUTH

The whole experience of being hit by a bullet is very interesting, and I think it is worth describing in detail.

It was at the corner of the parapet, at five o'clock in the morning. This was always a dangerous time because we had the dawn at our backs, and if you stuck your head above the parapet, it was clearly outlined against the sky. I was talking to the sentries preparatory to changing the guard. Suddenly, in the very middle of saying something, I felt—it is very hard to describe what I felt, though I remember it with the utmost vividness.

Roughly speaking, it was the sensation of being *at the center* of an explosion. There seemed to be a loud bang and a blinding flash of light all round me, and I felt a tremendous shock—no pain, only a violent shock, such as you get from an electric terminal; with it a sense of utter weakness, a feeling of being stricken and shriveled up to nothing. The sandbags in front of me receded into immense distance. I fancy you would feel much the same if you were struck by lightning. I knew immediately that I was hit, but because of the seeming bang and flash, I thought it was a rifle nearby that had gone off accidentally and shot me. All this happened in a space of time much less than a second. The next moment my knees crumpled up and I was falling, my head hitting the ground with a violent bang which, to my relief, did not hurt. I had a numb, dazed feeling, a consciousness of being very badly hurt, but no pain in the ordinary sense.

The American sentry I had been talking to had started forward. "Gosh! Are you hit?" People gathered round. There was the usual fuss—"Lift him up! Where's he hit? Get his shirt open!" etc., etc. The American called for a knife to cut my shirt open. I knew that there was one in my pocket and tried to get it out, but discovered that my right arm was paralyzed. Not being in pain, I felt a vague satisfaction. This ought to please my wife, I thought; she had always wanted me to be wounded, which would save me from being killed when the great battle came. It was only now that it occurred to me to wonder where I was hit, and how badly; I could feel nothing, but I was conscious that the bullet had struck me somewhere in the front of the body. When I tried to speak I found that I had no voice, only a faint squeak, but at the second attempt I managed to ask where I was hit. In the throat, they said. Harry Webb, our stretcher-bearer, had brought a bandage and one of the little bottles of alcohol they gave us for field-dressings. As they lifted me up, a lot of blood poured out of my mouth, and I heard a Spaniard behind me say that the bullet had gone clean through my neck. I felt the alcohol, which at ordinary times would sting like the devil, splash on to the wound as a pleasant coolness.

They laid me down again while somebody fetched a stretcher. As soon as I knew that the bullet had gone clean through my neck, I took it

1945: B-24 Liberator

THE DEATH OF THE BALL TURRET GUNNER

From my mother's sleep I fell into the State,
And I hunched in its belly till my wet fur froze.
Six miles from earth, loosed from its dream of life,
I woke to black flak and the nightmare fighters.
When I died they washed me out of the turret with a hose.

Randall Jarrell, *who published the poem in 1945, served as an Army
control tower operator in World War II.*

for granted that I was done for. I had never heard of a man or an animal getting a bullet through the middle of the neck and surviving it. The blood was dribbling out of the corner of my mouth. "The artery's gone," I thought. I wondered how long you last when your carotid artery is cut; not many minutes, presumably. Everything was very blurry. There must have been about two minutes during which I assumed that I was killed. And that too was interesting—I mean it is interesting to know what your thoughts would be at such a time. My first thought, conventionally enough, was for my wife. My second was a violent resentment at having to leave this world which, when all is said and done, suits me so well. I had time to feel this very vividly. The stupid mischance infuriated me. The meaninglessness of it! To be bumped off, not even in battle, but in this stale corner of the trenches, thanks to a moment's carelessness! I thought, too, of the man who had shot me—wondered what he was like, whether he was a Spaniard or a foreigner, whether he knew he had got me, and so forth. I could not feel any resentment against him. I reflected that as he was a Fascist, I would have killed him if I could, but that if he had been taken prisoner and brought before me at this moment I would merely have congratulated him on his good shooting.

It may be, though, that if you were really dying your thoughts would be quite different.

They had just got me on to the stretcher when my paralyzed right arm came to life and began hurting damnably. At the time I imagined that I must have broken it in falling; but the pain reassured me, for I knew that your sensations do not become more acute when you are dying. I began to feel more normal and to be sorry for the four poor devils who were sweating and slithering with the stretcher on their shoulders. It was a mile and a half to the ambulance, and vile going, over lumpy, slippery tracks. I knew what a sweat it was, having helped to carry a wounded man down a day or two earlier. The leaves of the silver poplars which, in places fringed our trenches, brushed against my face; I thought what a good thing it was to be alive in a world where silver poplars grow. But all the while the pain in my arm was diabolical, making me swear and then try not to swear, because every time I breathed too hard the blood bubbled out of my mouth.

From Homage to Catalonia, *the author's account of his service with the Republican militia in the Spanish Civil War. Orwell went to Spain in December 1936, rose to the rank of second lieutenant, and received the bullet from a fascist sniper near Huesca on May 20, 1937.*

'Scotland For Ever'; The Charge of the Scots Greys at Waterloo, June 18, 1815, by Elizabeth Butler, 1881.

A NATO soldier patrols the Kosovo/Macedonia border, 2001. Photograph by Andrew Testa.

c. 496: Tolbiac

CLOVIS CONVERTS TO CHRIST

Queen Clotild continued to pray that her husband might recognize the true God and give up his idol worship. Nothing could persuade him to accept Christianity. Finally war broke out against the Alamanni, and in this conflict he was forced by necessity to accept what he had refused of his own free will. It so turned out that when the two armies met on the battlefield, there was great slaughter and the troops of Clovis were rapidly being annihilated. He raised his eyes to heaven when he saw this, felt compunction in his heart, and was moved to tears. "Jesus Christ," he said, "you who Clotild maintains to be the son of the living God, you who deign to give help to those in travail and victory to those who trust in you—in faith, I beg the glory of your help. If you will give me victory over my enemies, and if I may have evidence of that miraculous power which the people dedicated to your name say that they have experienced, then I will believe in you and I will be baptized in your name. I have called upon my own gods, but, as I see only too clearly, they have no intention of helping me. I therefore cannot believe that they possess any power, for they do not come to the assistance of those who trust in them. I now call upon you. I want to believe in you, but I must first be saved from my enemies." Even as he said this, the Alamanni turned their backs and began to run away. As soon as they saw that their king was killed, they submitted to Clovis. "We beg you," they said, "to put an end to this slaughter. We are prepared to obey you." Clovis stopped the war. He made a speech in which he called for peace. Then he went home. He told the Queen how he had won a victory by calling on the name of Christ. This happened in the fifteenth year of his reign.

> **Gregory of Tours**, *from his* History of the Franks, *Book I.*

c. 1914: Ypres

You can be a virgin in horror the same as in sex. How, when I left the Place Clichy, could I have imagined such horror? Who could have suspected, before getting really into the war, all the ingredients that go to make up the rotten, heroic, good-for-nothing soul of man? And there I was, caught up in a mass flight into collective murder, into the fiery furnace…. Something had come up from the depths, and this is what happened.

The colonel was still as cool as a cucumber. I watched him as he stood on the embankment, taking little messages sent by the general, reading them without haste as the bullets flew all around him, and tearing them into little pieces. Did none of those messages include an order to put an immediate stop to this abomination? Did no top brass tell him there had been a misunderstanding? A horrible mistake? A misdeal? That somebody'd got it all wrong, that the plan had been for maneuvers, a sham battle, not a massacre! Not at all! "Keep it up, colonel! You're doing fine!" That's what General des Entrayes, the head of our division and commander over us all, must have written in those notes that were being brought every five minutes by a courier who looked greener and more shitless each time. I could have palled up with that boy, we'd have been scared together. But we had no time to fraternize.

So there was no mistake? So there was no law against people shooting at people they couldn't even see! It was one of the things you could do without anybody reading you the riot act. In fact, it was recognized and probably encouraged by upstanding citizens, like the draft, or marriage, or hunting!… No two ways about it. I was suddenly on the most intimate terms with war. I'd lost my virginity. You've got to be pretty much alone with her as I was then to get a good look at her, the slut, full face and profile. A war had been switched on between us and the other side, and now it was burning! Like the current between the two carbons of an arc lamp! And this lamp was in no hurry to go out! It would get us all, the colonel and everyone else; he looked pretty spiffy now, but he wouldn't roast up any bigger than me when the current from the other side got him between the shoulders.

There are different ways of being condemned to death. Oh! What wouldn't I have given to be in jail instead of here! What a fool I'd been! If only I had had a little foresight and stolen something or other when it would have been so easy and there was still time. I never think of anything. You come out of jail alive, out of a war you don't! The rest is blarney.

If only I'd had time, but I didn't. There was nothing left to steal. How pleasant it would be in a cozy little jailhouse, I said to myself, where the bullets couldn't get in. Where they never

> And is not war a youthful king,
>   A stately hero clad in mail?
> Beneath his footsteps laurels spring;
>   Him earth's majestic monarchs hail
> Their friend, their playmate! and his bold
>   bright eye
> Compels the maiden's love-confessing sigh.
>   —Samuel Taylor Coleridge, 1799

got in! I knew of one that was ready and waiting, all sunny and warm! I saw it in my dreams, the jailhouse of Saint-Germain to be exact, right near the forest. I knew it well, I'd often passed that way. How a man changes! I was a child in those days, and that jail frightened me. Because I didn't know what men are like. Never again will I believe what they say or what they think. Men are the thing to be afraid of, always, men and nothing else.

How much longer would this madness have to go on before these monsters dropped with exhaustion? How long could a convulsion like this last? Months? Years? How many? Maybe till everyone's dead? All these lunatics? Every last one of them? And seeing that events were taking such a desperate turn, I decided to stake everything on one throw, to make one last try, to see if I couldn't stop the war, just me, all by myself! At least in this one spot where I happened to be.

The colonel was only two steps away from me, pacing. I'd talk to him. Something I'd never done. This was a time for daring. The way things stood, there was practically nothing to lose. "What is it?" he'd ask me, startled, I imagined, at my bold interruption. Then I'd explain the situation as I saw it, and we'd see what he thought. The essential is to talk things over. Two heads are better than one.

I was about to take the decisive step when, at that very moment, who should arrive at the double but a dismounted cavalryman (as we said in those days), exhausted, shaky in the joints, holding his helmet upside-down in one hand like Belisarius, trembling, all covered with mud, his face even greener than the courier I mentioned before. He stammered and gulped. You'd have thought he was struggling to climb out of a tomb, and it had made him sick to his stomach. Could it be that this spook didn't like bullets any more than I did? That he saw them coming like me?

"What is it?" Disturbed, the colonel stopped him short; the glance he flung at that ghost was of steel.

It made our colonel very angry to see that wretched cavalryman so incorrectly clad and shitting in his pants with fright. The colonel had no use for fear, that was a sure thing. And especially that helmet held in hand like a bowler was really too much in a combat regiment like ours that was just getting into the war. It

Four terra cotta hand grenades used by the defenders of Constantinople against the Turks, late fifteenth century.

was as if this dismounted cavalryman had seen the war and taken his hat off in greeting.

Under the colonel's withering look the wobbly messenger snapped to attention, pressing his little finger to the seam of his trousers as the occasion demanded. And so he stood on the embankment, stiff as a board, swaying, the sweat running down his chinstrap; his jaws were trembling so hard that little abortive cries kept coming out of him, like a puppy dreaming. You couldn't make out whether he wanted to speak to us or whether he was crying.

Our Germans squatting at the end of the road had just changed instruments. Now they were having their fun with a machine-gun, sputtering like handfuls of matches, and all around us flew swarms of angry bullets, as hostile as wasps.

The man finally managed to articulate a few words:

"Colonel, sir, Sergeant Barousse has been killed."

"So what?"

"He was on his way to meet the bread wagon on the Etrapes road, sir."

"So what?"

"He was blown up by a shell!"

"So what, dammit!"

"That's what, colonel, sir."

"Is that all?"

"Yes, sir, that's all, colonel, sir."

"What about the bread?" the colonel asked.

That was the end of the dialogue, because, I remember distinctly, he barely had time to say, "What about the bread?" That was all. After that there was nothing but flame and noise.

Resource Wars

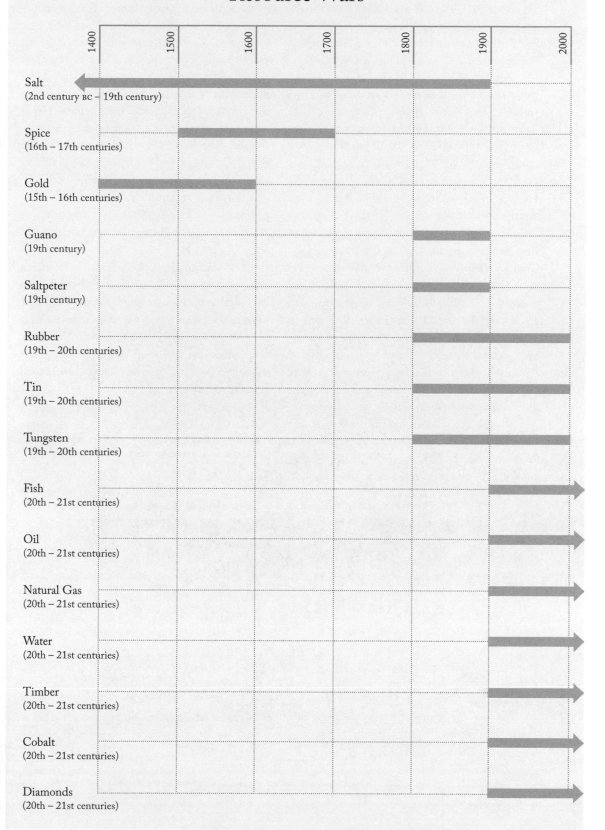

The kind of noise you wouldn't have thought possible. Our eyes, ears, nose, and mouth were so full of that noise I thought it was all over and I'd turned into noise and flame myself.

After a while, the flame went away, the noise stayed in my head, and my arms and legs trembled as if somebody were shaking me from behind. My limbs seemed to be leaving me, but then in the end they stayed on. The smoke stung my eyes for a long time, and the prickly smell of powder and sulfur hung on, strong enough to kill all the fleas and bedbugs in the whole world.

I thought of Sergeant Barousse, who had just gone up in smoke like the man told us. That was good news. Great, I thought to myself. That makes one less stinker in the regiment! He wanted to have me court-martialed for a can of meat. "It's an ill wind," I said to myself. In that respect, you can't deny it, the war seemed to serve a purpose now and then! I knew of three or four more in the regiment, real scum, that I'd have gladly helped to make the acquaintance of a shell, like Barousse.

As for the colonel, I didn't wish him any hard luck. But he was dead too. At first I didn't see him. The blast had carried him up the embankment and laid him down on his side, right in the arms of the dismounted cavalryman, the courier, who was finished too. They were embracing each other for the moment and for all eternity, but the cavalryman's head was gone, all he had was an opening at the top of the neck, with blood in it bubbling and glugging like jam in a kettle. The colonel's belly was wide open and he was making a nasty face about it. It must have hurt when it happened. Tough shit for him! If he'd beat it when the shooting started, it wouldn't have happened.

All that tangled meat was bleeding profusely.

Shells were still bursting to the right and left of the scene.

I'd had enough. I was glad to have such a good pretext for making myself scarce. I even hummed a tune and reeled like when you've been rowing a long way and your legs are wobbly. "Just one shell!" I said to myself. "Amazing how quick just one shell can clean things up. Could you believe it?" I kept saying to myself. "Could you believe it!"

From Journey to the End of Night, *a semiautobiographical novel drawn from the author's experiences as a soldier in the French cavalry during World War I.*

Thirty Years' War. Plate II from Jacques Callot's *Les misères et les malheurs de la guerre*, 1633.

Ifrael ex. Cum Priui. Reg.

A la fin ces l'oleurs infames et perdus ,
Comme fruits malheureux a cet arbre pendus

Monstrent bien que le crime (horrible et noire engeance)
Est luy mesme instrument de honte et de vengeance ,

Et que c'est le Destin des hommes vicieux
Desprouuer tost ou tard la iustice des Ci

1854: Balaclava

THE LIGHT BRIGADE DISAPPEARS
INTO THE SMOKE

The North Valley was a about a mile and quarter long and a little less than a mile wide. On the Fedioukine Hills, which enclosed the valley to the north, were drawn up eight battalions of infantry, four squadrons of cavalry, and fourteen guns; on the Causeway Heights to the south were the bulk of the eleven battalions, with thirty guns and a field battery which had captured the redoubts earlier in the day; at the end of the valley, facing the Light Brigade, the mass of the Russian cavalry which had been defeated by the Heavy Brigade was drawn up in three lines, with twelve guns unlimbered before them, strengthened by six additional squadrons of Lancers, three on each flank. The Light Brigade was not merely to run a gauntlet of fire: It was advancing into a deadly three-sided trap, from which there was no escape.

As the Brigade moved, a sudden silence fell over the battlefield. By chance for a moment, gun and rifle-fire ceased, and the watchers on the heights felt the pause was sinister. More than half a century afterwards old men recalled that as the Light Brigade moved to its doom, a strange hush fell, and it became so quiet that the jingle of bits and accoutrements could be clearly heard.

Before the Light Brigade had advanced fifty yards the hush came to an end: The Russian guns crashed out, and great clouds of smoke rose at the end of the valley. A moment later, an extraordinary and inexplicable incident took place. The advance was proceeding at a steady trot when suddenly Nolan, riding beside his friend Captain Morris in the first line, urged on his horse and began to gallop diagonally across the front. Morris thought that Nolan was losing his head with excitement, and, knowing that a mile and a quarter must be traversed before the guns were reached, shouted, "That won't do, Nolan! We've a long way to go and must be steady." Nolan took no notice; galloping madly ahead and to the right, he crossed in front of Lord Cardigan—an unprecedented breach of military etiquette—and, turning in his saddle, shouted and waved his sword as if he would address the Brigade, but the guns were firing with great crashes, and not a word could be heard. Had he suddenly realized that his interpretation of the order had been wrong, and that in his impetuosity he had direct-

> *Long peace, I find,*
> *But nurses dangerous humors up to strength,*
> *License and wanton rage, which war alone*
> *Can purge away.* —David Mallet, 1739

ed the Light Brigade to certain death? No one will ever know, because at that moment a Russian shell burst on the right of Lord Cardigan, and a fragment tore its way into Nolan's breast, exposing his heart. The sword fell from his hand, but his right arm was still erect, and his body remained rigid in the saddle. His horse wheeled and began to gallop back through the advancing Brigade, and then from the body there burst a strange and appalling cry, a shriek so unearthly as to freeze the blood of all who heard him. The terrified horse carried the body, still shrieking, through the 4th Light Dragoons, and then at last Nolan fell from the saddle, dead.

Lord Cardigan, looking strictly straight ahead and not aware of Nolan's death, was transported with fury. It was his impression that Nolan had been trying to take the command of the brigade away from him, to lead the charge himself; and so intense was his rage that when he was asked what he thought about as he advanced towards the guns, he replied that his mind was entirely occupied with anger against Nolan.

The watchers on the heights saw that the lines of horsemen, like toys down on the plain, were expanding and contracting with strange mechanical precision. Death was coming fast, and the Light Brigade was meeting death in perfect order; as a man or horse dropped, the riders on each side of him opened out; as soon as they had ridden clear, the ranks closed again. Orderly, as if on the parade ground, the Light

Brigade rode on, but its numbers grew every moment smaller and smaller as they moved down the valley. Those on the heights who could understand what that regular mechanical movement meant in terms of discipline and courage were intolerably moved, and one old soldier burst into tears. It was at this moment that Bosquet, the French general, observed, "C'est magnifique, mais ce n'est pas la guerre."

The fire grew fiercer; the first line was now within range of the guns at the end of the valley, as well as the fire pouring from both flanks. Round-shot, grape, and shells began to mow men down not singly, but by groups; the pace quickened and quickened again—the men could no longer be restrained, and the trot became a canter.

As batteries and massed riflemen on each flank began to tear gaps in their ranks and trooper after trooper came crashing to the ground, they had a new and horrible difficulty to face. The ground was strewn with casualties of the first line—not only dead men and dead horses, but horses and men not yet dead, able to crawl, to scream, to writhe. They had perpetually to avoid riding over men they knew, while riderless horses, some unhurt, some horribly injured, tried to force their way into the ranks.

And all the time, through the cheers, the groans, the ping of bullets whizzing through the air, the whirr and crash of shells, the earth-shaking thunder of galloping horses' hooves, when men were not merely falling one by one but being swept away in groups, words of command rang out as on the parade-ground, "Close in to your center. Back the right flank! Keep up, Private Smith. Left squadron, keep back. Look to your dressing." Until at last, as the ranks grew thinner and thinner, only one command was heard: "Close in! Close in! Close in to the center! Close in! Close in!"

Eight minutes had now passed since the advance began, and Lord Cardigan, with the survivors of the first line hard on his heels, galloping furiously but steadily, was within a few yards of the battery. The troopers could see the faces of the gunners, and Lord Cardigan selected the particular space between two guns where he intended to enter. One thought, wrote a survivor, was in all their minds: They were nearly out of it at last, and close on the accursed guns, and Lord Cardigan, still sitting rigid in his saddle, "steady as a church," waved his sword over his head. At that moment there was a roar, the earth trembled, huge flashes of flame shot out, and the smoke became so dense that darkness seemed to fall. The Russian gunners had fired a salvo from their twelve guns into the first line of the Light Brigade at a distance of eighty yards. The first line ceased to exist. To the second line, riding behind, it was as if the line had simply dissolved. Lord Cardigan's charger Ronald was blown sideways by the blast, a torrent of flame seemed to belch down his right side, and for a moment he thought he had lost a leg. He was, he estimated, only two or three lengths from the mouths of the guns. Then, wrenching Ronald's head round, he drove into the smoke and, charging into the space he had previously selected, was the first man into the battery. No roars, no great flashes of flame came from the guns—all was strangely, menacingly quiet. Nothing could be seen: The pall of smoke hung like a curtain over the end of the valley; only from time to time through their glasses the watchers saw riderless horses gallop out and men stagger into sight to fall prostrate among the corpses of their comrades littering the ground.

Fifty men only, blinded and stunned, had survived from the first line. Private Wightman of the 17th Lancers felt the frightful crash, saw his captain fall dead; then his horse made a "tremendous leap into the air," though what he jumped at Wightman never knew—the pall of smoke was so dense that he could not see his arm before him—but suddenly he was in the battery, and in the darkness there were sounds of fighting and slaughter. The scene was extraordinary: Smoke so obscured the sun that it was barely twilight, and in the gloom the British troopers, maddened with excitement, cut and thrust and hacked like demons, while the Russian gunners with superb courage fought to remove the guns.

At this moment, the second line swept down. The 11th Hussars outflanked the battery, as the 17th had done; the 8th Hussars had not yet come up, but the 4th Light Dragoons under Lord George Paget crashed into the battery. So great was the smoke and the confusion that Lord George did not see the battery until his regiment was on top of it. As they rode headlong down, one of his officers gave a "View halloo," and suddenly they were in and fighting among the guns. The Russian gunners, with great courage, persisted in their attempt to take the guns away, and the 4th Light Dragoons, mad with excitement, fell on them with savage frenzy. A cut-and-thrust,

or unhorsed were struggling towards the British lines; both his aides-de-camp had vanished; he had ridden never once looking back and had no idea of what the fate of his brigade had been. Nor had he any feeling of responsibility—in his own words, having "led the Brigade and launched them with due impetus, he considered his duty was done." The idea of trying to find out what had happened to his men or of rallying the survivors never crossed his mind. With extraordinary indifference to danger he had led the Light Brigade down the valley as if he were leading a charge in a review in Hyde Park, and he now continued to behave as if he were in a review in Hyde Park. He had, however, he wrote, some apprehension that for a general his isolated position was unusual, and he avoided any undignified

Prisoners of war. Detail of a victory parade from the Temple of Ishtar at Mari, Syria, 2400 BC.

hand-to-hand combat raged in which the British fought like tigers, one officer tearing at the Russians with his bare hands and wielding his sword in a delirium of slaughter. After the battle this officer's reaction was so great that he sat down and burst into tears. Brave as the Russians were, they were forced to give way; the Russian gunners were slaughtered, and the 4th Light Dragoons secured absolute mastery of every gun.

Lord Cardigan, however, looking up the valley over the scene of the charge, could see no sign of his brigade. The valley was strewn with dead and dying; small groups of men wounded

appearance of haste by riding back very slowly, most of the time at a walk. By another miracle he was untouched by the fire from the Causeway Heights, which, although the batteries on the Fedioukine Hills had been silenced by the French, was still raking the unfortunate survivors of the charge in the valley. As he rode, he continued to brood on Nolan's behavior, and on nothing else. The marvelous ride, the dauntless valor of the Light Brigade and their frightful destruction, his own miraculous escape from death, made no impression on his mind; Nolan's insubordination occupied him exclusively, and when he reached the point where the Heavy Brigade was halted, he rode up to General Scarlett and immediately broke into accusations of Nolan, furiously complaining of Nolan's insubordination, his ride across the front of the brigade, his attempt to assume command and, Lord Cardigan finished contemptuously, "Imagine the fellow screaming like a woman when he was hit." General Scarlett checked him: "Say no more, my lord; you have just ridden over Captain Nolan's dead body."

The retreat was worse than the advance.

"Killer Tunes"

From a 1991 list of sixty-seven songs the BBC classified as having "lyrics that need thought in scheduling" during the Persian Gulf War:

....

Abba – "Under Attack"

The Animals – "We Gotta Get out of This Place"

Joan Baez – "The Night They Drove
            Old Dixie Down"

Bangles – "Walk Like an Egyptian"

Pat Benatar – "Love Is a Battlefield"

Blondie – "Atomic"

Cher – "Bang Bang (My Baby Shot Me Down)"

Eric Clapton – "I Shot the Sheriff"

Cutting Crew – "I Just Died in
              Your Arms Tonight"

Dire Straits – "Brothers in Arms"

Duran Duran – "View to a Kill"

Jose Feliciano – "Light My Fire"

Roberta Flack – "Killing Me Softly
               with His Song"

Elton John – "Saturday Night's
            Alright for Fighting"

John Lennon – "Give Peace a Chance"

Bob Marley – "Buffalo Soldier"

Donny Osmond – "Soldier of Love"

Bruce Springsteen – "I'm on Fire"

Cat Stevens – "I'm Gonna Get Me a Gun"

Stevie Wonder – "Heaven Help Us All"

Men and horses were utterly exhausted and almost none was unhurt. Troopers who had become attached to their horses refused to leave them behind, and wounded and bleeding men staggered along, dragging with them wounded and bleeding beasts. Horses able to move were given up to wounded men; Major de Salis of the 8th Hussars retreated on foot, leading his horse with a wounded trooper in the saddle. All formation had been lost, and it was a rabble who limped painfully along. The pace was heartbreakingly slow; most survivors were on foot; little groups of men dragged along step by step, leaning on each other. The wreckage of men and horses was piteous. "What a scene of havoc was this last mile—strewn with the dead and dying and all friends!" wrote Lord George Paget. Men recognized their comrades, "some running, some limping, some crawling," saw horses in the trappings of their regiments, "in every position of agony struggling to get up, then floundering back again on their mutilated riders."

When the last survivors had trailed in, the remnants of the Light Brigade reformed on a slope looking southward over Balaclava. The charge had lasted twenty minutes from the moment the trumpet sounded the advance to the return of the last survivor. Lord Cardigan rode forward. "Men, it is a mad-brained trick, but it is no fault of mine," he said in his loud, hoarse voice. A voice answered, "Never mind, my lord; we are ready to go again," and the roll call began, punctuated by the melancholy sound of pistol shots as the farriers went round dispatching ruined horses.

Some seven hundred horsemen had charged down the valley, and 195 had returned. The 17th Lancers was reduced to thirty-seven troopers, the 13th Light Dragoons could muster only two officers and eight mounted men; five hundred horses had been killed.

> **Cecil Woodham-Smith**, *from* The Reason Why.
> *When Lord Cardigan returned to England in January 1855, he received a hero's welcome. An adoring crowd gathered on the pier at Dover gave "three cheers for Balaclava."*

378: Adrianople

THE ROMAN EMPIRE GIVES WAY TO THE GOTHS

After a march of eight miles over rough country under a burning midday sun, our troops came within sight of the enemy's wagons, which, as our scouts had reported, were drawn up in a regular circle. While the enemy in their usual way were raising a wild and doleful yell, the Roman generals marshaled their line of battle.

The opposing lines came into collision like ships of war and pushed each other to and fro, heaving under the reciprocal motion like the waves of the sea. Our left wing penetrated as far as the very wagons, and would have gone further if it had received any support, but it was abandoned by the rest of the cavalry, and under pressure of numbers gave way and collapsed like a broken dike. This left the infantry unprotected and so closely huddled together that a man could hardly wield his sword or draw back his arm once he had stretched it out. Dust rose in such clouds as to hide the sky, which rang with frightful shouts. In consequence it was impossible to see the enemy's missiles in flight and dodge them; all found their mark and dealt death on every side. The barbarians poured on in huge columns, trampling down horse and man and crushing our ranks so as to make an orderly retreat impossible. Our men were too close-packed to have any hope of escape, so they resolved to die like heroes, faced the enemy's swords, and struck back at their assailants. On both sides helmets and breast-plates were split in pieces by blows from the battle-axe. You might see a lionhearted savage, who had been hamstrung or had lost his right hand or been wounded in the side, grinding his clenched teeth and casting defiant glances around in the very throes of death. In this mutual slaughter, so many were laid low that the field was covered with the bodies of the slain, while the groans of the dying and severely wounded filled all who heard them with abject fear.

In this scene of total confusion, the infantry, worn out by toil and danger, had no strength or sense left to form a plan. Most had had their spears shattered in the constant collisions, so they made do with their drawn swords and plunged into the dense masses of the foe, regardless of their lives and aware that there was no hope of escape. The ground was so drenched with blood that they slipped and fell, but they strained every nerve to sell their lives dearly, and faced their opponents with such resolution that some perished

A dead enemy always smells good.
—*Alus Vitellius, 69*

at the hands of their own comrades. In the end, when the whole field was one dark pool of blood and they could see nothing but heaps of slain wherever they turned their eyes, they trampled without scruple on the lifeless corpses.

The sun, which was high in the sky, scorched the Romans who were weak from hunger, parched with thirst, and weighed down by the burden of their armor. Finally, our line gave way under the overpowering pressure of the barbarians, and as a last resort our men took to their heels in a general scramble for their lives.

The barbarians' eyes flashed fire as they pursued their dazed foe, whose blood ran cold with terror. Some fell without knowing who struck them, some were crushed by sheer weight of numbers, and some were killed by their own comrades. They could neither gain ground by resistance nor obtain mercy by giving way. Besides, many lay blocking the way half dead, unable to endure the agony of their wounds, and the carcasses of slaughtered horses covered the ground in heaps. At last a moonless night brought an end to these irreparable losses, which cost Rome so dear. It is certain that hardly a third of our army escaped.

Ammianus Marcellinus, Res Gestae, *a chronicle of the late Roman Empire by the contemporary historian. Emperor Valens died in the Battle of Adrianople, and Rome was never again strong enough to ward off the arrival of immigrant barbarians.*

1527: Rome

CRUEL AND INSATIABLE GREED

Meanwhile the rest of the Roman people, as well as the merchants, prelates, courtiers, and foreigners, all ran back and forth in great confusion and terror looking for some refuge. Running through the streets as if they were lost, unable to leave Rome because the gates were barred, they entered the strongest places or those they considered the safest.

Since it is an especially noteworthy fact, I must include here that in this calamity for themselves and for their unlucky city none of those appointed to be officers of the Church made any attempt to cut the bridges or to organize the defense of the walls of Trastevere. They did not, as they should have, resist with all their strength the attack of their cruel enemy or resolve to die manfully defending themselves with weapons in their hands. Instead, running like everyone else, they increased the panic in Rome and gave the enemy confidence of absolute victory.

When the Spanish troops realized that all the defenders had fled and that they were tru-ly in control of the city, they began to capture houses (along with everyone and everything that was in them) and to take prisoners. The Germans, however, were obeying the articles of war and cutting to pieces anyone they came upon (an act that is very necessary in the first hours of a victory). They were quickly persuaded, however, by the Spanish captains that since the city was abandoned by its defenders and that great riches must have been hidden in it, it would be a grave mistake not to keep alive anyone who might be able to show them where treasures were hidden, or give them the names of people outside Rome who would pay their ransoms.

How many courtiers, how many genteel and cultivated men, how many refined prelates, how many devoted nuns, virgins, or chaste wives with their little children became the prey of these cruel foreigners! How many calixes, crosses, statues, and vessels of silver and gold were stolen from the altars, sacristies, and other holy places where they were stored. How many rare and venerable relics, covered with gold and silver, were despoiled by bloody, homicidal hands and hurled with impious derision to the earth. The heads of St. Peter, St. Paul, St.

The Battle of San Romano, first panel, by Paolo Uccello, c. 1456

Andrew, and many other saints; the wood of the Cross, the Thorns, the Holy Oil, and even consecrated Hosts were shamefully trodden underfoot in that fury.

In the street you saw nothing but thugs and rogues carrying great bundles of the richest vestments and ecclesiastical ornaments and huge sacks full of all kinds of vessels of gold and silver—testifying more to the riches and empty pomp of the Roman Curia than to the humble poverty and true devotion of the Christian religion. Great numbers of captives of all sorts were to be seen, groaning and screaming, being swiftly led to makeshift prisons. In the streets there were many corpses. Many nobles lay there cut to pieces, covered with mud and their own blood, and many people only half dead lay miserably on the ground.

My purpose is to show what sad and unlucky ends those governments come to which rule and maintain themselves in a culture of lust, greed, and ambition, rather than in military severity, beloved poverty, and just moderation. I confess that I cannot hold back my tears when I consider what torment and suffering human beings receive from their fellow humans, and how often we are the causes of our own misery and not Fortune (even though the majority of mortals blame her). Nonetheless I will force myself to describe some part of the pitiable events occurring in Rome in the very recent past.

If anyone had been walking through the streets of Rome by day or night, he would have heard not sighs and tearful laments, but the pitiful cries and screams of hapless prisoners coming from every house and building. The grandest nobles, the richest and most refined prelates, cardinals, courtiers, merchants, and Roman citizens who fell into their hands were all treated more cruelly and with less respect in proportion to their rank; and they tortured them with greater thirst for ransom.

Many were suspended by their arms for hours at a time; others were led around by ropes tied to their testicles. Many were branded with hot irons in various parts of their bodies. Some endured extreme thirst; others were prevented from sleeping. A very cruel and effective torture was to pull out their back teeth. Some were made to eat their own ears, or nose, or testicles roasted; and others were subjected to bizarre and unheard of torments that affect me too strongly even to think of them, let alone to describe them in detail.

A priest was shamelessly and cruelly killed because he refused to administer the most holy sacrament to a mule in clerical vestments. I will not describe what happened to the noble and beautiful young matrons, to virgins and nuns, in order not to shame anyone. The majority were ransomed, and anyone can easily imagine for himself what must have happened when these women found themselves in the hands of such lustful people as the Spaniards. Rather than submit to their conquerors, many noble and pure virgins supposedly stabbed themselves or leapt from some high point into the Tiber. I, however, have never heard that anyone has been able to positively identify a woman of such virtue and chastity. This should not be surprising considering how corrupt Rome is at present, how full of abominable vices and entirely lacking in the virtues it possessed in Antiquity.

One cannot imagine, therefore, an unbearable form of torture that their prisoners did not experience and endure many times for the sake of cruel and insatiable greed. How patiently these torments were borne by refined and delicate prelates and effeminate courtiers is easy to imagine if one realizes with what difficulty in good times they bore not the ills of the body, but the bite of a fly. And because many of these barbarians feared that their prisoners had not revealed to them all the money and valuables that they had hidden away, they forced their prisoners, even if they were high-ranking nobles, to empty with their own hands the sewers and other disgusting places where human excrement and the like were disposed of. Anyone can imagine how much pain and suffering that must have given to those who had always been accustomed to having their houses, their clothes, their bodies, and especially their boots perfumed with sweet and alluring scents.

The immense riches of the Roman nobility, preserved in their families for many centuries, were destroyed in an hour. The incredible profits that had been accumulated and multiplied unjustly and dishonestly through years of usury, theft, simony, and other immoral means by courtiers and merchants fell in an instant into the hands of these barbarians. But why do I bother to recount the details of various fortunes or possessions that fell in such short time into the hands of these savage foreigners? Everybody knows that money, merchandise, and delicacies from all over Europe and much of the rest of the world came pouring into that city every hour to satisfy the insatiable appetites and the illicit desires of its many licentious prelates and courtiers.

Those Germans, who had arrived only a short time before with Captain George von Frundsberg, now wore silks and brocades; huge gold chains hung across their chests and shoulders; and their arms were covered with bracelets inset with jewels of enormous value. Dressed up like mock popes and cardinals, they went for pleasure rides through Rome on beautiful hackneys and mules. Their wives and concubines, proud and richly dressed, accompanied them. The women's heads, necks, and breasts were covered with the largest pearls and the most perfect jewels pried from pontifical miters and sacred reliquaries. Their pages and servants had helmets of heavy gold and the barrels of their arquebuses were made of solid gold stripped from the altars and holy places of Rome. It would not have been possible to believe that these were the same people who had crossed the Po a few months before. Then they were exhausted, shoeless, and so poorly dressed that some of them were unable to keep even their private parts covered.

By the same token, no one would now recognize the cardinals, patriarchs, archbishops, bishops, protonotaries, generals, provincials, guardians, abbots, vicars, and all the rest of the ridiculous and infinite tribe of modern religious titleholders, who dishonor and burden the Christian religion. Now many of these men wore torn and disgraceful habits, were marked by cuts and bruises all over their bodies from the indiscriminate whippings and beatings they had received. Some had thick and greasy beards. Some had their faces branded; and some were missing teeth; others were without noses or ears. Some were castrated and so depressed and terrified that they failed to show in any way the vain and effeminate delicacy and lasciviousness that they had put on with such excessive energy for so many years in their earlier, happy days.

I will not write of the anguish and confusion that those in Castel Sant'Angelo are enduring. With the pope, there are thirteen cardinals, innumerable prelates, lords, noblewomen, merchants, couriers, and soldiers, all in terror and despairing of their safety. Since they are completely surrounded and very carefully watched by their enemies, I have little knowledge of what is going on inside. We can imagine, though (since they know that they cannot escape), that they spend their time blaming Jacopo Salviati, the datary, Signor Renzo, Cardinal Armellini, and perhaps the pontiff himself, in sharp and venomous words for their obvious and multiple mistakes.

One can easily imagine the anguish and torment of the pope, constantly seeing and hearing such a scourge of punishment raised against himself and against Rome. Like the rest of those under siege, he is suffering in fear that he will soon fall into the hands of cruel enemies, obviously thirsting for his blood. And though he enjoyed great honors and sweet pleasures in the past, now he is paying for them with humiliation and pitiful distress. If he ever considered himself a wise and glorious prince, now he must acknowledge himself to be the most unfortunate and the most abject pontiff who ever lived. And since it is his fault that the Church, Rome, and Italy all find themselves in such extreme danger, we can easily imagine that he often looks toward the sky with tears in his eyes.

Luigi Guicciardini, *from* The Sack of Rome. *A witness to the events in question, Gucciardini served as a senior official in the Vatican entourage of Pope Clement VII.*

German infantrymen pursue Soviet forces through a burning Russian village, 1941.

1676: New England

CASUALTY REPORT

In Narragansett, not one House left standing.

At Warwick, but one.

At Providence, not above three.

At Potuxit, none left.

Very few at Seaconicke.

At Swansey, two, at most.

Marlborough, wholly laid in Ashes, except two or three Houses.

Grantham and Nashaway, all ruined but one House or two.

Many Houses burnt at Springfield, Scituate, Lancaster, Brookefield, and Northampton.

The greatest Part of Rehoboth and Taunton destroyed.

Great Spoil made at Hadley, Hatfield, and Chelmsford.

Deerfield wholly, and Westfield much, ruined.

At Sudbury, many Houses burnt, and some at Hingham, Weymouth, and Braintree.

Besides particular Farms and Plantations, a great Number not be reckoned up, wholly laid waste, or very much damnified.

And as to Persons, it is generally thought, that of the English there hath been lost, in all, Men, Women, and Children, above Eight Hundred since the War began: of whom many have been destroyed with exquisite Torments and most inhumane Barbarities; the Heathen rarely giving Quarter to those that they take, but if they were Women, they first forced them to sastisfie their filthy Lusts and then murdered them, either cutting off the Head, ripping open the Belly, or skulping the Head of Skin and Hair, and hanging them up as Trophies; wearing Men's Fingers as Bracelets about their Necks and Stripes of their Skins which they dresse for Belts. They knockt one Youth of the Head, and laying him for dead, they flead (or skulp'd) his Head of Skin and Hair. After which the Boy wonderfully revived, and is now recovered, only he hath Nothing but the dry Skull, neither Skin nor Hair on his Head. Nor have our Cattle escaped the Cruelty of these worse than Brute and Savage Beasts: for what Cattle they took they seldom killed outright: or if they did, would eat but little of the Flesh, but rather cut their Bellies, and letting them go several Days, trailing their Guts after them, putting out their Eyes, or cutting off one Leg, etc.

Nathaniel Saltonstall, *from "A True but Brief Account of Our Losses Sustained Since This Cruel and Mischievous War Began." The losses were inflicted on the colonies of Massachusetts and Rhode Island by various Native American tribes, among them the Pokanoket, the Nipmuck, and the Squakheag, in what was known as King Philip's War (1675-1676). Saltonstall, a magistrate of Haverhill, Massachusetts, was selected in 1692 to preside over the Salem Witch Trials. He resigned in disgust.*

70: Jerusalem

UNHOLY SLAUGHTER

While the Sanctuary was burning, looting went on right and left and all who were caught were put to the sword. There was no pity for age, no regard for rank; little children and old men, laymen and priests alike were butchered; every class was held in the iron embrace of war, whether they defended themselves or cried for mercy. Through the roar of the flames as they swept relentlessly on could be heard the groans of the falling: Such were the height of the hill and the vastness of the blazing edifice that the entire city seemed to be on fire, while as for the noise, nothing could be imagined more shattering or more horrifying. There was the war cry of the Roman legions as they converged; the yells of the partisans encircled with fire and sword; the panic flight of the people cut off above into the arms of the enemy, and their shrieks as the end approached. The cries from the hill were answered from the crowded streets; and now many who were wasted with hunger and beyond speech found strength to moan and wail when they saw the Sanctuary in flames. Back from Peraea and the mountains round about came the echo in a thunderous bass.

Yet more terrible than the din were the sights that met the eye. The Temple Hill, enveloped in flames from top to bottom, appeared to be boiling up from its very roots; yet the sea of flame was nothing to the ocean of blood, or the companies of killers to the armies of killed: Nowhere could the ground be seen between the corpses, and the soldiers climbed over heaps of bodies as they chased the fugitives.

The Romans, judging it useless to spare the outbuildings now that the Sanctuary was in flames, set fire to them all—what remained of the colonnades and all the gates except two: one on the east end, the other on the south, both of which they later demolished. They also burnt the treasuries which housed huge sums of money, huge quantities of clothing, and other precious things; here, in fact, all the wealth of the Jews was piled up, for the rich had dismantled their houses and brought the contents here for safe keeping. Next they came to the last surviving colonnade of the outer court. On this women and children and a mixed crowd of citizens had found a refuge—six thousand in all. Before Caesar could reach a decision about them or instruct his officers, the soldiers, carried away by their fury, fired the colonnade from below; as a result, some flung themselves out of the flames to their death, others perished in the blaze. Of that vast number there escaped not one.

Next day the Romans drove the terrorists from the Lower City and burnt the whole place as far as Siloam. They were glad enough to see the town destroyed but got precious little loot, as the whole area had been cleaned out by the partisans before they withdrew to the Upper City. These men felt no remorse for the mischief they had done; they boasted as if they were proud of it. When they saw the city burning, they laughed heartily and said they were happily awaiting the end; for, with the people slaughtered, the Sanctuary burnt to the ground, and the town blazing, they were leaving nothing to the enemy. Yet to the very last, Josephus never wearied of appealing to them to spare what was left of the city, though however much he might say against their savagery and impiety, however much advice he might give them for their own good, he got nothing but ridicule in return. As they could not very well surrender because of their oath and were unable now to fight the Romans on equal terms, they were like caged animals, so used to killing that they thirsted for blood. They scattered through the outskirts of the city and lay in wait among the ruins for would-be deserters. Many in fact were caught, and as hunger had left them too weak even to run away, all were butchered and their bodies thrown to the dogs. But any kind of death was more bearable than starvation, so that although they had no hope now of mercy from the Romans, they still fled to them, falling into the murderous hands of the partisans with their eyes open. Not one spot in the whole city was empty: every single one had its corpse, the victim of hunger or faction.

Masters now of the walls, the Romans set up their standards on the towers and with clapping and singing celebrated their victory, having found the end of the war much easier than the beginning. They had surmounted the last wall without losing a man—it seemed too good to be true—and when they found no one to oppose them, they could make nothing of it. They poured into the streets sword in hand, cut down without mercy all who came within reach, and burnt the houses of any who took refuge indoors, occupants and all. Many they raided, and as they entered in search of plunder, they found whole families dead and the rooms full of the victims of starvation; horrified by the sight, they emerged empty-handed. Pity for those who had died in this way was matched by no such feeling for the living: They ran every man through whom they met and blocked the narrow streets with corpses, deluging the whole city with gore so that many of the fires were quenched by the blood of the slain. At dusk the slaughter ceased, but in the night the fire gained the mastery, and on the eighth of Gorpiaios, the sun rose over Jerusalem in flames—a city that during the siege had suffered such disasters that if she had enjoyed as many blessings from her foundation, she would have been the envy of the world, and a city that deserved these terrible misfortunes on no other account than that she produced a generation such as brought about her ruin.

As the soldiers were now growing weary of bloodshed and survivors were still appearing in large numbers, Caesar gave orders that only men who offered armed resistance were to be killed, and everyone else taken alive. But as well as those covered by the orders, the aged and infirm were slaughtered: Men in their prime who might be useful were herded into the Temple and shut up in the Court of the Women. To guard them, Caesar appointed one of his freedmen, and his friend Fronto to decide each man's fate according to his deserts. Those who had taken part in sedition and terrorism informed against each other, and Fronto executed the lot. Of the youngsters he picked out the tallest and handsomest to be kept for the triumphal procession; of the rest, those over seventeen were put in irons and sent to hard labor in Egypt, while great numbers were presented by Titus to the provinces to perish in the theaters by the sword or by wild beasts; those under seventeen were sold. During the days in which Fronto was sorting them out, starvation killed eleven thousand of the prisoners, some because the guards hated them too bitterly to allow them any food, others because they would not

Sudanese Liberation Army soldiers walk past a dead body, Darfur, 2004. Photograph by Lynsey Addario.

accept it when offered; in any case, there was not even enough corn to fill so many mouths.

All the prisoners taken from beginning to end of the war totalled 97,000; those who perished in the long siege, 1,100,000. Of these the majority were Jews by race but not Jerusalem citizens: They had come together from the whole country for the Feast of Unleavened Bread and

> *War is sweet to those who don't know it.*
> —*Desiderius Erasmus, 1508*

had suddenly been caught up in the war, so that first the overcrowding meant death by pestilence, and later hunger took a heavier toll.

But now fate had decreed that one prison should confine the whole nation and that a city solid with men should be held fast in war's embrace. No destruction ever wrought by God or man approached the wholesale carnage of this war. Every man who showed himself was either killed or captured by the Romans, and then those in the sewers were ferreted out, the ground was torn up, and all who were trapped were killed. There too were found the bodies of more than two thousand, some killed by their own hand, some by one another's, but most by starvation. So foul a stench of human flesh greeted those who charged in that many turned back at once. Others were so avaricious that they pushed on, climbing over the piles of corpses; for many valuables were found in the passages, and all scruples were silenced by the prospect of gain. The Romans now fired the outlying districts of the town and demolished the walls.

So fell Jerusalem in the second year of Vespasian's reign, on the eighth of Gorpiaios, captured five times before and now, for the second time, utterly laid waste.

Josephus, *from* History of the Jewish War. *Although born a Jew and aligned with the cause of Jewish freedom from Roman rule, Josephus moved to Rome after the sack of Jerusalem and became a favorite scholar at court during the ascendancies of the emperors Vespasian, Titus, and Domitian.*

1542: Hispaniola

ASYMMETRIC WARFARE

The island of Hispaniola was the first to witness the arrival of Europeans and the first to suffer the wholesale slaughter of its people and the devastation and depopulation of the land. It all began with the Europeans taking native women and children both as servants and to satisfy their own base appetites; then, not content with what the local people offered them of their own free will (and all offered as much as they could spare), they started taking for themselves the food the natives contrived to produce by the sweat of their brows, which was in all honesty little enough. Since what a European will consume in a single day normally supports three native households of ten persons each for a whole month, and since the newcomers began to subject the locals to other vexations, assaults, and iniquities, the people began to realize that these men could not, in truth, have descended from the heavens. Some of them started to conceal what food they had, others decided to send their women and children into hiding, and yet others took to the hills to get away from the brutal and ruthless cruelty that was being inflicted on them. The Christians punched them, boxed their ears, and flogged them in order to track down the local leaders, and the whole shameful process came to a head when one of the European commanders raped the wife of the paramount chief of the entire island. It was then that the locals began to think up ways of driving the Europeans out of their lands and to take up arms against them. Their weapons, however, were flimsy and ineffective both in attack and in defence (and, indeed, war in the Americas is no more deadly than our jousting, or than many European children's games), and, with their horses and swords and lances, the Spaniards easily fended them off, killing them and committing all kind of atrocities against them.

They forced their way into native settlements, slaughtering everyone they found there, including small children, old men, pregnant women,

---

and even women who had just given birth. They hacked them to pieces, slicing open their bellies with their swords as though they were so many sheep herded into a pen. They even laid wagers on whether they could manage to slice a man in two at a stroke, or cut an individual's head from his body, or disembowel him with a single blow of their axes. They grabbed suckling infants by the feet and, ripping them from their mothers' breasts, dashed them headlong against the rocks. Others, laughing and joking all the while, threw them over their shoulders into a river, shouting, "Wriggle, you little perisher." They slaughtered anyone and everyone in their path, on occasion running through a mother and her baby with a single thrust of their swords. They spared no one, erecting especially wide gibbets on which they could string their victims up with their feet just off the ground and then burn them alive thirteen at a time, in honor of our Savior and the twelve apostles, or tie dry straw to their bodies and set fire to it. Some they chose to keep alive and sim-ply cut their wrists, leaving their hands dangling, saying to them, "Take this letter," meaning that their sorry condition would act as a warning to those hiding in the hills. The way they normally dealt with the native leaders and nobles was to tie them to a kind of griddle consisting of sticks resting on pitchforks driven into the ground and then grill them over a slow fire, with the result that they howled in agony and despair as they died a lingering death.

It once happened that I myself witnessed their grilling of four or five local leaders in this fashion (and I believe they had set up two or three other pairs of grills alongside so that they might process other victims at the same time), when the poor creatures' howls came between the Spanish commander and his sleep. He gave orders that the prisoners were to be throttled, but the man in charge of the execution detail, who was more bloodthirsty than the average com-mon hangman (I know his identity and even met some relatives of his in Seville), was loath to

Heroic Feat! Against the Dead! by Francisco de Goya y Lucientes. Plate 39 from *The Disasters of War,* 1810–14.

cut short his private entertainment by throttling them, and so he personally went round ramming wooden bungs into their mouths to stop them making such a racket and deliberately stoked the fire so that they would take just as long to die as he himself chose. I saw all these things for myself and many others besides. And, since all those who could do so took to the hills and mountains in order to escape the clutches of these merciless and inhuman butchers, these mortal enemies of human kind trained hunting dogs to track them down—wild dogs who would savage a native to death as soon as look at him, tearing him to shreds and devouring his flesh as though he were a pig. These dogs wrought havoc among

the natives and were responsible for much carnage. And when, as happened on the odd occasion, the locals did kill a European, as, given the enormity of the crimes committed against them, they were in all justice fully entitled to, the Spanish came to an unofficial agreement among themselves that for every European killed one hundred natives would be executed.

> **Bartolomé de las Casas,** *from* A Brief Account of the Destruction of the Indies. *A Dominican priest eventually named Bishop of Chiapas in Mexico, las Casas, a Spaniard, was one of the few Europeans in the sixteenth-century Americas who publicly condemned the brutal mistreatment of the Indians by the importers of an advanced civilization.*

Battle between the Sioux and the Blackfoot (detail).

1758: Pennsylvania Frontier

MARY JEMISON CAUGHT UP IN THE FRENCH AND INDIAN WAR

The party that took us consisted of six Indians and four Frenchmen, who immediately commenced plundering and took what they considered most valuable, consisting principally of bread, meal, and meat. Having taken as much provision as they could carry, they set out with their prisoners in great haste, for fear of detection, and soon entered the woods. On our march that day, an Indian went behind us with a whip, with which he frequently lashed the

children to make them keep up. In this manner we traveled till dark without a mouthful of food or a drop of water, although we had not eaten since the night before. Whenever the little children cried for water, the Indians would make them drink urine or go thirsty. At night they encamped in the woods without fire and without shelter, where we were watched with the greatest vigilance. Extremely fatigued and very hungry, we were compelled to lie upon the ground, supperless and without drop of water to satisfy the cravings of our appetites. As in the daytime, so the little ones were made to drink urine in the night if they cried for water. Fatigue alone brought us a little sleep for the refreshment of our weary limbs, and at the dawn of day we were again started on our march in the same order that we had proceeded the day before.

About sunrise we were halted, and the Indians gave us a full breakfast of provision that they had brought from my father's house. Each of us, being very hungry, partook of this bounty of the Indians, except Father, who was so much overcome with his situation—so much exhausted by anxiety and grief—that silent despair seemed fastened upon his countenance, and he could not be prevailed upon to refresh his sinking nature by the use of a morsel of food. Our repast being finished, we again resumed our march, and before noon passed a small fort that I heard my father say was called Fort Canagojigge. That was the only time that I heard him speak from the time we were taken till we were finally separated the following night.

Towards evening we arrived at the border of a dark and dismal swamp which was covered with small hemlocks, or some other evergreen and other bushes, into which we were conducted; and having gone a short distance, we stopped to encamp for the night. Here we had some bread and meat for supper, but the dreariness of our situation, together with the uncertainty under which we all labored, as to our future destiny, almost deprived us of the sense of hunger, and destroyed our relish for food.

Mother, from the time we were taken, had manifested a great degree of fortitude and encouraged us to support our troubles without complaining; and by her conversation, seemed to make the distance and time shorter, and the way more smooth. But Father lost all his ambition in the beginning of our trouble, and continued apparently lost to every care—absorbed in melancholy. Here, as before, she insisted on the necessity of our eating; and we obeyed her, but it was done with heavy hearts.

As soon as I had finished my supper, an Indian took off my shoes and stockings, and put a pair of moccasins on my feet, which my mother observed, and believing that they would spare my life, even if they should destroy the other captives, addressed me as near as I can remember, in the following words:

"My dear little Mary, I fear that the time has arrived when we must be parted forever. Your life, my child, I think will be spared; but we shall probably be tomahawked here in this lonesome place by the Indians. O! how can I part with you, my darling? What will become of my sweet little Mary? O! how can I think of your being continued in captivity without a hope of your being

I shall always respect war hereafter. The cost of life, the dreary havoc of comfort and time, are overpaid by the vistas it opens of eternal life, eternal law, reconstructing and uplifting society—breaks up the old horizon, and we see through the rifts a wider vista.
—Ralph Waldo Emerson, 1864

rescued? O! that death had snatched you from my embraces in your infancy; the pain of parting then would have been pleasing to what it now is, and I should have seen the end of your troubles! Alas, my dear! my heart bleeds at the thoughts of what awaits you; but, if you leave us, remember, my child, your own name, and the name of your father and mother. Be careful and not forget your English tongue. If you shall have an opportunity to get away from the Indians, don't try to escape; for if you do, they will find and destroy you. Don't forget, my little daughter, the prayers that I have learned you—say them often; be a good child, and God will bless you. May God bless you, my child, and make you comfortable and happy."

During this time, the Indians stripped the shoes and stockings from the little boy that belonged to the woman who was taken with us, and put moccasins on his feet, as they had done before on mine. I was crying. An Indian took the little boy and myself by the hand, to lead us off from the company, when my mother exclaimed, "Don't cry, Mary—Don't cry, my child. God will bless you! Farewell—farewell!"

The Indian led us some distance into the bushes, or woods, and there lay down with us to spend the night. The recollection of parting with my tender mother kept me awake, while the tears constantly flowed from my eyes. A number of times in the night the little boy begged of me earnestly to run away with him and get clear of the Indians, but remembering the advice I had so lately received, and knowing the dangers to which we should be exposed in traveling without a path and without a guide through a wilderness unknown to us, I told him that I would not go and persuaded him to lie still till morning.

Early the next morning, the Indians and Frenchmen that we had left the night before

came to us, but our friends were left behind. It is impossible for anyone to form a correct idea of what my feelings were at the sight of those savages, whom I supposed had murdered my parents and brothers, sister, and friends, and left them in the swamp to be devoured by wild beasts! But what could I do? A poor little defenseless girl, without the power or means of escaping; without a home to go to, even if I could be liberated; without a knowledge of the direction or distance to my former place of residence; and without a living friend to whom to fly for protection, I felt a kind of horror, anxiety, and dread, that, to me, seemed insupportable. I durst not cry—I durst not complain, and to inquire of them the fate of my friends (even if I could have mustered resolution) was beyond my ability, as I could not speak their language, nor they understand mine. My only relief was in silent, stifled sobs.

My suspicions as to the fate of my parents proved too true, for soon after I left them they were killed and scalped and mangled in the most shocking manner.

Having given the little boy and myself some bread and meat for breakfast, they led us on as fast as we could travel, and one of them went behind and with a long staff, picked up all the grass and weeds that we trailed down by going over them. By taking that precaution they avoided detection, for each weed was so nicely placed in its natural position that no one would have suspected that we had passed that way. It is the custom of Indians when scouting, or on private expeditions, to step carefully and where no impression of their feet can be left—shunning wet or muddy ground. They seldom take hold of a bush or limb and never break one; and by observing those precautions and that of setting up the weeds and grass which they necessarily lop, they completely elude the sagacity of their pursuers and escape that punishment which they are conscious they merit from the hand of justice.

After a hard day's march we encamped in a thicket, where the Indians made a shelter of boughs, and then built a good fire to warm and dry our benumbed limbs and clothing, for it had rained some through the day. Here we were again fed as before. When the Indians had finished their supper, they took from their baggage a number of scalps and went about preparing them for the market, or to keep without spoiling, by straining them over small hoops which they prepared for that purpose, and then drying and scraping them by the fire. Having put the scalps, yet wet and bloody, upon the hoops, and stretched them to their full extent, they held them to the fire till they were partly dried, and then with their knives, commenced scraping off the flesh; and in that way they continued to work, alternately drying and scraping them, till they were dry and clean. That being done, they combed the hair in the neatest manner, and then painted it and the edges of the scalps yet on the hoops, red. Those scalps I knew at the time must have been taken from our family by the color of the hair. My mother's hair was red, and I could easily distinguish my father's and the children's from each other. That sight was most appalling, yet I was obliged to endure it without complaining.

From the Narrative of the Life of Mary Jemison. *Abducted at the age of fifteen by Shawnee Indians and French soldiers, Jemison was adopted by the Seneca tribe and married to a Seneca man in 1765. She lived the rest of her life among Indians and published her story in 1824 at the age of eighty-one.*

C. 440 BC: Scythia

HERODOTUS DRINKS FROM
THE CUP OF VICTORY

As regards war, the Scythian custom is for every soldier to drink the blood of the first man he kills. The heads of all enemies killed in battle are taken to the king, a head being a sort of ticket by which a soldier is admitted to his share of the loot—no head, no loot. He strips the skin off the head by making a circular cut round the ears and shaking out the skull; he then scrapes the flesh off the skin with the rib of an ox and, when it is clean, works it in his fingers until it is supple and fit to be used as a sort of handkerchief. He hangs these handkerchiefs on the bridle of his horse and is very proud of them. The finest fellow is the man who has the greatest number. Many Scythians sew a number of scalps together and make cloaks out of them, like the ones peasants wear; and often, too, they take the skin, nails and all, off the right hands and arms of dead enemies and use it to cover their quivers with—having discovered the fact that human skin is not only tough, but white, as white as almost any skin. Sometimes they flay a whole body, and stretch the skin on a wooden frame which they carry around with them when they ride. They have a special way of dealing with the actual skulls—not with all of them, but only those of their worst enemies: They saw off the part below the eyebrows and, after cleaning out what remains, stretch a piece of rawhide round it on the outside. If a man is poor, he is content with that, but a rich man goes further and gilds the inside of the skull as well. In either case, the skull is then used to drink from. They treat the skulls of their kinsmen in the same way, in cases where quarrels have occurred and a man has been beaten in a fight in the presence of the king. When important visitors arrive, these skulls are passed round and the host tells the story of them: how they were once his relatives and made war against him, and how he defeated them—all of which passes for a proof of courage. Once a year the governor of each district mixes a bowl of wine, from which every Scythian who has killed his man in battle has the right to drink. Those who have no dead enemy to their credit are not allowed to touch the wine, but have to sit by themselves in disgrace—the worst indeed—which they can suffer. Any man, on the contrary, who has killed a great many enemies, has two cups and drinks from both of them at once.

From the Histories. *On his travels through the ancient Caucasus, Herodotus encountered the Scythians somewhere in the vicinity of what is now southern Russia.*

Battle between two warriors on horseback, c. 1480.

1415: Agincourt

JOHN KEEGAN REVISITS
THE BATTLEFIELD

They must have received at least two orders: the first to draw their bows, the second to loose their strings. How the orders were synchronized between different groups of archers is an unanswerable question, but when the shout went up or the banner down, four clouds of arrows would have streaked out of the English line to reach a height of one hundred feet before turning in flight to plunge at a steeper angle on and among the French men-at-arms opposite. We can suppose that the armor served its purpose effectively in this, the opening moment of Agincourt. But one should not dismiss the moral effect of the arrow strike. The singing of the arrows would not have moved ahead of their flight, but the sound of their impact must have been extraordinarily cacophonous, a weird clanking and banging on the bowed heads and backs of the French men-at-arms. If any of the horses in the flanking squadrons were hit, they were likely to have been hurt, however, even at this extreme range, for they were armored only on their faces and chests, and the chisel-pointed head of the cloth-yard arrow would have penetrated the padded cloth hangings which covered the rest of their bodies. Animal cries of pain and fear would have risen above the metallic clatter.

One or two volleys would have been insult enough. On the arrival of the first arrows, the two large squadrons of horse on either flank mounted, walked their horses clear of the line, and broke into a charge.

It is not difficult to picture the beginning of the charge; the horsemen booting their mounts to form line, probably two or three rows deep, so

Byzantines battle the Arabs, 842. Byzantine miniature, c. eleventh century.

that, riding knee to knee, they would have presented a front of two or three hundred lances, more or less equaling in width the line of the archers opposite, say, three hundred yards. We can imagine them setting off, sitting (really standing) "long" in their high-backed, padded saddles, legs straight and thrust forward, toes down in the heavy stirrups, lance under right arm, left free to manage the reins (wearing plate armor obviated the need to carry a shield); and we can see them in motion, riding at a pace which took them across all but the last fifty of the two or three hundred yards they had to cover in forty seconds or so, and then spurring their horses to ride down on the archers at the best speed they could manage—twelve or fifteen miles an hour.

So far so good. The distance between horses and archers narrows. The archers, who have delivered three or four volleys at the bowed heads and shoulders of their attackers, get off one more flight. More horses—some have already gone down or broken back with screams of pain—stumble and fall, tripping their neighbors, but the mass drive on and… and what? It is at this moment that we have to make a judgment about the difference between what happens in a battle and what happens in a violent accident. A horse, in the normal course of events, will not gallop at an obstacle it cannot jump or see a way through, and it cannot jump or see a way through a solid line of men. Even less will it go at the sort of obviously dangerous obstacles which the archers' stakes presented. Equally, a man will not stand in the path of a running horse: He will run himself, or seek shelter, and only if exceptionally strong-nerved and knowing in its ways, stand his ground. Nevertheless, accidents happen. Men, miscalculating or slow-footed, and horses, confused or maddened, do collide, with results almost exclusively unpleasant for the man. We cannot therefore say, however unnatural and exceptional we recognize collisions between man and horse to be, that nothing of that nature occurred between the archers and the French cavalry at Agincourt. For the archers were trained to "receive cavalry," the horses trained to charge home, while it was the principal function of the

riders to insist on the horses doing that against which their nature rebelled. The horses had then found themselves on top of the stakes too late to refuse the obstacle, and a short, violent, and noisy collision had resulted.

The charge, momentarily terrifying for the English, had been a disaster for the enemy. And, as they rode off, the archers, with all the violent anger that comes with release from sudden danger, bent their bows and sent fresh flights of

If matched armies encounter one another, the one who does so in sorrow is sure to conquer.
—Lao Tzu, sixth century BC

arrows after them, bringing down more horses and maddening others into uncontrolled flight.

But the results of the rout went beyond the demoralization of the survivors. For as their horses galloped back, they met the first division of dismounted men-at-arms marching out to attack the English center. Perhaps eight thousand strong, and filling the space between the woods eight to ten deep, they could not easily or quickly open their ranks to let the fugitives through. But those that barged in, an occurrence to which the chroniclers testify, broke up the rhythm of the advance and knocked some men to the ground, an unpleasant experience when the soil is wet and trampled and one is wearing sixty or seventy pounds of sheet metal on the body.

This interruption in an advance which should have brought the French first division to within weapons' length of the English in three or four minutes at most gave Henry's men-at-arms ample time to brace themselves for the encounter. It also gave the archers, both those in the large groups on the wings and the two smaller groups in the central wedges, the chance to prolong their volleying of arrows into the French ranks. The range was progressively shortened by the advance, and the arrows, coming in on a flat trajectory in sheets of five thousand at ten-second intervals, must have begun to cause casualties among the French foot. For though they bowed their heads and hunched their shoulders, presenting a continuous front of deflecting surface to the storm, some of the arrows must have found the weak spots in the visor and at the shoulders and, as the range dropped right down, might even have penetrated armor itself.

Their charge, however, won an initial success, for before it the English men-at-arms fell back "a spear's length." What distance the chronicler means by that traditional phrase we cannot judge, and all the less because the French had cut down their lances in anticipation of fighting on foot. It probably implies "just enough to take the impetus out of the onset of the French," for we must imagine

> *War is a game, but unfortunately the cards, counters, and fishes suffer by an ill run more than the gamesters.* —Horace Walpole, 1788

them, although puffed by the effort of a jostling tramp across three hundred yards of wet plowland, accelerating over the last few feet into a run calculated to drive the points of their spears hard onto the enemy's chests and stomachs. The object would have been to knock over as many of them as possible, and so to open gaps in the ranks and isolate individuals who could then be killed or forced back onto the weapons of their own comrades; "sowing disorder" is a shorthand description of the aim. To avoid its achievement, the English, had they been more numerous, might have started forward to meet the French before they developed impulsion; since they were so outnumbered, it was individually prudent and tactically sound for the men most exposed to trot backwards before the French spearpoints, thus "wrongfooting" their opponents (a spearman times his thrust to coincide with the forward step of his left foot). The English, at the same time, would have been thrusting their spears at the French and, as movement died out of the two hosts, we can visualize them divided, at a distance of ten or fifteen feet, by a horizontal fence of waving and stabbing spear shafts.

In this fashion, the clash of the men-at-arms might have petered out, as it did on so many medieval battlefields, without a great deal more hurt to either side—though the French would have continued to suffer casualties from the fire of the archers, as long as they remained within range and the English had arrows to shoot at them (the evidence implies they must now have been running short). We can guess that three factors deterred the antagonists from drawing off from each other. One was the English fear of quitting their solid position between the woods and behind the archers' stakes for the greater dangers of the open field; the second was the French certainty of victory; the third was their enormous press of numbers.

This was disastrous, for it is vital to recognize, if we are to understand Agincourt, that all infantry actions, even those fought in the closest of close order, are not, in the last resort, combats of mass against mass, but the sum of many combats of individuals—one against one, one against two, three against five. This must be so, for the very simple reason that the weapons which individuals wield are of very limited range and effect, as they remain ever since missile weapons have become the universal equipment of the infantryman. At Agincourt, where the man-at-arms bore lance, sword, dagger, mace, or battleaxe, his ability to kill or wound was restricted to the circle centered on his own body, within which his reach allowed him to club, slash, or stab. Prevented by the throng at their backs from dodging, side-stepping, or retreating from the blows and thrusts directed at them by their English opponents, the individual French men-at-arms must shortly have begun to lose their man-to-man fights, collecting blows on the head or limbs which, even through armor, were sufficiently bruising or stunning to make them drop their weapons or lose their balance or footing. Within minutes, perhaps seconds, of hand-to-hand fighting being joined, some of them would have fallen, their bodies lying at the feet of their comrades, further impeding the movement of individuals and thus offering an obstacle to the advance of the whole column.

Seeing the French falling at the heads of the columns, while those on the flanks still flinched away from the final flights of arrows, the archers seized the chance that confusion and irresolution offered. Drawing swords, swinging heavier weapons—axes, bills, or the mallets they used to hammer in their stakes—they left their staked-out positions and ran down to assault the men in armor.

While an archer swung or lunged at a man-at-arms' front, another dodged his sword-arm to land him a mallet-blow on the back of the head or an axe-stroke behind the knee. Either would have toppled him and, once sprawling, he would have been helpless; a thrust into his face if he were wearing a bascinet, into the slits of his visor if he were wearing a closed helmet, or through the mail of his armpit or groin would have killed him outright or left him to bleed to death. Each act of execution need have taken only a few seconds, time enough for a flurry of thrusts clumsily parried, a fall, two or three figures to kneel over another on the ground, a few butcher's blows, a cry *in extremis*.

Nevertheless, very large numbers of Frenchmen had, on promise of ransom, been taken captive, presumably from the moment when the English sensed that the battle was going their way. Their removal from the field, the deaths of others, and the moral and by now no doubt incipient physical collapse of those left had opened up sufficient space for the English to abandon their close order and penetrate their enemy's ranks.

This advance brought them eventually—we are talking of an elapsed time of perhaps only half an hour since the first blows were exchanged—into contact with the second line. They must themselves have been tiring by this time. For the excitement, fear, and physical exertion of fighting hand-to-hand with heavy weapons in plate armor quickly drained the body of its energy, despite the surge of energy released under stress by glandular activity. Even so, they were not repulsed by the onset of the second line. Indeed, its intervention seems to have made no appreciable im-

pact on the fighting. There is a modern military cliché, "Never reinforce failure," which means broadly that to thrust reinforcements in among soldiers who have failed in an attack, feel themselves beaten, and are trying to run away is merely to waste the newcomers' energies in a struggle against the thrust of the crowd and to risk infecting them with its despair. And it was indeed in congestion and desperation that the second line appear to have met the English. The chroniclers do not specify exactly what passed between them, presumably because it was so similar to what had gone on before during the defeat of the first line. Though we may guess that a large number of the second line, as soon as they became aware of the disaster, turned their backs and ran off the way they had come; some were dragged out by their pages or servants.

> From The Face of Battle. *A twentieth-century military historian sets up the pieces on a fifteenth-century chessboard.*

Between the Devil and the Deep-Blue Sea

A U.S. serviceman's chances of death in battle:

Revolutionary War: 1 in 50 (2 percent)

War of 1812: 1 in 127 (0.8 percent)

Indian Wars: 1 in 106 (0.9 percent)

Mexican-American War: 1 in 45 (2.2 percent)

Civil War: 1 in 15 (6.7 percent)

Spanish-American War: 1 in 798 (0.1 percent)

World War I: 1 in 89 (1.1 percent)

World War II: 1 in 56 (1.8 percent)

Korean War: 1 in 171 (0.6 percent)

Vietnam War: 1 in 185 (0.5 percent)

Persian Gulf War: 1 in 3,162 (0.03 percent)

1944: Peleliu

BLOOD AND FLIES

The sun bore down on us like a giant heat lamp. Once I saw a misplaced phosphorous grenade explode on the coral from the sun's intense heat. We always shaded our stacked mortar shells with a piece of ammo box to prevent this.

Occasional rains that fell on the hot coral merely evaporated like steam off hot pavement. The air hung heavy and muggy. Everywhere we went on the ridges, the hot humid air reeked with the stench of death. A strong wind was no relief; it simply brought the horrid odor from an adjacent area. Japanese corpses lay where they fell among the rocks and on the slopes. It was impossible to cover them. Usually there was no soil that could be spaded over them, just the hard, jagged coral. The enemy dead simply rotted where they had fallen. They lay all over the place in grotesque positions with puffy faces and grinning buck-toothed expressions.

It is difficult to convey to anyone who has not experienced it the ghastly horror of having your sense of smell saturated constantly with the putrid odor of rotting human flesh day after day, night after night. This was something the men of an infantry battalion got a horrifying dose of during a long, protracted battle such as Peleliu. In the tropics the dead became bloated and gave off a terrific stench within a few hours after death.

Soviet ski troops advance through Finland, 1939-40.

Whenever possible we removed Marine dead to the rear of the company's position. There they were usually laid on stretchers and covered with ponchos which stretched over the head of the corpse down to the ankles. I rarely saw a dead Marine left uncovered with his face exposed to sun, rain, and flies. Somehow it seemed indecent not to cover our dead. Often though, the dead might lie on the stretchers for some time and decompose badly before the busy graves registration crews could take them for burial in the division cemetery near the airfield.

During the fighting around the Umurbrogol Pocket, there was a constant movement of one weary, depleted Marine company being relieved by another slightly less weary, depleted company. We seemed to rotate from one particularly dangerous part of the line to one slightly less so and back again continuously.

There were certain areas we moved into and out of several times as the campaign dragged along its weary, bloody course. In many such areas I became quite familiar with the sight of some particular enemy corpse, as if it were a landmark. It was gruesome to see the stages of decay proceed from just killed, to bloated, to maggot-infested rotting, to partially exposed bones—like some biological clock marking the inexorable passage of time. On each occasion my company passed such a landmark, we were fewer in number.

Each time we moved into a different position, I could determine the areas occupied by each rifle company as we went into that sector of the line. Behind each company position lay a pile of ammo and supplies and the inevitable rows of dead under their ponchos. We could determine how bad that sector of the line was by the number of dead. To see them so always filled me with anger at the war and the realization of the senseless waste. It depressed me far more than my own fear.

Added to the awful stench of the dead of both sides was the repulsive odor of human excrement everywhere. It was all but impossible to practice simple, elemental field sanitation

on most areas of Peleliu because of the rocky surface. Field sanitation during maneuvers and combat was the responsibility of each man. In short, under normal conditions, he covered his own waste with a scoop of soil. At night when he didn't dare venture out of his foxhole, he simply used an empty grenade canister or ration can, threw it out of his hole, and scooped dirt over it next day if he wasn't under heavy enemy fire.

But on Peleliu, except along the beach areas and in the swamps, digging into the coral rock was nearly impossible. Consequently, thousands of men—most of them around the Umurbrogol Pocket in the ridges, many suffering with severe diarrhea, fighting for weeks on an island two miles by six miles—couldn't practice basic field sanitation. This fundamental neglect caused an already putrid tropical atmosphere to become inconceivably vile.

Added to this was the odor of thousands of rotting, discarded Japanese and American rations. At every breath one inhaled hot, humid air heavy with countless repulsive odors. I felt as though my lungs would never be cleansed of all those foul vapors. It may not have been that way down on the airfield and in other areas where the service troops were encamped, but around the infantry in the Umurbrogol Pocket, the stench varied only from foul to unbearable.

In this garbage-filled environment the flies, always numerous in the tropics anyway, underwent a population explosion. This species was not the unimposing common housefly (the presence of one of which in a restaurant is enough to cause most Americans today to declare the place unfit to serve food to the public). Peleliu's most common fly was the huge blowfly or bluebottle fly. This creature has a plump, metallic, greenish-blue body, and its wings often make a humming sound during flight.

The then new insecticide DDT was sprayed over the combat areas on Peleliu for the first time anywhere. It supposedly reduced the adult fly population while Marines were still fighting on the ridges, but I never noticed that the flies became fewer in number.

With human corpses, human excrement,

and rotting rations scattered across Peleliu's ridges, those nasty insects were so large, so glutted, and so lazy that some could scarcely fly. They could not be waved away or frightened off a can of rations or a chocolate bar. Frequently they tumbled off the side of my canteen cup into my coffee. We actually had to shake the food to dislodge the flies, and even then they sometimes refused to move. I usually had to balance my

Come back with your shield or on it.
—Spartan proverb

can of stew on my knee, spooning it up with my right hand while I picked the sluggish creatures off the stew with my left. They refused to move or to be intimidated. It was revolting, to say the least, to watch big fat blowflies leave a corpse and swarm into our C rations.

Even though none of us had much appetite, we still had to eat. A way to solve the fly problem was to eat after sunset or before sunrise when the insects were inactive. Chow had to be unheated then, because no sterno tablets or other form of light could be used after dark. It was sure to draw enemy sniper fire.

Each morning just before sunrise, when things were fairly quiet, I could hear a steady humming sound like bees in a hive as the flies became active with the onset of daylight. They rose up off the corpses, refuse, rocks, brush, and wherever else they had settled for the night like a swarm of bees. Their numbers were incredible.

Large land crabs crawled all over the ridges at night, attracted by corpses. Their rustling through dry debris often was indistinguishable from prowling enemy soldiers. We responded by tossing a grenade at the sound.

In addition to rotting corpses and organic waste, the litter of smashed and worn-out equipment of every type became more abundant as the battle dragged on and the size of the Umurbrogol Pocket shrank slowly. The ridges and ravines were littered with the flotsam of fierce combat. Debris of battle was everywhere and became more noticeable as the weeks dragged on.

I still see clearly the landscape around one particular position we occupied for several days. It was a scene of destruction and desolation that no fiction could invent. The area was along the southwestern border of the pocket where ferocious fighting had gone on since the second day of battle (16 September). The 1st Marines, the 7th Marines, and now the 5th Marines, all in their turn, had fought against this same section of ridges. Our exhausted battalion, 3/5, moved into the line to relieve another slightly more exhausted battalion. It was the same old weary shuffling of one tired, depleted outfit into the line to relieve another whose sweating men trudged out of their positions, hollow-eyed, stooped, grimy, bearded zombies.

The Company K riflemen and machine gunners climbed up the steep ridge and into the crevices and holes of the company we relieved. Orders were given that no one must look over the crest of the ridge, because enemy rifle and machine-gun fire would kill instantly anyone who did.

As usual the troops pulling out gave our men "the dope" on the local conditions: what type fire to expect, particular danger spots, and possible infiltration routes at night.

My mortar went into a gun pit occupied by one of the 60mm mortars of the company we were relieving. The gun pit was among coral rocks about twenty yards from the foot of the ridge. An extremely youthful Marine was just buckling the leather strap around the bipod and tube of his 60mm mortar as I walked up near the position and put down my heavy ammo bag. I sat on my helmet and started talking to him as the rest of our squad moved into their positions. As the young man looked up, I was struck by the agonized expression on his face. He didn't seem happy, the way he should have, about being relieved.

"You guys watch out for the Japs at night. Two of the bastards got into this gun pit last night and cut up our gunner and assistant gunner," he said.

He told me in a strained voice that the crew was so occupied firing the mortar during the previous night that two Japanese who slipped through the line on the ridge managed to creep up close to the pit without detection. They jumped in and cut up the two men working the mortar before nearby mortar ammo carriers killed them. The wounded Marines had been evacuated, but one of them had died, and the other was in poor condition. The bodies of the Japanese had been thrown into some nearby bushes.

The man telling me of the tragedy and another crouching beside the gun pit had been ammo carriers but had now assumed new duties as gunner and assistant. I noticed that as the new gunner folded and strapped his gun to leave, he seemed reluctant to touch the bottom or sides of the emplacement. When he left and we came closer to the gun pit to set up our mortar, I saw why. The white coral sides and bottom were spattered and smeared with the dark red blood of his two comrades.

After we got our gun emplaced, I collected up some large scraps of cardboard from ration and ammo boxes and used them to cover the bottom of the pit as well as I could. Fat, lazy blowflies were reluctant to leave the blood-smeared rock.

I had long since become used to the sight of blood, but the idea of sitting in that blood-stained gun pit was a bit too much for me. It seemed almost like leaving our dead unburied to sit on the blood of a fellow Marine spilled out on the coral. I noticed that my buddy looked approvingly at my efforts as he came back from getting orders for our gun. Although we never discussed the subject, he apparently felt as I did. As I looked at the stains on the coral, I recalled some of the eloquent phrases of politicians and newsmen about how "gallant" it is for a man to "shed his blood for his country," and "to give his life's blood as a sacrifice," and so on. The words seemed so ridiculous. Only the flies benefited.

Eugene Sledge, *from* With the Old Breed, *the author's remembrance of his service in the U.S. Marine Corps during World War II. The battle for control of Peleliu, a small island in the Pacific Ocean of no strategic importance, lasted seventy days and produced an honor roll of 1,529 American dead.*

1917: Hindenburg Trench

SIEGFRIED SASSOON IN NO MAN'S LAND

At 9:00 P.M. the company fell in at the top of the ruined street of Saint Martin. Two guides from the outgoing battalion awaited us. We were to relieve some Northumberland Fusiliers in the Hindenburg Trench—the companies going up independently.

It was a gray evening, dry and windless. The village of Saint Martin was a shattered relic; but even in the devastated area one could be conscious of the arrival of spring, and as I took up my position in the rear of the moving column, there was something in the sober twilight which could remind me of April evenings in England and the Butley cricket field where a few of us had been having our first knock at the nets. The cricket season had begun.... But the company had left the shell-pitted road and was going uphill across open ground. Already the guides were making the pace too hot for the rear platoon; like most guides they were inconveniently nimble owing to their freedom from accoutrement, and insecurely confident that they knew the way. The muttered message, "Pass it along—steady the pace in front," was accompanied by the usual muffled clinkings and rattlings of arms and equipment. Unwillingly retarded, the guides led us into the deepening dusk. We hadn't more than two miles to go, but gradually the guides grew less authoritative. Several times they stopped to get their bearings. Leake fussed and fumed, and they became more and more flurried. I began to suspect that our progress was circular.

At a midnight halt the hill still loomed in front of us; the guides confessed that they had lost their way, and Leake decided to sit down and wait for daylight. (There were few things more uncomfortable in the life of an officer than to be walking in front of a party of men all of whom knew that he was leading them in the wrong direction.) With Leake's permission I blundered experimentally into the gloom, fully expecting to lose both myself and the company. By a lucky accident, I soon fell headlong into a sunken road and found myself among a small party of sappers who could tell me where I was. It was a case of, "Please, can you tell me the way to the Hindenburg Trench?" Congratulating myself on my cleverness, I took one of the sappers back to poor benighted B Company, and we were led to our battalion rendezvous.

We were at the end of a journey which had begun twelve days before, when we started from Camp Thirteen. Stage by stage, we had marched to the life-denying region which from far away had threatened us with the blink and growl of its bombardments. Now we were groping and stumbling along a deep ditch to the place appointed for us in that zone of inhuman havoc. There must have been some hazy moonlight, for I remember the figures of men huddled against the sides of communication trenches; seeing them in some sort of ghastly glimmer—(was it, perhaps, the diffused whiteness of a sinking flare beyond the ridge?) I was doubtful whether they were asleep or dead, for the attitudes of many were like death, grotesque and distorted. But this is nothing new to write about, you will say; just a weary company, squeezing past dead or drowsing men while it sloshes and stumbles to a front line trench. Nevertheless, that night relief had its significance for me, though in human experience it had been multiplied a millionfold. I, a single human being with my little stock of earthly experience in my head, was entering once again the veritable gloom and disaster of the thing called Armageddon. And I saw it then, as I see it now—a dreadful place, a place of horror and desolation which no imagination could have invented. Also it was a place where a man of strong spirit might know himself utterly powerless against death and destruction, and yet stand up and defy gross darkness and stupefying shell fire, discovering in himself the invincible resistance of an animal or an insect, and an endurance which he might, in after days, forget or disbelieve.

Anyhow, there I was, leading that little procession of Flintshire Fusiliers, many of whom had never seen a front line trench before. At that juncture they asked no compensation for their efforts except a mug of hot tea. The tea would have been a miracle, and we didn't get it till next morning, but there was some comfort in the fact that it wasn't raining.

It was nearly four o'clock when we found ourselves in the Hindenburg Main Trench. After telling me to post the sentries, Leake disappeared down some stairs to the Tunnel. The company we were relieving had already departed, so there was no one to give me any information. At first I didn't even know for certain that we were in the front line. The trench was a sort of gully: deep, wide, and unfinished looking. The sentries had to clamber up a bank of loose earth before they could see over the top. Our company was only about eighty strong and its sector was fully six hundred yards. The distance between the sentry posts made me aware of our inadequacy in that wilderness. I had no right to feel homeless, but I did; and if I had needed to be reminded of my forlorn situation as a living creature, I could have done it merely by thinking of a field cashier. Fifty franc notes were comfortable things, but they were no earthly use up here, and the words "field cashier" would have epitomized my remoteness from snugness and security and from all assurance that I should be alive and kicking the week after next. But it would soon be Sunday morning; such ideas weren't wholesome, and there was a certain haggard curiosity attached to the proceedings, combined with the self-dramatizing desperation which enabled a good many of us to worry our way through much worse emergencies than mine.

Out in No Man's Land there was no sign of any German activity. The only remarkable thing was the unbroken silence. I was in a sort of twilight, for there was a moony glimmer in the low-clouded sky; but the unknown territory in front was dark, and I stared out at it like a man looking from the side of a ship. Returning to my own sector I met a runner with a verbal message from Battalion HQ. B Company's front was to be thoroughly patrolled at once. Realizing the futility of sending any of my few spare men out on patrol (they'd been walking about for seven hours and were dead beat), I lost my temper, quietly and inwardly. Shirley and Rees were nowhere to be seen, and it wouldn't have been fair to send them out, inexperienced as they were. So I stumped along to our right-flank post, told them to pass it along that a patrol was going out from right to left, and then started sulkily out for a solitary stroll in No Man's Land. I felt more annoyed with Battalion Headquarters than with the enemy. There was no wire in front of the trench, which was, of course, constructed for people facing the other way. I counted my steps; two hundred steps straight ahead; then I began to walk the presumptive six hundred footsteps to the left. But it isn't easy to count your steps in the dark among shell holes, and after a problematic four hundred I lost confidence in my automatic pistol, which I was grasping in my right-hand breeches pocket. Here I am, I thought, alone out in this god forsaken bit of ground, with quite a good chance of bumping into a Boche strong-post. Apparently there was only one reassuring action which I could per-

form; so I expressed my opinion of the war by relieving myself (for it must be remembered that there are other reliefs beside battalion reliefs). I insured my sense of direction by placing my pistol on the ground with its muzzle pointing the way I was going. Feeling less lonely and afraid, I finished my patrol without having met so much as a dead body, and regained the trench exactly opposite our left-hand post after being huskily challenged by an irresolute sentry, who, as I realized at the time, was the greatest danger I had encountered. It was now just beginning to be more daylight than darkness, and when I stumbled down a shaft to the underground trench, I left the sentries shivering under a red and rainy-looking sky.

By ten o'clock I was above ground again, in charge of a fatigue party. We went halfway back to Saint Martin, to an ammunition dump, whence we carried up boxes of trench mortar bombs. I carried a box myself, as the conditions were vile and it seemed the only method of convincing the men that it had to be done. We were out nearly seven hours; it rained all day

A soldier fires a blunderbuss. From the *Bellifortis* manuscript, fifteenth century.

and the trenches were a morass of gluelike mud. The unmitigated misery of that carrying party was a typical infantry experience of discomfort without actual danger. Even if the ground had been dry, the boxes would have been too heavy for most of the men; but we were lucky in one way: The wet weather was causing the artillery

A German soldier fires his bazooka, 1945. Photograph taken by the German Army.

to spend an inactive Sunday. It was a yellow, corpselike day, more like November than April, and the landscape was desolate and treeless. What we were doing was quite unexceptional; millions of soldiers endured the same sort of thing and got badly shelled into the bargain. Nevertheless I can believe that my party, staggering and floundering under its loads, would have made an impressive picture of "Despair." The background, too, was appropriate. We were among the debris of the intense bombardment of ten days before, for we were passing along and across the Hindenburg Outpost Trench, with its belt of wire (fifty yards deep in places); here and there these rusty jungles had been flattened by tanks. The Outpost Trench was about two hundred yards from the Main Trench, which was now our front line. It had been solidly made, ten feet deep, with timbered firesteps, splayed sides,

and timbered steps at intervals to front and rear and to machine-gun emplacements. Now it was wrecked as though by earthquake and eruption. Concrete strong-posts were smashed and tilted sideways; everywhere the chalky soil was pocked and pitted with huge shell holes; and wherever we looked the mangled effigies of the dead were our *memento mori*. Shell-twisted and dismembered, the Germans maintained the violent attitudes in which they had died. The British had mostly been killed by bullets or bombs, so they looked more resigned. But I can remember a pair of hands (nationality unknown) which protruded from the soaked ashen soil like the roots of a tree turned upside down; one hand seemed to be pointing at the sky with an accusing gesture. Each time I passed that place, the protest of those fingers became more expressive of an appeal to God in defiance of those who made the war. Who made the war? I laughed hysterically as the thought passed through my mud-stained mind. But I only laughed mentally, for my box of Stokes-gun ammunition left me no breath to spare for an angry guffaw. And the dead were the dead; this was no time to be pitying them or asking silly questions about their outraged lives. Such sights must be taken for granted, I thought, as I gasped and slithered and stumbled with my disconsolate crew. Floating on the surface of the flooded trench was the mask of a human face which had detached itself from the skull.

From Memoirs of an Infantry Officer, *the poet's account of his years as a British officer in World War I. Sassoon's near suicidal heroism on the Western Front inspired his fellow soldiers to award him the nickname "Mad Jack." During the war his public statements of pacifism prompted higher-ranking military authorities to place him in an asylum for the temporarily insane.*

1969: My Lai

THE "PINKVILLE" INCIDENT

In late April 1968, I was awaiting orders for a transfer from HHC, 11th Brigade, to Company E, 51st Inf. (LRP), when I happened to run into Pfc. "Butch" Gruver, whom I had known in Hawaii. Gruver told me he had been assigned to C Company, 1st of the 20th, until April 1, when he transferred to the unit that I was headed for. During the course of our conversation, he told me the first of many reports I was to hear of "Pinkville."

"Charlie" Company 1/20 had been assigned to Task Force Barker in late February 1968 to help conduct "search and destroy" operations on the Batangan Peninsula, Barker's area of operation. The task force was operating out of L.F. Dottie, located five or six miles north of Quang Ngai city on Vietnamese National Highway 1. Gruver said that Charlie Company had sustained casualties, primarily from mines and booby traps, almost everyday from the first day they arrived on the peninsula. One village area was particularly troublesome and seemed to be infested with booby traps and enemy soldiers. It was located about six miles northeast of Quang Ngai city at approximate coordinates B.S. 728795. It was a notorious area, and the men of Task Force Barker had a special name for it: They called it "Pinkville." One morning in the latter part of March, Task Force Barker moved out from its firebase headed for "Pinkville." Its mission: destroy the trouble spot and all of its inhabitants.

When "Butch" told me this I didn't quite believe that what he was telling me was true, but he assured me that it was and went on to describe what had happened. The other two companies that made up the task force cordoned off the village so that Charlie Company could move through to destroy the structures and kill the inhabitants. Any villagers who ran from Charlie Company were stopped by the encircling companies. I asked "Butch" several times if all the people were killed. He said that he thought they were, men, women, and children. He re-

called seeing a small boy, about three or four years old, standing by the trail with a gunshot wound in one arm. The boy was clutching his wounded arm with his other hand while blood trickled between his fingers. He was staring around himself in shock and disbelief at what he saw. "He just stood there with big eyes staring around like he didn't understand; he didn't believe what was happening. Then the captain's RTO [radio operator] put a burst of 16 [M-16 rifle] fire into him." It was so bad, Gruver said, that one of the men in his squad shot himself in the foot in order to be medivaced out of the area so that he would not have to participate in the slaughter. Although he had not seen it, Gruver had been told by people he considered trustworthy that one of the company's officers, Second Lieutenant Kally (this spelling may be incorrect) had rounded up several groups of villagers (each group consisting of a minimum of twenty persons of both sexes and all ages). According to the story, Kally then machine-gunned each group. Gruver estimated that the population of the village had been three to four hundred people and that very few, if any, escaped.

Terry and Doherty had been in the same squad, and their platoon was the third platoon of C Company to pass through the village. Most of the people they came to were already dead. Those that weren't were sought out and shot. The platoon left nothing alive, neither livestock nor people. Around noon, the two soldiers' squads stopped to eat. "Billy and I started to get our chow," Terry said, "but close to us was a bunch of Vietnamese in a heap, and some of them were moaning. Kally had been through before us, and all of them had been shot, but many weren't dead. It was obvious that they weren't going to get any medical attention, so Billy and I got up and went over to where they were. I guess we sort of finished them off." Terry went on to say that he and Doherty then returned to where their packs were and ate lunch.

It was June before I spoke to anyone who had something of significance to add to what I had already been told of the "Pinkville" incident. It was the end of June 1968 when I ran into Sergeant Larry La Croix at the USO in Chu Lai. La Croix had been in Second Lt. Kally's platoon on the day Task Force Barker swept through "Pinkville." What he told me verified the stories of the others, but he also had something new to add. He had been a witness to Kally's gunning down of at least three separate groups of villagers. "It was terrible. They were slaughtering the villagers like so many sheep." Kally's men were dragging people out of bunkers and hootches and putting them together in a group. The people in the group were men, women, and children of all ages. As soon as he felt that the group was big enough, Kally ordered an M-60 [machine-gun] set up and the people killed. La Croix said that he bore witness to this procedure at least three times. The three groups were of different sizes: one of about twenty people, one of about thirty people, and one of about forty people. When the first group was put together Kally ordered Pfc. Torres to man the machine-gun and open fire on the villagers that had been grouped together. This Torres did, but before everyone in the group was down, he ceased fire and refused to fire again. After ordering Torres to recommence firing several times, Lieutenant Kally took over the M-60 and finished shooting the remaining villagers in that first group himself. Sergeant La Croix told me that Kally didn't bother to order anyone to take the machine-gun when the other two groups of villagers were formed. He simply manned it himself and shot down all villagers in both groups.

> **Ron Ridenhour**, *from a letter written on March 29, 1969, to the American military command in Vietnam. Ridenhour, a helicopter gunner in country with the 51st Infantry, was telling an old story that he had heard from a friend. The letter, sent also to officials at the Pentagon and to thirty members of Congress, led to the investigation of the murder of five hundred Vietnamese civilians in the village of My Lai on March 16, 1968.*

The Battle of Trafalgar, as Seen from the Mizen Starboard Shrouds of the Victory, by Joseph Mallord William Turner, 1806–1808.

1861: Virginia

In one of the late movements of our troops in the valley (near Upperville, I think) a strong force of Moseby's mounted guerillas attack'd a train of wounded and the guard of cavalry convoying them. The ambulances contain'd about sixty wounded, quite a number of them officers of rank. The rebels were in strength, and the capture of the train and its partial guard after a short snap was effectually accomplish'd. No sooner had our men surrender'd, the rebels instantly commenced robbing the train and murdering their prisoners, even the wounded. Here is the scene or a sample of it, ten minutes after. Among the wounded officers in the ambulances were one, a lieutenant of regulars, and another of higher rank. These two were dragg'd out on the ground on their backs, and were now surrounded by the guerillas, a demoniac crowd, each member of which was stabbing them in different parts of their bodies. One of the officers had his feet pinn'd firmly to the ground by bayonets stuck through them and thrust into the ground. These two officers, as afterwards found on examination, had receiv'd about twenty such thrusts, some of them through the mouth, face, etc. The wounded had all been dragg'd (to give a better chance also for plunder) out of their wagons; some had been effectually dispatch'd, and their bodies were lying there lifeless and bloody. Others, not yet dead, but horribly mutilated, were moaning or groaning. Of our men who surrender'd, most had been thus maim'd or slaughter'd.

At this instant a force of our cavalry, who had been following the train at some interval, charged suddenly upon the secesh captors, who proceeded at once to make the best escape they could. Most of them got away, but we gobbled two officers and seventeen men in the very acts just described. The sight was one which admitted of little discussion, as may be imagined. The seventeen captur'd men and two officers were put under guard for the night, but it was decided there and then that they should die. The next morning the two officers were taken in the town, separate places, put in the centre of the street, and shot. The seventeen men were taken to an open ground, a little one side. They were placed in a hollow square, half-encompass'd by two of our cavalry regiments, one of which regiments had three days before found the bloody corpses of three of their men hamstrung and hung up by the heels to limbs of trees by Moseby's guerillas, and the other had not long before had twelve men, after surrendering, shot and then hung by the neck to limbs of trees, and jeering inscriptions pinn'd to the breast of one of the corpses, who had been a sergeant. Those three, and those twelve, had been found, I say, by these environing regiments. Now, with revolvers, they form'd the grim cordon of the seventeen prisoners. The latter were placed in the midst of the hollow square, unfasten'd, and the ironical remark made to them that they were now to be given "a chance for themselves." A few ran for it. But what use? From every side the deadly pills came. In a few minutes the seventeen corpses strew'd the hollow square. I was curious to know whether some of the Union soldiers, some few (some one or two at least of the youngsters), did not abstain from shooting on the helpless men. Not one. There was no exultation, very little said, almost nothing, yet every man there contributed his shot.

Multiply the above by scores, aye, hundreds—verify it in all the forms that different circumstances, individuals, places, could afford—light it with every lurid passion, the wolf's, the lion's lapping thirst for blood—the passionate, boiling volcanoes of human revenge for comrades, brothers slain—with the light of burning farms and heaps of smutting, smouldering black embers—and in the human heart everywhere black, worse embers—and you have an inkling of this war.

From Specimen Days in America, *the poet's recollection of his travels during the Civil War. Whitman served as a "psychological nurse" in Washington's Army hospitals.*

1805: Cape Trafalgar

ENGLAND EXPECTS, NELSON CONFIDES

As the moment approached, the tension grew almost unbearable: The waiting had been so long. Men suddenly remembered something quite mundane: They were hungry, and the battle was going to start exactly at dinnertime. Some captains had foreseen it and ordered the cooks to have the beef and biscuit ready an hour early; others less wise ordered cheese up from the holds, and a half ration of rum. Officers, whose cabins had been dismantled, ate where they

An Amazon fights the cavalry. Greek, fourth century BC.

stood or grouped round the rudder head, which they used as a table. Some captains called their junior lieutenants up from the gun decks for a final word—mostly to tell them to hold their fire. Captain Hargood of the *Belleisle* pointed out the black bulk of the *Santa Ana*: "Gentlemen, I have only to say that I shall pass close under the stern of that ship. Put in two round shot and then a grape, and give her *that*."

And Nelson also felt the tension and the need for a final word. He said to Blackwood, who had been his most constant companion all the morning, "I will now amuse the fleet with a signal. Do you not think there is one yet wanting?" Blackwood said everyone seemed to know exactly what to do. Nelson thought for a moment, and then said, "Suppose we telegraph, 'Nelson confides that every man will do his duty.'" Somebody suggested "England" instead of "Nelson," and Nelson accepted the change

with pleasure. With an air of boyish gaiety, he called the flag lieutenant: "Mr. Pasco, I wish to say to the fleet, 'England confides that every man will do his duty.' You must be quick, for I have one more to make, which is for close action." Pasco asked to be allowed to use "expects" instead of "confides" because "expects" was in Popham's signal book, but "confides" would have to be spelt. "That will do, Pasco, make it directly," Nelson said. And at 11:35 the most famous battle signal ever made was hoisted to the yards and mastheads of the *Victory*.

"England expects that every man will do his duty." The phrase inspired generations of Englishmen. Yet it was not received with unanimous joy in the fleet. Ships cheered it, but in some of them the cheer itself had a dutiful ring about it. Collingwood, seeing the flags, said, "I wish Nelson would stop signaling. We know well enough what to do"—but when the whole signal was read to him, he approved it cordially enough. In the *Euryalus*, nobody bothered to repeat it to the crew; and in the *Ajax*, the officer who was sent to read it out on the gun decks heard sailors muttering, "Do my duty? I've always done my duty; haven't you, Jack?"

Nelson's first instinct had been right, as it always was in matters of that kind. "England" was too impersonal; "expects" was too mandatory. Nelson's confidence would have meant much more to the fleet than England's expectation. "Nelson confides"—they would have cheered that all right; that was what they would have liked to hear. England was far away; England was not the navy, and this was a naval occasion. But Nelson was there, he was with them, one of them: he was their pride.

When the flags were hauled down, his last signal was hoisted: "Engage the enemy more closely." It flew at the masthead until it was shot away.

David Howarth, *from* Trafalgar: The Nelson Touch. *On October 21, 1805, southwest of Spain's Cape Trafalgar, the British fleet defeated a force of French and Spanish ships in the decisive naval battle of the Napoleonic War. Admiral Lord Horatio Nelson died of wounds aboard his flagship, HMS* Victory.

c. 1943: Majdanek

The warm, damp changing room was quiet and gloomy; the only light came through some small rectangular windows.

Benches made from thick bare planks disappeared into the half-darkness. A low partition ran down the middle of the room to the wall opposite the entrance; the men were undressing on one side, the women and children on the other.

This division didn't cause any anxiety: people were still able to see each other and call out, "Manya, Manya, are you there?" "Yes, yes, I can see you." One man shouted out, "Matilda, bring a flannel so you can rub my back for me!" Most people felt a sense of relief.

Serious-looking men in gowns walked up and down the rows, keeping order and giving out sensible advice: Socks, footcloths, and stockings should be placed inside your shoes, and you mustn't forget the number of your row and place.

People's voices sounded quiet and muffled.

But Sofya Levinton noticed something else. It was as though the body of a whole people, previously covered over by layers of rags, was laid bare in these naked bodies of all ages: the skinny little boy with the big nose over whom an old woman had shaken her head and said, "Poor little Hassid!" the fourteen-year-old girl who was admired even here by hundreds of eyes; the feeble and deformed old men and women who aroused everyone's pitying respect; men with strong backs covered in hair; women with large breasts and prominently veined legs. It was as though she felt, not just about herself, but about her whole people: "Yes, here I am." This was the naked body of a people: young and old, robust and feeble, with bright curly hair and with pale gray hair.

Sofya looked at her own broad, white shoulders; no one had ever kissed them—only her mother, long ago when she was a child. Then, with a feeling of meekness, she looked

at David. Had she really, only a few minutes ago, forgotten about him and leapt furiously at an SS guard? "A foolish young Jew and an old Russian pupil of his once preached the doctrine of nonviolence," she thought. "But that was before Fascism." No longer ashamed of the maternal feelings that had been aroused in her—virgin though she was—she bent down and took David's narrow little face in her large

> *War is the health of the state.*
> *—Randolph Bourne, 1918*

hands. It was as though she had taken his warm eyes into her hands and kissed them.

"Yes, my child," she said, "we've reached the bathhouse."

Behind the partition, a man with a thick black beard, wearing torn pajama bottoms instead of underpants, called out, his eyes and his false teeth glittering, "Manechka, there's a bathing-costume for sale here. Shall we buy it?"

Musya Borisovna smiled at the joke; her low-cut shift revealed her breasts, and she was covering them with one hand.

Sofya Levinton knew that these witticisms were anything but an expression of strength. It was just that terror became less terrible if you laughed at it.

Rebekka Bukhman's beautiful face looked thin and exhausted; she turned her huge, feverish eyes aside and ran her fingers through her thick curls, hiding away her rings and earrings.

She was in the grip of a cruel, blind life-force. Helpless and unhappy though she was, Fascism had reduced her to its own level: Nothing could break her determination to survive. Even now she no longer remembered how, with these same hands, she had squeezed her child's throat, afraid that its crying would reveal their hiding place.

But as Rebekka Bukhman gave a long sigh, like an animal that had finally reached the safety of a thicket, she caught sight of a woman in a gown cutting Musya Borisovna's curls with a pair of scissors. Beside her someone else was cutting a little girl's hair. A silky black stream fell silently onto the concrete floor. There was hair everywhere; it was as though the women were washing their legs in streams of bright and dark water.

The woman in the gown unhurriedly took Rebekka's hand away and seized the hair at the back of her head; the tips of her scissors clinked

against the rings. Without stopping work, she deftly ran her fingers through Rebekka's hair, removed the rings and whispered, "Everything will be returned to you." Then, still more quietly, she whispered, "*Ganz ruhig*—Quiet. The Germans are listening."

Rebekka at once forgot the woman's face; she had no eyes, no lips, just a blue-veined, yellowish hand.

A gray-haired man appeared on the other side of the partition; his spectacles sat askew on his crooked nose and he looked like a sick, unhappy demon. He glanced up and down the benches. Articulating each syllable like someone used to speaking to the deaf, he asked:

"Mother, Mother, how are you?"

A little wrinkled old woman, recognizing her son's voice amid the general hubbub, guessed what he meant and answered:

"My pulse is fine, no irregularity at all, don't worry!"

Someone next to Sofya Levinton said:

"That's Helman. He's a famous doctor."

A naked young woman was holding a thick-lipped little girl in white knickers by the hand and screaming:

"They're going to kill us, they're going to kill us!"

"Quiet, quiet! Calm her down, she's mad," said the other women. They looked round— there were no guards in sight. Their eyes and ears were able to rest in the quiet semidarkness.

What pleasure there was, a pleasure they hadn't experienced for months on end, in taking off their half-rotten socks, stockings, and foot-cloths, in being free of clothes that had become almost wooden with dirt and sweat. The hair-cutters finished their job and went away; the women breathed still more freely. Some began to doze, others checked the seams on their clothes for lice, still others started to chat quietly among themselves.

"A pity we haven't got a pack of cards!" said one voice. "We could play Fool."

At this moment, Kaltluft, a cigar between his teeth, was picking up the telephone receiver; the storeman was loading a motor-cart with jars of "Zyklon B" that had red labels on them like pots of jam; and the special unit orderly was sitting in the office, waiting for the red indicator lamp on the wall to light up.

Suddenly the order "Stand up!" came from each end of the changing room.

Germans in black uniforms were standing at the end of the benches. Everyone made their way into a wide corridor, lit by dim ceiling-lamps covered by ovals of thick glass. The muscular strength of the smoothly curving concrete sucked in the stream of people. It was quiet; the only sound was the rustle of bare feet.

Before the war, Sofya Levinton had once said to Yevgenia Nikolaevna Shaposhnikova, "If one man is fated to be killed by another, it would be interesting to trace the gradual convergence of their paths. At the start they might be miles away from one another—I might be in Pamir picking alpine roses and clicking my camera, while this other man, my death, might be eight thousand miles away, fishing for ruff in a little stream after school. I might be getting ready to go to a concert and he might be at the railway station buying a ticket to go and visit his mother-in-law—and yet eventually we are bound to meet, we can't avoid it…"

Sofya looked up at the ceiling: the thick concrete would never again allow her to listen to a storm or glimpse the overturned dipper of the Great Bear…. She was walking in bare feet towards a bend in the corridor, and the corridor was noiselessly, stealthily floating towards her. The movement went on by itself, without violence; it was as if she were gliding along in a dream, as if everything inside her and round her had been smeared with glycerine…

The door to the gas chamber opened gradually and yet suddenly. The stream of people flowed through. An old couple, who had lived together for fifty years and had been separated in the changing room, were again walking side by side; the machinist's wife was carrying her baby, now awake; a mother and son looked over everyone's heads, scrutinizing not space but time. Sofya Levinton caught a glimpse of the doctor's face; right beside her she saw Musya Borisovna's kind eyes, then the horror-filled gaze of Rebekka Bukhman. There was Lusya Shterental—nothing could lessen the beauty of her young eyes, her nose, her neck, her half-open mouth; and there was old Lapidus walking beside her with his wrinkled blue lips. Again, Sofya Levinton hugged David's shoulders. Never before had she felt such tenderness for people.

Rebekka Bukhman, now walking at Sofya's side, gave a sudden scream—the scream of someone who is being turned into ashes.

A man with a length of hosepipe was standing beside the entrance to the gas chamber. He wore a brown shirt with a zip-fastener and short sleeves. It was seeing his childish, mindless, drunken smile that had caused Rebekka Bukhman to let out that terrible scream.

His eyes slid over Sofya Levinton's face. There he was; they had met at last!

Sofya felt her fingers itching to seize hold of the neck that seemed to creep up from his open collar. The man with the smile raised his club. Through the ringing of bells and the crunch of broken glass in her head, she heard the words: "Easy now, you filthy Yid!"

She just managed to stay on her feet. With slow, heavy steps, still holding David, she crossed the steel threshold.

David passed his hand over the steel frame of the door; it felt cool and slippery. He caught sight of a light gray blur that was the reflection of his own face. The soles of his bare feet told him that the floor here was colder than in the corridor—it must have just been washed.

Taking short, slow steps, he walked into a concrete box with a low ceiling. He couldn't see any lamps, but there was a gray light in the chamber, a stonelike light that seemed unfit for living beings—it was as though the sun were shining through a concrete sky.

Think not that I am come to send peace on earth: I came not to send peace, but a sword.
                                        —Matthew 10:34

People who had always stayed together now drifted apart, began to lose one another. David glimpsed the face of Lusya Shterental. When he had first seen it in the goods-wagon, he had felt the sweet sadness of being in love. A moment later a short woman with no neck was standing where Lusya had been. She was replaced by an old man with blue eyes and white fluff on his neck, then by a young man with a fixed wide-eyed stare.

This wasn't how people moved. It wasn't even how the lowest form of animal life moved. It was a movement without sense or purpose, with no trace of a living will behind it. The stream of people flowed into the chamber; the people going in pushed the people already inside, the latter pushed their neighbors, and all these countless shoves and pushes with elbows, shoulders, and stomachs gave rise to a form of movement identical in every respect to the streaming of molecules.

The crowd grew steadily denser; people began to move more and more slowly, their steps shorter and shorter. No one was controlling the movement of people in the concrete box. The Germans didn't care whether the people in the chamber stood still or moved in senseless zigzags and half-circles. The naked boy went on taking tiny, senseless steps. The curve traced by his slight body no longer coincided with the curve traced by Sofya Levinton's large heavy body; they were being pulled apart. She shouldn't have held him

145

by the hand; they should have been like those two women—mother and daughter—clasping each other convulsively, with all the melancholy obstinacy of love, cheek to cheek and breast to breast, fusing into one indivisible body.

Now there were even more people, packed in so tightly they no longer obeyed the laws of molecular movement. The boy screamed as he lost hold of Sofya Levinton's hand. But immediately Sofya Levinton receded into the past. Nothing existed except the present moment. Beside him, mouths were breathing, bodies were touching each other, people's thoughts and feelings fusing together.

David had been caught by a subcurrent which, thrown back by the wall, was now flowing towards the door. He glimpsed three people joined together: two men and an old woman—she was defending her children; they were supporting their mother. Suddenly a new, quite different movement arose beside David. The noise was new too, quite distinct from the general shuffling and muttering.

"Let me through!" A man with strong, muscular arms, head bent forward over a thick neck, was forcing his way through the solid mass of bodies. Hew wanted to escape the hypnotic concrete rhythm; his body was rebelling, blindly, thoughtlessly, like the body of a fish on a kitchen table. Soon he became quiet again, choking, taking tiny steps like everyone else.

This disruption changed people's trajectories; David found himself beside Sofya Levinton again. She clasped the boy to her with the peculiar strength familiar to the Germans who worked there—when they emptied the chamber, they never attempted to separate bodies locked in a close embrace.

There were screams from near the entrance; seeing the dense human mass inside, people were refusing to go through the door.

David watched the door close: Gently, smoothly, as though drawn by a magnet, the steel door drew closer to its steel frame. Finally they became one.

High up, behind a rectangular metal grating in the wall, David saw something stir. It looked like a gray rat, but he realized it was a fan beginning to turn. He sensed a faint, rather sweet smell.

The shuffling quietened down; all you could hear were occasional screams, groans, and barely audible words. Speech was no longer of any use to people, nor was action; action is directed towards the future and there no longer was any future. When David moved his head and neck, it didn't make Sofya Levinton want to turn and see what he was looking at.

Her eyes—which had read Homer, *Izvestia*, *Huckleberry Finn*, and Mayne Reid, that had looked at good people and bad people, that had seen the geese in the green meadows of Kursk, the stars above the observatory at Pulkovo, the glitter of surgical steel, the *Mona Lisa* in the Louvre, tomatoes and turnips in the bins at market, the blue water of Issyk-Kul—her eyes were no longer of any use to her. If someone had blinded her, she would have felt no sense of loss.

She was still breathing, but breathing was hard work and she was running out of strength. The bells ringing in her head became deafening; she wanted to concentrate on one last thought, but was unable to articulate this thought. She stood there—mute, blind, her eyes still open.

The boy's movements filled her with pity. Her feelings towards him were so simple that she no longer needed words and eyes. The half-dead boy was still breathing, but the air he took in only drove life away. His head was turning from side to side; he still wanted to see. He could see people settling onto the ground; he could see mouths that were toothless and mouths with white teeth and gold teeth; he could see a thin stream of blood flowing from a nostril. He could see eyes peering through the glass. He still needed his voice—he would have asked Aunt Sonya about those wolflike eyes. He still even needed thought. He had taken only a few steps in the world. He had seen the prints of children's bare heels on hot, dusty earth, his mother lived in Moscow, the moon looked down and people's eyes looked up at it from below, a teapot was boiling on the gas-ring.... This world, where a chicken could run without its head, where there was milk in the morning and frogs he could get to dance by holding their front feet—this world still preoccupied him.

All this time David was being clasped by strong warm hands. He didn't feel his eyes go dark, his heart become empty, his mind grow dull and blind. He had been killed; he no longer existed.

Sofya Levinton felt the boy's body subside in her arms. Once again she had fallen behind him. In mine-shafts where the air becomes poisoned, it is always the little creatures, the birds and mice, that die first. This boy, with his slight, birdlike body, had left before her.

"I've become a mother," she thought.

That was her last thought.

Her heart, however, still had life in it: It contracted, ached, and felt pity for all of you, both living and dead; Sofya Osipovna felt a wave of nausea. She pressed David, now a doll, to herself; she became dead, a doll.

> **Vasily Grossman**, *from his novel* Life and Fate. *The facility at Majdanek in eastern Poland was one of the two Nazi extermination centers that released Zyklon-B into its gas chambers. From 1941 to 1945, between 80,000 and 110,000 prisoners there were gassed.*

Battle of Pavia, 1525 (detail), by Bernard van Orley.

1945: Nagasaki

TOTEM POLE

We took off at 3:50 this morning and headed northwest on a straight line for the Empire. The night was cloudy and threatening, with only a few stars here and there breaking through the overcast. The weather report had predicted storms ahead part of the way but clear sailing for the final and climactic stages of our odyssey.

By 5:50 it was real light outside. We had lost our lead ship, but our navigator informs me that we had arranged for that contingency. We have an assembly point in the sky above the little island of Yakoshima, southeast of Kyushu, at 9:10. We are to circle there and wait for the rest of our formation.

Our genial bombardier comes over to invite me to take his front-row seat in the transparent nose of the ship, and I accept eagerly. From that vantage point in space, seventeen thousand feet above the Pacific, one gets a view of hundreds of miles on all sides, horizontally and vertically. At that height the vast ocean below and the sky above seem to merge into one great sphere.

I was on the inside of that firmament, riding above the giant mountains of white cumulus clouds, letting myself be suspended in infinite space. One hears the whirl of the motors behind, but it soon becomes insignificant against the immensity all around and is before long swallowed by it. There comes a point where space also swallows time, and one lives through eternal moments filled with an oppressive loneliness, as though all life had suddenly vanished from the earth and you are the only one left, a lone survivor traveling endlessly through interplanetary space.

Somewhere beyond these vast mountains of white clouds ahead of me there lies Japan, the land of our enemy. In about four hours from now one of its cities, making weapons of war for use against us, will be wiped off the map by the greatest weapon ever made by man. In one-tenth of a millionth of a second, a fraction of time immeasurable by any clock, a whirlwind from the skies will pulverize thousands of its buildings and tens of thousands of its inhabitants.

Does one feel any pity or compassion for the poor devils about to die? Not when one thinks of Pearl Harbor and of the Death March on Bataan.

The captain informs me that we are about to start our climb to bombing altitude.

He manipulates a few knobs on his control panel to the right of him, and I alternately watch the white clouds and ocean below me and the altimeter on the bombardier's panel. We reached our altitude at nine o'clock. We were then over Japanese waters, close to their mainland.

We reached Yakoshima at 9:12 and there, about four thousand feet ahead of us, was *The Great Artiste* with its precious load.

We started circling. We saw little towns on the coastline, heedless of our presence. We kept on circling, waiting for the third ship in our formation.

It was 9:56 when we began heading for the coastline. Our weather scouts had sent us code messages, informing us that both the

Explosion of a 19-megaton nuclear bomb in the Nevada desert, 1952.

primary target as well as the secondary were clearly visible.

We flew southward down the channel and at 11:33 crossed the coastline and headed straight for Nagasaki about a hundred miles to the west. Here again we circled until we found an opening in the clouds. It was 12:01 and the goal of our mission had arrived.

We heard the prearranged signal on our radio, put on our arc-welder's glasses and watched tensely the maneuverings of the strike ship about half a mile in front of us.

"There she goes!" someone said.

Out of the belly of *The Great Artiste* what looked like a black object came downward.

The captain swung around to get out of range; but even though we were turning away in the opposite direction, and despite the fact that it was broad daylight in our cabin, all of us became aware of a giant flash that broke through the dark barrier of our arc-welder's lenses and flooded our cabin with an intense light.

We removed our glasses after the first flash but the light still lingered on, a bluish-green light that illuminated the entire sky all around. A tremendous blast wave struck our ship and made it tremble from nose to tail. This was followed by four more blasts in rapid succession, each resounding like the boom of cannon fire hitting our plane from all directions.

Observers in the tail of our ship saw a giant ball of fire rise as though from the bowels of the earth, belching forth enormous white smoke rings. Next they saw a giant pillar of purple fire, ten thousand feet high, shooting skyward with enormous speed.

By the time our ship had made another turn in the direction of the atomic explosion, the pillar of purple fire had reached the level of our altitude. Only about forty-five seconds had passed. Awestruck, we watched it shoot upward like a meteor coming from the earth instead of from outer space, becoming ever more alive as it climbed skyward through the white clouds. It was no longer smoke, or dust, or even a cloud of fire. It was a living thing, a new species of being, born right before our incredulous eyes.

At one stage of its evolution, covering millions of years in terms of seconds, the entity assumed the form of a giant square totem pole, with its base about three miles long, tapering off to about a mile at the top. Its bottom was brown, its center was amber, its top white. But it was a living totem pole, carved with many grotesque masks grimacing at the earth.

An honorable peace is attainable only by an efficient war. —*Henry Clay, 1813*

Then, just when it appeared as though the thing had settled down into a state of permanence, there came shooting out of the top a giant mushroom that increased the height of the pillar to a total of 45,000 feet. The mushroom top was even more alive than the pillar, seething and boiling in a white fury of creamy foam, sizzling upwards and then descending earthward, a thousand Old Faithful geysers rolled into one.

It kept struggling in an elemental fury, like a creature in the act of breaking the bonds that held it down. In a few seconds it had freed itself from its gigantic stem and floated upward with tremendous speed, its momentum carrying into the stratosphere to a height of about sixty thousand feet.

But no sooner did this happen when another mushroom, smaller in size than the first one, began emerging out of the pillar. It was as though the decapitated monster was growing a new head.

As the first mushroom floated off into the blue, it changed its shape into a flowerlike form, its giant petal curving downward, creamy white outside, rose-colored inside. It still retained that shape when we last gazed at it from a distance of about two hundred miles.

William Laurence, *special to the* New York Times, *published on September 9, 1945. The bomb known as "Fat Man" exploded 1,650 feet above Nagasaki with a force equivalent to 21,000 tons of TNT, obliterating the city and killing an estimated 70,000 of its citizens. Laurence's reporting received a Pulitzer Prize.*

Dresden, c.1946.

POSTMORTEMS

2007: Washington

JESSICA LYNCH SPEAKS TRUTH TO POWER

I have been asked here today to address "misinformation from the battlefield." Quite frankly, it is something that I have been doing since I returned from Iraq. However, I want to note for the record, I am not politically motivated in my appearance here today. I lived the war in Iraq. Today I have family and friends still serving in Iraq. My support for our troops is unwavering.

I believe this is not a time for finger pointing. It is time for the truth, the whole truth, versus misinformation and hype.

Because of the misinformation, people try to discount the realities of my story, including me as part of the hype. Nothing could be further from the truth. My experiences have caused a personal struggle of sorts for me. I was given opportunities not extended to my fellow soldiers—and I embraced those opportunities to set the record straight. It is something I have done since 2003, and something I imagine I will have to do for the rest of my life. I have answered criticisms for being paid to tell my story. Quite frankly, the injuries I have will last a lifetime and I had a story to tell, a story that needed to be told so people would know the truth.

I want to take a minute to remind the committee of my true story. I was a soldier.

In July 2001, I enlisted in the Army with my brother. We had different reasons as to why we joined, but we both wanted to serve our country. I loved my time in the Army, and I am grateful for the opportunity to have served this nation during a time of crisis.

In 2003, I received word that my unit had been deployed. I was part of a hundred-mile long convoy going to Baghdad to support the Marines. I drove the five-ton water-buffalo truck. Our unit drove the heaviest vehicles. The sand was thick—our vehicles just sank. It would take us hours to travel the shortest distance. We decided to divide our convoy so the lighter vehicles could reach our target. But then came the city of An Nasiriyah and a day I will never forget.

The truck I was driving broke down. I was picked up by my roommate and best friend, Lori Piestewa, who was driving our First Sergeant, Robert Dowdy. We also picked up two other soldiers from a different unit to get them out of harm's way.

As we drove through An Nasiriyah, trying to get turned around to try to leave the city, the signs of hostility were increasing with people with weapons on rooftops and the street watching our entire group.

The vehicle I was riding in was hit by a rocket-propelled grenade and slammed into the back of another truck in the convoy. Three people in the vehicle were killed upon impact. Lori and I were taken to a hospital where she later died and I was held for nine days. In all, eleven soldiers died that day, six others from the unit, plus two others were taken prisoner.

Russia has two generals she can trust: General Janvier and General Février.
—*Nicholas I of Russia, 1853*

Following the ambush, my injuries were extensive. When I awoke in the Iraqi hospital, I was not able to move or feel anything below my waist. I suffered a six-inch gash in my head. My fourth and fifth lumbars were overlapping, causing pressure on my spine. My right humerus bone was broken. My right foot was crushed. My left femur was shattered. The Iraqis in the hospital tried to help me by removing the bone and replacing it with a metal rod. The rod they used was a model from the 1940s for a man and was too long. Following my rescue, the doctors in Landstuhl, Germany, found in a physical exam that I had been sexually assaulted. Today, I continue to deal with bladder, bowel, and kidney problems as a result of my injuries. My left leg still has no feeling from the knee down, and I am required to wear a brace so that I can stand and walk.

When I awoke, I did not know where I was. I could not move or fight or call for help. The nurses at the hospital tried to soothe me and tried unsuccessfully at one point to return me to American troops.

Then on April 1, while various units created diversions around Nasiriyah, a group came to the hospital to rescue me. I could hear them speaking in English, but I was still very afraid. Then a soldier came into my room, he tore the American flag from his uniform and pressed into my hand, and he told me, "We're American soldiers, and we're here to take you home." As I held his hand, I told him, "Yes, I am an American soldier too."

When I remember those difficult days, I remember the fear, I remember the strength. I remember the hand of a fellow American soldier reassuring me that I was okay now.

At the same time, tales of great heroism were being told. My parent's home in Wirt County was under siege of the media all repeating the story of the little girl Rambo from the hills who went down fighting.

It was not true.

I have repeatedly said, when asked, that if the stories about me helped inspire our troops and rally a nation, then perhaps there was some good. However, I am still confused as to why they chose to lie and tried to make me a legend when the real heroics of my fellow soldiers that day were, in fact, legendary. People like Lori Piestewa and First Sergeant Dowdy who picked up fellow soldiers in harm's way, or people like Patrick Miller and Sergeant Donald Walters, who *actually* fought until the very end.

The bottom line is the American people are capable of determining their own ideals for heroes, and they don't need to be told elaborate tales.

My hero is my brother Greg who continues to serve this country today. My hero is my friend Lori who died in Iraq but set an example for a generation of Hopi and Native American women and little girls everywhere about the important contributions just one soldier can make in the fight for freedom. My hero is every American who says, "My country needs me," and answers the call to fight.

I had the good fortune and opportunity to come home, and I told the truth. Many other soldiers, like Pat Tillman, do not have the opportunity.

The truth of war is not always easy to hear, but it is always more heroic than the hype.

Testimony before the House Committee on Oversight and Government Reform, April 24, 2007. The dispatches released by the American military and embellished by the American media had decorated PFC Lynch with counterfeit medals for valor.

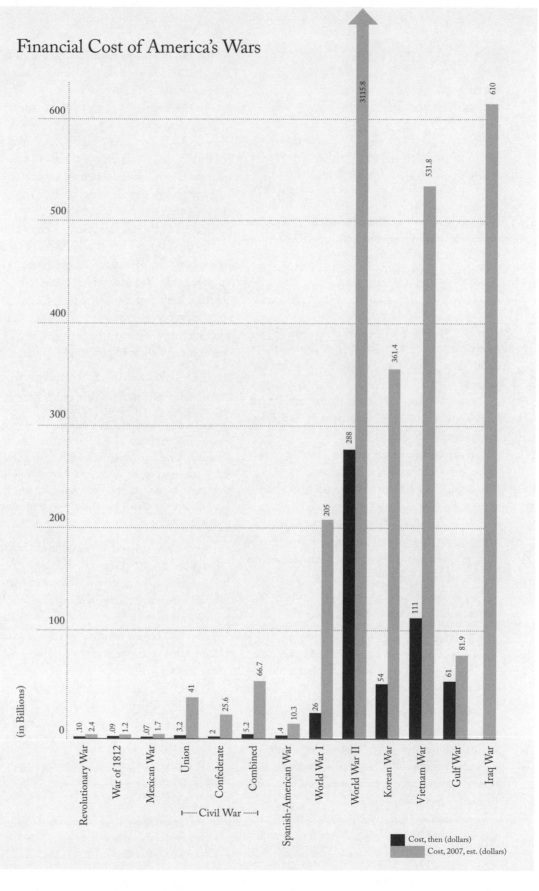

Financial Cost of America's Wars

(in Billions)

War	Cost, then (dollars)	Cost, 2007, est. (dollars)
Revolutionary War	.10	2.4
War of 1812	.09	1.2
Mexican War	.07	1.7
Union	3.2	41
Confederate	2	25.6
Combined	5.2	66.7
Spanish–American War	.4	10.3
World War I	26	205
World War II	288	3115.8
Korean War	54	361.4
Vietnam War	111	531.8
Gulf War	61	81.9
Iraq War		610

⊢······· Civil War ·······⊣

■ Cost, then (dollars)
▨ Cost, 2007, est. (dollars)

1921: Arlington

JOHN DOS PASSOS AT THE
TOMB OF THE UNKNOWN

Whereasthe Congressoftheunitedstates byaconcurrentresolutionadoptedon the4th dayofmarch lastauthorizedthe Secretary ofwar to cause to be brought to theunitedstatesthe body of an Americanwhowasamemberoftheamerican expeditionaryforcesineurope wholost hislifeduringtheworldwarandwhose identityhasnotbeenestablished for burial inthememorialamphitheatreofthe nationalcemetaryatarlingtonvirginia

In the tarpaper morgue at Châlons-sur-Marne in the reek of chloride of lime and the dead, they picked out the pine box that held all that was left of

enie menie minie moe plenty other pine boxes stacked up there containing what they'd scraped up of Richard Roe

and other person or persons unknown. Only one can go. How did they pick John Doe?

Make sure he aint a dinge, boys,

make sure he aint a guinea or a kike,

how can you tell a guy's a hundredpercent when all you've got's a gunnysack full of bones, bronze buttons stamped with the screaming eagle and a pair of roll puttees?

…and the gagging chloride and the puky dirtstench of the yearold dead…

The day withal was too meaningful and tragic for applause. Silence, tears, songs and prayer, muffled drums and soft music were the instrumentalities today of national approbation.

John Doe was born (thudding din of blood in love into the shuddering soar of a man and a woman alone indeed together lurching into

and ninemonths sick drowse waking into scared agony and the pain and blood and mess of birth). John Doe was born

and raised in Brooklyn, in Memphis, near the lakefront in Cleveland, Ohio, in the stench of the stockyards in Chi, on Beacon Hill, in

an old brick house in Alexandria Virginia, on Telegraph Hill, in a halftimbered Tudor cottage in Portland the city of roses,

in the Lying-In Hospital old Morgan endowed on Stuyvesant Square,

across the railroad tracks, out near the country club, in a shack cabin tenement apartmenthouse exclusive residential suburb;

scion of one of the best families in the social register, won first prize in the baby parade at Coronado Beach, was marbles champion of the Little Rock grammarschools, crack basketballplayer at the Booneville High, quarterback at the State Reformatory, having saved the sheriff's kid from drowning in the Little Missouri River was invited to Washington to be photographed shaking hands with the President on the White House steps—

though this was a time of mourning, such an assemblage necessarily has about it a touch of color. In the boxes are seen the court uniforms of foreign diplomats, the gold braid of our own and foreign fleets and armies, the black of the conventional mourning dress of American statesmen, the varicolored furs and outdoor wrapping garments of mothers and sisters come to mourn, the drab and blue of soldiers and sailors, the glitter of musical instruments and the white and black of a vested choir

—busboy harveststiff hogcaller boyscout champeen cornshucker of Western Kansas bellhop at the United States Hotel at Saratoga Springs office boy callboy fruiter telephone lineman longshoreman lumberjack plumber's helper,

worked for an exterminating company in Union City, filled pipes in an opium joint in Trenton, N. J.

Y.M.C.A. secretary, express agent, truckdriver, fordmechanic, sold books in Denver Colorado: Madam would you be willing to help a young man work his way through college?

President Harding, with a reverence seemingly more significant because of his high temporal station, concluded his speech:

We are met today to pay the impersonal tribute;
the name of him whose body lies before us took
flight with his imperishable soul…

as a typical soldier of this representative democracy he fought and died believing in the indisputable justice of his country's cause...

by raising his right hand and asking the thousands within the sound of his voice to join in the prayer:

Our Father which art in heaven hallowed be thy name...

Naked he went into the army;

they weighed you, measured you, looked for flat feet, squeezed your penis to see if you had clap, looked up your anus to see if you had piles, counted your teeth, made you cough, listened to your heart and lungs, made you read the letters on the card, charted your urine and your intelligence,

gave you a service record for a future (imperishable soul)

and an identification tag stamped with your serial number to hang around your neck, issued O D regulation equipment, a condiment can and a copy of the articles of war.

Atten'SHUN suck in your gut you c——r wipe that smile off your face eyes right wattja tink dis is a choirch-social? Forwar-D'ARCH.

John Doe

and Richard Roe and other person or persons unknown

drilled hiked, manual of arms, ate slum, learned to salute, to soldier, to loaf in the latrines, forbidden to smoke on deck, overseas guard duty, forty men and eight horses, shortarm inspection and the ping of shrapnel and the shrill bullets combing the air and the sorehead woodpeckers the machineguns mud cooties gasmasks and the itch.

Say feller tell me how I can get back to my outfit.

John Doe had a head

for twentyodd years intensely the nerves of the eyes the ears the palate the tongue the fingers the toes the armpits, the nerves warmfeeling under the skin charged the coiled brain with hurt sweet warm cold mine must dont sayings print headlines:

Thou shalt not the multiplication table

The village of Tama burns after an attack, Sudan, 2005. Photograph by Lynsey Addario.

long division, Now is the time for all good men knocks but once at a young man's door, It's a great life if Ish gebibbel, The first five years'll be the Safety First, Suppose a hun tried to rape your my country right or wrong, Catch 'em young, What he dont know wont treat 'em rough, Tell 'em nothing, He got what was coming to him he got his, This is a white man's country, Kick the bucket, Gone west, If you dont like it you can croaked him

Say buddy cant you tell me how I can get back to my outfit?

Cant help jumpin when them things go off, give me the trots them things do. I lost my identification tag swimmin in the Marne, roughhousin with a guy while we was waitin to be deloused, in bed with a girl named Jeanne (Love moving picture wet French postcard dream began with saltpeter in the coffee and ended at the propho station)—

Say soldier for chrissake cant you tell me how I can get back to my outfit?

John Doe's
heart pumped blood:
alive thudding silence of blood in your ears
down in the clearing in the Oregon forest where the punkins were punkincolor pouring into the blood through the eyes and the fallcolored trees and the bronze hoopers were hopping through the dry grass, where tiny striped snails hung on the underside of the blades and the flies hummed, wasps droned, bumblebees buzzed, and the woods smelt of wine and mushrooms and apples, homey smell of fall pouring into the blood,
and I dropped the tin hat and the sweaty pack and lay flat with the dogday sun licking my throat and adamsapple and the tight skin over the breastbone.

The shell had his number on it.

The blood ran into the ground.

The service record dropped out of the filing cabinet when the quartermaster sergeant got blotto that time they had to pack up and leave the billets in a hurry.

The identification tag was in the bottom of the Marne.

The blood ran into the ground, the brains oozed out of the cracked skull and were licked up by the trenchrats, the body swelled and raised a generation of bluebottle flies,
and the incorruptible skeleton,
and the scraps of dried viscera and skin bundled in khaki

they took to Châlons-sur-Marne
and laid it out neat in a pine coffin
and took it home to God's Country on a battleship
and buried it in a sarcophagus in the Memorial Amphitheatre in the Arlington National Cemetery
and draped the Old Glory over it
and the bugler played taps
and Mr. Harding prayed to God and the diplomats and the generals and the admirals and the brasshats and the politicians and the handsomely dressed ladies out of the society column of the *Washington Post* stood up solemn
and thought how beautiful sad Old Glory God's Country it was to have the bugler play taps and the three volleys made their ears ring.

Where his chest ought to have been they pinned
the Congressional Medal, the D.S.C., the Medaille Militaire, the Belgian Croix de Guerre, the Italian gold medal, the Vitutea Militara sent by Queen Marie of Rumania, the Czechoslovak war cross, the Virtuti Militari of the Poles, a wreath sent by Hamilton Fish Jr., of New York, and a little wampum presented by a deputation of Arizona redskins in warpaint and feathers. All the Washingtonians brought flowers.

Woodrow Wilson brought a bouquet of poppies.

From 1919, *the second volume of the* USA *trilogy. President Warren Harding officiated over the internment of America's Unknown Soldier at Arlington National Cemetery on Armistice Day, 1921. Eleven years later, Dos Passos wrote an epitaph.*

1944: New York

plato told

him:he couldn't
believe it(jesus

told him;he
wouldn't believe
it)lao

tsze
certainly told
him,and general
(yes

mam)
sherman;
and even
(believe it
or

not)you
told him:i told
him;we told him
(he didn't believe it,no

sir)it took
a nipponized bit of
the old sixth

avenue
el;in the top of his head:to tell

him

The final lines of e. e. cummings'
poem refer to Manhattan's dis-
mantled Sixth Avenue elevated
tracks, which were bought as
scrap metal by Imperial Japan
three years before the bombing of
Pearl Harbor.

1764: Paris

VOLTAIRE DEFINES WAR AS THE WORK OF A DEFORMED IMAGINATION

Famine, plague, and war are the three most celebrated ingredients of this world of ours. In the category of famine can be included all the bad food to which scarcity obliges us to resort, abridging our life in the hope of sustaining it. In plague are comprised all the contagious diseases, which number two or three thousand. These two gifts come to us from providence. But war, which unites all these benefits, comes to us from the

Sometime they'll give a war and nobody will come. —Carl Sandburg, 1936

imaginations of three or four hundred persons scattered over the surface of this globe under the names of princes or ministers; and it is perhaps for this reason that in many a dedication they are called the living images of divinity.

A genealogist proves to a prince that he is the direct descendant of a count whose relatives had made a family pact three or four hundred years ago with a house whose very name has left no memory. This house had remote pretensions to a province whose last owner had just died of apoplexy. The prince and his council conclude without difficulty that the province belongs to him by divine right. This province, which is some hundreds of leagues distant, protests in vain that it does not know him, that it has no wish to be governed by him, that one must at least have a people's consent before legislating for it. These discourses do not even reach the ears of the prince whose rights are incontestable. He immediately finds a great number of men who have nothing to do nor to lose. He dresses them in heavy blue cloth at 110 *sous* the ell, puts a heavy white cord round their hats, makes them turn right and left, and marches to glory.

The other princes who hear of this escapade take part in it, each according to his means, and occupy a small piece of land with more merce-

nary murderers than Genghis Khan, Tamerlane, Bajazet ever dragged in their train.

Fairly distant peoples hear that there is going to be fighting, and that five or six *sous* a day can be earned if they care to take part. They at once divide themselves into two troops like harvesters and go off to sell their services to anyone who wants to employ them. These multitudes go for one another, not only without having any interest in the proceedings, but even without knowing what they are about.

Five or six belligerent powers can be seen at once, now three against three, now two against four, now one against five, all equally hating each other, uniting and fighting with each other turn and turn about, all agreed on a single point, to do as much harm as possible.

What is marvelous about this infernal undertaking is that each chief of murderers has his banners blessed and solemnly invokes God before he sets off to exterminate his neighbors. If a chief has had the good fortune to have only two or three thousand men butchered, he does not thank God for it. But when about ten thousand have been exterminated by fire and sword, and, by a crowning grace, some town has been destroyed from top to bottom, then they sing a rather long four-part song, composed in a language unknown to all those who fought, besides being crammed with barbarisms. The same song serves for marriages and births, as well as murders, which is unpardonable.

Natural religion has a thousand times prevented citizens from committing crimes. A well-bred soul has no wish to commit them. A tender soul is afraid of them, remembering a just and vengeful god. But artificial religion encourages all the cruelties done in association, conspiracies, seditions, robbery, ambushes, attacks on towns, pillages, murders. Each one marches gaily off to crime under the banner of his saint.

A certain number of orators are everywhere paid to celebrate these bloodstained days. Some wear long black jackets, doubled by abridged cloaks; others have shirts over gowns; some wear two slings of motley cloth over their shirts. All talk for a long time. When it is about a battle in Veteravia, they refer to what was done of old in Palestine.

The rest of the year these people declaim against the vices. They prove by three points and by antitheses that ladies who lightly spread a little rouge on their fresh cheeks will be the eternal objects of the eternal vengeance of the eternal; that *Polyeucte* and *Athalie* are the works of the demon; that a man who has two hundred crowns' worth of seafood served at his table in Lent infallibly brings about his salvation, and that a poor man who eats two and half *sous'* worth of mutton goes forever to all the devils.

Out of five or six thousand declamations of this kind, there are three or four at most, composed by a Gaul called Massillon, that an upright man can read without disgust. But among all these discourses there are hardly two in which the orator dares to protest against this scourge and this crime of war, which comprises all scourges and all crimes. The wretched orators speak ceaselessly against love, which is mankind's only consolation and the only way of perpetuating it. They say nothing about the abominable efforts we make to destroy it.

Wretched physicians of souls, you declaim for five quarters of an hour about some pin-prick, and you say nothing about the disease that tears us into a thousand pieces! Philosophical moralists, burn all your books. So long as the whim of a few men causes thousands of our brothers to be honorably butchered, the portion of mankind devoted to heroism will be the most frightful thing in the whole of nature.

What becomes of and what do I care about humanity, benevolence, modesty, temperance, tenderness, wisdom, piety, when half a pound of lead shot from six hundred paces shatters my body, and I die at the age of twenty in agony beyond words, in the midst of five or six thousand dying men, while my eyes, opening for the last time, see the town in which I was born destroyed by sword and fire, and the last sounds I hear are the cries of women and children expiring under the ruins, all for the alleged benefit of a man I do not know?

What is worst is that war is an inevitable scourge. If we examine the matter, we find that all men have worshipped the god Mars.

The article, "La Guerre," appeared in Voltaire's Philosophical Dictionary. *Condemned as heresy throughout Europe, the book was printed in Geneva absent the name of its author.*

The Invincible Soldier, by B.V. Cerbakov.

World's Largest Land Armies (in troops):

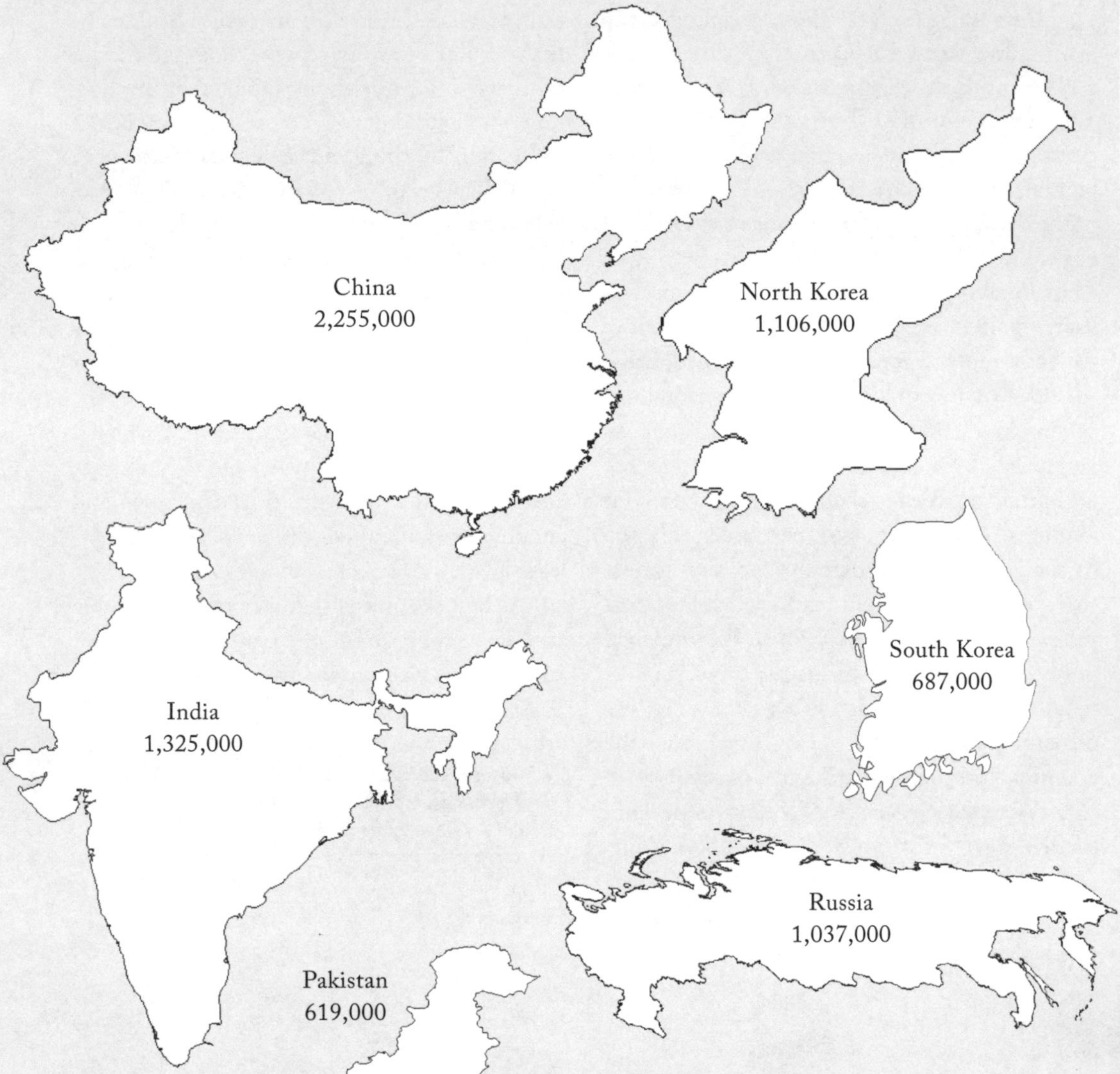

China
2,255,000

North Korea
1,106,000

India
1,325,000

South Korea
687,000

Russia
1,037,000

Pakistan
619,000

Iran
545,000

United States
1,426,713

Turkey
514,850

Vietnam
484,000

1932: Paris/Vienna

WHY WAR

July

Dear Mr. Freud:

The proposal of the League of Nations and its International Institute of Intellectual Co-operation at Paris that I should invite a person, to be chosen by myself, to a frank exchange of views on any problem that I might select affords me a very welcome opportunity of conferring with you upon a question which, as things now are, seems the most insistent of all the problems civilization has to face. This is the problem: Is there any way of delivering mankind from the menace of war? It is common knowledge that, with the advance of modern science, this issue has come to mean a matter of life and death for civilization as we know it; nevertheless, for all the zeal displayed, every attempt at its solution has ended in a lamentable breakdown.

I believe, moreover, that those whose duty it is to tackle the problem professionally and practically are growing only too aware of their impotence to deal with it, and have now a very lively desire to learn the views of men who, absorbed in the pursuit of science, can see world problems in the perspective distance lends. As for me, the normal objective of my thought affords no insight into the dark places of human will and feeling. Thus, in the inquiry now proposed, I can do little more than to seek to clarify the question at issue and, clearing the ground of the more obvious solutions, enable you to bring the light of your far-reaching knowledge of man's instinctive life to bear upon the problem.

How is it possible for a small clique to bend the will of the majority, who stand to lose and suffer by a state of war, to the service of their ambitions? An obvious answer to this question would seem to be that the minority, the ruling class at present, has the schools and press, usually the Church as well, under its thumb. This enables it to organize and sway the emotions of the masses and makes its tool of them.

Yet even this answer does not provide a complete solution. Another question arises from it: how is it that these devices succeed so well in rousing men to such wild enthusiasm, even to sacrifice their lives? Only one answer is possible. Because man has within him a lust for hatred and destruction. In normal times, this passion exists in a latent state; it emerges only in unusual circumstances; but it is a comparatively easy task to call it into play and raise it to the power of a collective psychosis. Here lies,

> *Ask any soldier. To kill a man is to merit a woman.* —Jean Giraudoux, 1935

perhaps, the crux of all the complex factors we are considering, an enigma that only the expert in the lore of human instincts can resolve.

And so we come to our last question. Is it possible to control man's mental evolution so as to make him proof against the psychosis of hate and destructiveness? Here I am thinking by no means only of the so-called uncultured masses. Experience proves that it is rather the so-called intelligentsia that is most apt to yield to these disastrous collective suggestions, since the intellectual has no direct contact with life in the raw but encounters it in its easiest, synthetic form—upon the printed page.

I know that in your writings we may find answers, explicit or implied, to all the issues of this urgent and absorbing problem. But it would be of the greatest service to us all were you to present the problem of world peace in the light of your most recent discoveries, for such a presentation well might blaze the trail for new and fruitful modes of action.

Yours very sincerely,
A. Einstein

September

Dear Mr. Einstein:

You are amazed that it is so easy to infect men with the war fever, and you surmise that man has in him an active instinct for hatred and destruction, amenable to such stimulations. I entirely agree with you. I believe in the existence of this instinct and have been recently at pains to study its manifestations. In this connection may I set out a fragment of that knowledge of the instincts, which we psychoanalysts, after so many tentative essays and gropings in the dark, have compassed? We assume that human instincts are of two kinds: those that conserve and unify, which we call "erotic" (in the meaning Plato gives to Eros in his Symposium), or else "sexual" (explicitly extending the popular connotation of "sex"); and, secondly, the instincts to destroy and kill, which we assimilate as the aggressive or destructive instincts. These are, as you perceive, the well known opposites, Love and Hate, transformed into theoretical entities; they are, perhaps, another aspect of those eternal polarities, attraction and repulsion, which fall within your province. But we must be chary of passing overhastily to the notions of good and evil.

Only exceptionally does an action follow on the stimulus of a single instinct, which is *per se* a blend of Eros and destructiveness. As a rule, several motives of similar composition concur to bring about the act. Thus, when a nation is summoned to engage in war, a whole gamut of human motives may respond to this appeal—high and low motives, some openly avowed, others slurred over. The lust for aggression and destruction is certainly included; the innumerable cruelties of history and man's daily life confirm its prevalence and strength. The stimulation of these destructive impulses by appeals to idealism and the erotic instinct naturally facilitate their release. Musing on the atrocities recorded on history's page, we feel that the ideal motive has often served as a camouflage for the lust of destruction; sometimes, as with the cruelties of the Inquisition, it seems that, while the ideal motives occupied the foreground of consciousness, they drew their strength from the destructive instincts submerged in the unconscious. Both interpretations are feasible.

All this may give you the impression that our theories amount to species of mythology and a gloomy one at that! But does not every natural science lead ultimately to this—a sort of mythology? Is it otherwise today with your physical sciences?

The upshot of these observations, as bearing on the subject in hand, is that there is no likeli-

Campagne de France, 1814, by Ernest Meissonier, 1864.

hood of our being able to suppress humanity's aggressive tendencies. In some happy corners of the earth, they say, where nature brings forth abundantly whatever man desires, there flourish races whose lives go gently by, unknowing of aggression or constraint. This I can hardly credit; I would like further details about these happy folk. The Bolshevists, too, aspire to do away with human aggressiveness by insuring the satisfaction of material needs and enforcing equality between man and man. To me this hope seems vain. Meanwhile, they busily perfect their armaments, and their hatred of outsiders is not the least of the factors of cohesion among themselves. In any case, as you too have observed, complete suppression of man's aggressive tendencies is not an issue; what we may try is to divert it into a channel other than that of warfare.

From our "mythology" of the instincts, we may easily deduce a formula for an indirect method of eliminating war. If the propensity for war be due to the destructive instinct, we have always its counteragent, Eros, to our hand. All that produces ties of sentiment between man and man must serve us as war's antidote. These ties are of two kinds. First, such relations as those toward a beloved object, void though they be of sexual intent. The psychoanalyst need feel no compunction in mentioning "love" in this connection; religion uses the same language: Love thy neighbor as thyself. A pious injunction, easy to enounce, but hard to carry out! The other bond of sentiment is by way of identification. All that brings out the significant resemblances between men calls into play this feeling of community, identification, whereon is founded, in large measure, the whole edifice of human society.

In your strictures on the abuse of authority, I find another suggestion for an indirect attack on the war impulse. That men are divided into the leaders and the led is but another manifestation of their inborn and irremediable inequality. The second class constitutes the vast majority; they need a high command to make decisions for them, to which decisions they usually bow without demur. In this context we would point out that men should be at greater pains than

heretofore to form a superior class of independent thinkers, unamenable to intimidation and fervent in the quest of truth, whose function it would be to guide the masses dependent on their lead. There is no need to point out how little the rule of politicians and the Church's ban on liberty of thought encourage such a new creation. The ideal conditions would obviously be found in a community where every man subordinated his instinctive life to the dictates of reason. Nothing less than this could bring about so thorough and so durable a union between men, even if this involved the severance of mutual ties of sentiment. But surely such a hope is utterly utopian,

War to the castles; peace to the cottages.
— Nicolas Chamfort, 1790

as things are. The other indirect methods of preventing war are certainly more feasible, but entail no quick results. They conjure up an ugly picture of mills that grind so slowly that, before the flour is ready, men are dead of hunger.

As you see, little good comes of consulting a theoretician, aloof from worldly contact, on practical and urgent problems! Better it were to tackle each successive crisis with means that we have ready to our hands. However, I would like to deal with a question which, though it is not mooted in your letter, interests me greatly. Why do we, you and I and many another, protest so vehemently against war, instead of just accepting it as another of life's odious importunities? For it seems a natural thing enough, biologically sound and practically unavoidable. I trust you will not be shocked by my raising such a question. For the better conduct of an inquiry, it may be well to don a mask of feigned aloofness. The answer to my query may run as follows: Because every man has a right over his own life and war destroys lives that were full of promise, it forces the individual into situations that shame his manhood, obliging him to murder fellow men, against his will; it ravages material amenities, the fruits of human toil, and much besides. Moreover, wars, as now conducted, afford no scope for acts of heroism according to the old ideals and, given the high perfection of modern arms, war today would mean the sheer extermination of one of the combatants, if not of both. This is so true, so obvious, that we can but wonder why the conduct of war is not banned by general consent. Doubtless, either of the points I have just made is open to debate. It may be asked if the community, in its turn, cannot claim a right over the individual lives of its members. Moreover, all forms of war cannot be indiscriminately condemned; so long as there are nations and empires, each prepared callously to extermi-

> Join the Army, see the world, meet interesting
> people, and kill them. —Pacifist slogan, 1970s

nate its rival, all alike must be equipped for war. But we will not dwell on any of these problems; they lie outside the debate to which you have invited me. I pass on to another point, the basis, as it strikes me, of our common hatred of war. It is this: we cannot do otherwise than hate it. Pacifists we are, since our organic nature wills us thus to be. Hence, it comes easy to us to find arguments that justify our standpoint.

How long have we to wait before the rest of men turn pacifist? Impossible to say, and yet perhaps our hope that these two factors—man's cultural disposition and a well-founded dread of the form that future wars will take—may serve to put an end to war in the near future, is not chimerical. But by what ways or byways this will come about, we cannot guess. Meanwhile, we may rest on the assurance that whatever makes for cultural development is working also against war.

With kindest regards and, should this exposé prove a disappointment to you, my sincere regrets,

Yours,
Sigmund Freud

> From Why War?, an exchange of letters between
> **Albert Einstein** and **Sigmund Freud**, published by
> the League of Nations in 1933.

1906: Stanford

WILLIAM JAMES PROPOSES
THE MORAL EQUIVALENT OF WAR

The war against war is going to be no holiday excursion or camping party. The military feelings are too deeply grounded to abdicate their place among our ideals until better substitutes are offered than the glory and shame that come to nations as well as to individuals from the ups and downs of politics and the vicissitudes of trade. There is something highly paradoxical in the modern man's relation to war. Ask all our millions, north and south, whether they would vote now (were such a thing possible) to have our war for the Union expunged from history, and the record of a peaceful transition to the present time substituted for that of its marches and battles, and probably hardly a handful of eccentrics would say yes. Those ancestors, those efforts, those memories and legends are the most ideal part of what we now own together, a sacred spiritual possession worth more than all the blood poured out. Yet ask those same people whether they would be willing in cold blood to start another civil war now to gain another similar possession, and not one man or woman would vote for the proposition. In modern eyes, precious though wars may be, they must not be waged solely for the sake of the ideal harvest. Only when forced upon one, only when an enemy's injustice leaves us no alternative, is a war now thought permissible.

Modern war is so expensive that we feel trade to be a better avenue to plunder; but modern man inherits all the innate pugnacity and all the love of glory of his ancestors. Showing war's irrationality and horror is of no effect upon him. The horrors make the fascination. War is the *strong* life; it is life *in extremis*; war taxes are the only ones men never hesitate to pay, as the budgets of all nations show us.

Our ancestors have bred pugnacity into our bone and marrow, and thousands of years of peace won't breed it out of us. The popular imagination fairly fattens on the thought of wars. Let public opinion once reach a certain fighting pitch, and no ruler can withstand it. In the Boer War, both governments began with bluff but couldn't stay there—the military tension was too much for them. In 1898, our people had read the word "war" in letters three inches high for three months in every newspaper. The pliant politician McKinley was swept away by their eagerness, and our squalid war with Spain became a necessity.

"Peace" in military mouths today is a synonym for "war expected." The word has become a pure provocative, and no government wishing peace sincerely should allow it ever to be printed in a newspaper. Every up-to-date dictionary should say that "peace" and "war" mean the same thing, now *in posse*, now *in actu*. It may even reasonably be said that the intensely sharp competitive *preparation* for war by the nations *is the real war*, permanent, unceasing; and that the battles are only a sort of public verification of the mastery gained during the "peace" interval.

So far as the central essence of this feeling goes, no healthy-minded person, it seems to me, can help to some degree partaking of it. Militarism is the great preserver of our ideals of hardihood, and human life with no use for hardihood would be contemptible. Without risks or prizes for the darer, history would be insipid indeed; and there is a type of military character which everyone feels that the race should never cease to breed, for everyone is sensitive to its superiority. The duty is incumbent on mankind of keeping military characters in stock—of keeping them, if not for use, then as ends in themselves and as pure pieces of perfection—so that Roosevelt's weaklings and mollycoddles may not end by making everything else disappear from the face of nature.

Pacifists ought to enter more deeply into the aesthetical and ethical point of view of their opponents. Do that first in any controversy, *then move the point*, and your opponent will follow. So long as antimilitarists propose no substitute for war's disciplinary function, no *moral equivalent* of war, analogous, as one might say, to the mechanical equivalent of heat, so long they fail to realize the full inwardness of the situation. And, as a rule, they do fail.

The duties, penalties, and sanctions pictured in the utopias they paint are all too weak and tame to touch the military-minded. Tolstoy's pacifism is the only exception to this rule, for it is profoundly pessimistic as regards all this world's values, and makes the fear of the Lord furnish the moral spur provided elsewhere by the fear of the enemy. But our socialistic peace-advocates all believe absolutely in this world's values; and instead of the fear of the Lord and the fear of the enemy, the only fear they reckon with is the fear of poverty if one be lazy. This weakness pervades all the socialistic literature with which I am acquainted. Meanwhile, men at large still live as they always have lived, under a pain-and-fear economy—for those of us who live in an ease-economy are but an island in the stormy ocean—and the whole atmosphere of present-day utopian literature tastes mawkish

Rwanda, 1994. Photograph by David Turnley.

and dishwatery to people who still keep a sense for life's more bitter flavors. It suggests, in truth, ubiquitous inferiority.

Inferiority is always with us, and merciless scorn of it is the keynote of the military temper. "Dogs, would you live forever?" shouted Frederick the Great. "Yes," say our utopians, "let us live forever, and raise our level gradually." The best thing about our "inferiors" today is that they are as tough as nails, and physically and morally almost as insensitive. Utopianism would see them soft and squeamish, while militarism would keep their callousness, but transfigure it into a meritorious characteristic needed by "the service" and redeemed by that from the suspicion of inferiority. All the qualities of a man acquire dignity when he knows that the service of the collectivity that owns him needs them. If proud of the collectivity, his own pride rises in proportion. No collectivity is like an army for nourishing such pride; but it has to be confessed that the only sentiment which the image of pacific cosmopolitan industrialism is capable of arousing in countless worthy breasts is shame at the idea of belonging to *such* a collectivity. Where is the savage "yes" and "no," the unconditional duty? Where is the conscription? Where is the blood tax? Where is anything that one feels honored by belonging to?

I devoutly believe in the reign of peace and in the gradual advent of some sort of socialistic equilibrium. The fatalistic view of the war-function is to me nonsense, for I know that war-making is due to definite motives and subject to prudential checks and reasonable criticisms, just like any other form of enterprise. And when whole nations are the armies, and the science of destruction vies in intellectual refinement with the sciences of production, I see that war becomes absurd and impossible from its own monstrosity.

All these beliefs of mine put me squarely into the antimilitarist party. But I do not believe that peace either ought to be, or will be, permanent on this globe, unless the states, pacifically organized, preserve some of the old elements of army discipline. A permanently successful peace economy cannot be a simple pleasure

Roman relief sculpture of Amazon warriors.

economy. In the more or less socialistic future toward which mankind seems drifting, we must still subject ourselves collectively to those severities which answer to our real position upon this only partly hospitable globe. We must make new energies and hardihoods continue the manliness to which the military mind so faithfully clings. Martial virtues must be the enduring cement; intrepidity, contempt of softness, surrender of private interest, obedience to command must still remain the rock upon which states are built.

Let me illustrate my idea more concretely. There is nothing to make one indignant in the mere fact that life is hard, that men should toil and suffer pain. The planetary conditions once for all are such, and we can stand it. But that so many men, by mere accidents of birth and opportunity, should have a life of *nothing else* but toil and pain and hardness and inferiority imposed upon them, should have *no* vacation, while others natively no more deserving never get any taste of this campaigning life at all—*this* is capable of arousing indignation in reflective minds. It may end by seeming shameful to all of us that some of us have nothing but campaigning, and others nothing but unmanly ease. If now—and this is my idea—there were, instead of military conscription, a conscription of the whole youthful population, to form for a certain number of years a part of the army enlisted against *Nature*, the injustice would tend to be evened out, and numerous other goods to the commonwealth would follow. The military ideals of hardihood and discipline would be wrought into the growing fiber of the people; no one would remain blind, as the luxurious classes now are blind, to man's relations to the globe he lives on and to the permanently sour and hard foundations of his higher life. To coal and iron mines, to freight trains, to fishing fleets in December, to dishwashing, clothes-washing, and window-washing, to road-building and tunnel-making, to foundries and stoke-holes, and to the frames of skyscrapers would our gilded youths be drafted off, according to their choice, to get the childishness knocked out of them, and to come back into society with healthier sympathies and soberer ideas. They would have paid their blood tax, done their own part in the immemorial human warfare against nature; they would tread the earth more proudly, the women would value them more highly, they would be better fathers and teachers of the following generation.

War hath no fury like a noncombatant.
— *Charles Edward Montague, 1922*

Such a conscription, with the state of public opinion that would have required it, and the many moral fruits it would bear, would preserve in the midst of a pacific civilization the manly virtues which the military party is so afraid of seeing disappear in peace. We should get toughness without callousness, authority with as little criminal cruelty as possible, and painful work done cheerily because the duty is temporary and threatens not, as now, to degrade the whole remainder of one's life. I spoke of the "moral equivalent" of war. So far, war has been the only force that can discipline a whole community, and until an equivalent discipline is organized, I believe that war must have its way. But I have no serious doubt that the ordinary prides and shames of social man, once developed to a certain intensity, are capable of organizing such a moral equivalent as I have sketched, or some other just as effective for preserving manliness of type. It is but a question of time, of skillful propagandism, and of opinion-making men seizing historic opportunities.

The martial type of character can be bred without war. Strenuous honor and disinterestedness abound everywhere. Priests and medical men are in a fashion educated to it, and we should all feel some degree of its imperative if we were conscious of our work as an obligatory service to the state. We should be *owned*, as soldiers are by the army, and our pride would rise accordingly. We could be poor, then, without humiliation, as army officers now are.

It would be simply preposterous if the only force that could work ideals of honor and standards of efficiency into English or American natures should be the fear of being killed by the Germans or the Japanese. Great indeed is fear; but it is not, as our military enthusiasts believe and try to make us believe, the only stimulus known for awakening the higher ranges of men's spiritual energy. The amount of alteration in public opinion which my utopia postulates is vastly less than the difference between the mentality of those black warriors who pursued Stanley's party on the Congo with their cannibal war cry of "Meat! Meat!" and that of the "general staff" of any civilized nation. History has seen the latter interval bridged over: The former one can be bridged over much more easily.

From a lecture delivered at Stanford University during James' year as a visiting scholar on leave from Harvard. The brother of the novelist Henry James, William was among the most eminent of America's late nineteenth-century philosophers.

Corinthian-type helmet, Bulgaria. Photograph by Erich Lessing.

c. 1916: Western Front

"BED 26, AMPUTATED THIGH"

I sit by Kemmerich's bed. He is sinking steadily. Around us is great commotion. A hospital train has arrived, and the wounded fit to be moved are being selected. The doctor passes by Kemmerich's bed without once looking at him.

"Next time, Franz," I say.

He raises himself on the pillow with his elbows. "They have amputated my leg."

He knows it too then. I nod and answer, "You must be thankful you've come off with that."

He is silent.

I resume, "It might have been both legs, Franz. Wegeler has lost his right arm. That's much worse. Besides, you will be going home." He looks at me. "Do you think so?"

"Of course."

"Do you think so?" he repeats.

"Sure, Franz. Once you've got over the operation."

He beckons me to bend down. I stoop over him and he whispers, "I don't think so."

"Don't talk rubbish; Franz, in a couple of days you'll see for yourself. What is it anyway—an amputated leg? Here they patch up far worse things than that."

He lifts one hand. "Look here though, these fingers."

"That's the result of the operation. Just eat decently and you'll soon be well again. Do they look after you properly?"

He points to a dish that is still half full. I get excited. "Franz, you must eat. Eating is the main thing. That looks good too."

He turns away. After a pause he says slowly, "I wanted to become a head forester once."

"So you may still," I assure him. "There are splendid artificial limbs now; you'd hardly know there was anything missing. They are fixed onto the muscles. You can move the fingers and work and even write with an artificial hand. And besides, they will always be making new improvements."

For a while he lies still. Then he says, "You can take my lace-up boots with you for Müller."

I nod and wonder what to say to encourage him. His lips have fallen away, his mouth has become larger, his teeth stick out and look as though they were made of chalk. The flesh melts, the forehead bulges more prominently, the cheekbones protrude. The skeleton is working itself through. The eyes are already sunken in. In a couple of hours it will be over.

He is not the first that I have seen thus; but we grew up together and that always makes it a bit different. I have copied his essays. At school he used to wear a brown coat with a belt and shiny sleeves. He was the only one of us, too, who could do the giant's turn on the horizontal bar. His hair flew in his face like silk when he did it. Kantorek was proud of him. But he couldn't stand cigarettes. His skin was very white; he had something of the girl about him.

I glance at my boots. They are big and clumsy, the breeches are tucked into them, and standing up one looks well built and powerful in these great drainpipes. But when we go bathing and strip, suddenly we have slender legs again and slight shoulders. We are no longer soldiers but little more than boys; no one would believe that we could carry packs. It is a strange moment when we stand naked; then we become civilians, and almost feel ourselves to be so. When bathing, Franz Kemmerich looked as slight and frail as a child. There he lies now—but why? The whole world ought to pass by this bed and say, "That is Franz Kemmerich, nineteen and a half years old, he doesn't want to die. Let him not die!"

My thoughts become confused. This atmosphere of carbolic and gangrene clogs the lungs, it is a thick gruel, it suffocates.

It grows dark. Kemmerich's face changes color, it lifts from the pillow and is so pale that it gleams. The mouth moves slightly. I draw near to him. He whispers, "If you find my watch, send it home—"

I do not reply. It is no use any more. No one can console him. I am wretched with helplessness. This forehead with its hollow temples, this mouth that now seems all teeth, this sharp

nose! And the fat, weeping woman at home to whom I must write. If only the letter were sent off already!

Hospital orderlies go to and fro with bottles and pails. One of them comes up, casts a glance at Kemmerich and goes away again. You can see he is waiting; apparently he wants the bed.

The great nations have always acted like gangsters, and the small nations like prostitutes.
—Stanley Kubrick, 1963

I bend over Franz and talk to him as though that could save him: "Perhaps you will go to the convalescent home at Klosterberg, among the villas, Franz. Then you can look out from the window across the fields to the two trees on the horizon. It is the loveliest time of the year now, when the corn ripens; at evening, the fields in the sunlight look like mother-of-pearl. And the lane of poplars by the Klosterbach, where we used to catch sticklebacks! You can build an aquarium again and keep fish in it, and you can go without asking anyone, you can even play the piano if you want to."

I lean down over his face which lies in the shadow. He still breathes, lightly. His face is wet, he is crying. What a fine mess I have made of it with my foolish talk!

"But Franz"—I put my arm round his shoulder and put my face against his. "Will you sleep now?"

He does not answer. The tears run down his cheeks. I would like to wipe them away, but my handkerchief is too dirty.

An hour passes. I sit tensely and watch his every movement in case he may perhaps say something. What if he were to open his mouth and cry out! But he only weeps, his head turned aside. He does not speak of his mother or his brothers and sisters. He says nothing; all that lies behind him; he is entirely alone now with his little life of nineteen years, and cries because it leaves him. This is the most disturbing and hardest parting that I ever have seen, although it was pretty bad too with Tiedjen, who called for his mother—a big bear of a fellow who, with wild eyes full of terror, held off the doctor from his bed with a dagger until he collapsed.

Suddenly Kemmerich groans and begins to gurgle.

I jump up, stumble outside and demand, "Where is the doctor? Where is the doctor?"

As I catch sight of the white apron I seize hold of it: "Come quick, Franz Kemmerich is dying."

He frees himself and asks an orderly standing by, "Which will that be?"

He says, "Bed Twenty-Six, amputated thigh."

He sniffs, "How should I know anything about it; I've amputated five legs today"; he shoves me away, says to the hospital orderly, "You see to it," and hurries off to the operating room.

I tremble with rage as I go along with the orderly. The man looks at me and says, "One operation after another since five o'clock this morning. You know, today alone there have been sixteen deaths—yours is the seventeenth. There will probably be twenty altogether—"

I become faint; all at once I cannot do any more. I won't revile any more, it is senseless; I could drop down and never rise up again.

We are by Kemmerich's bed. He is dead. The face is still wet from the tears. The eyes are half open and yellow like old horn buttons. The orderly pokes me in the ribs, "Are you taking his things with you?" I nod.

He goes on, "We must take him away at once; we want the bed. Outside they are lying on the floor."

I collect Kemmerich's things and untie his identification disc. The orderly asks about the paybook. I say that it is probably in the orderly room, and go. Behind me they are already hauling Franz on to a waterproof sheet.

> **Erich Maria Remarque**, *from his novel* All Quiet on the Western Front. *The book enjoyed popular and critical success when it was published in Germany in 1929. Four years later, the Nazi government classified it as Jewish propaganda and prohibited its sale and distribution.*

1905 : New York

WAR PRAYER

It was a time of great and exalting excitement. The country was up in arms, the war was on, in every breast burned the holy fire of patriotism; the drums were beating, the bands playing, the toy pistols popping, the bunched firecrackers hissing and spluttering; on every hand and far down the receding and fading spread of roofs and balconies, a fluttering wilderness of flags flashed in the sun; daily the young volunteers marched down the wide avenue gay and fine in their new uniforms, the proud fathers and mothers and sisters and sweethearts cheering them with voices choked with happy emotion as they swung by; nightly the packed mass meetings listened, panting, to patriot oratory which stirred the deepest deeps of their hearts and which they interrupted at briefest intervals with cyclones of applause, the tears running down their cheeks the while; in the churches the pastors preached devotion to flag and country and invoked the God of Battles, beseeching His aid in our good cause in outpouring of fervid eloquence which moved every listener. It was indeed a glad and gracious time, and the half-dozen rash spirits that ventured to disapprove of the war and cast a doubt upon its righteousness straightway got such a stern and angry warning that for their personal safety's sake, they quickly shrank out of sight and offended no more in that way.

Sunday morning came—next day the battalions would leave for the front; the church was filled; the volunteers were there, their young faces alight with martial dreams—visions of the stern advance, the gathering momentum, the rushing charge, the flashing sabers, the flight of the foe, the tumult, the enveloping smoke, the fierce pursuit, the surrender!—then home from the war, bronzed heroes, welcomed, adored, submerged in golden seas of glory! With the volunteers sat their dear ones, proud, happy, and envied by the neighbors and friends who had no sons and brothers to send forth to the field of honor, there to win for the flag or, failing, die the noblest of noble deaths. The service proceeded; a war chapter from the Old Testament was read; the first prayer was said; it was followed by an organ burst that shook the building, and with one impulse the house rose, with glowing eyes and beating hearts, and poured out that tremendous invocation:

"God the all-terrible! Thou who ordainest,
Thunder thy clarion and lightning thy sword!"

Then came the "long" prayer. None could remember the like of it for passionate pleading and moving and beautiful language. The burden of its supplication was that an ever merciful and benignant Father of us all would watch over our noble young soldiers and aid, comfort, and encourage them in their patriotic work; bless them, shield them in the day of battle and the hour of peril, bear them in His mighty hand, make them strong and confident, invincible in the bloody onset; help them to crush the foe, grant to them and to their flag and country imperishable honor and glory.

An aged stranger entered and moved with slow and noiseless step up the main aisle, his eyes fixed upon the minister, his long body clothed in a robe that reached to his feet, his head bare, his white hair descending in a frothy cataract to his shoulders, his seamy face unnaturally pale, pale even to ghastliness. With all eyes following him and wondering, he made his silent way; without pausing, he ascended to the preacher's side and stood there, waiting. With shut lids, the preacher, unconscious of his presence, continued with his moving prayer and at last finished it with the words, uttered in fervent appeal, "Bless our arms, grant us the victory, O Lord our God, Father and Protector of our land and flag!"

The stranger touched his arm, motioned him to step aside—which the startled minister did—and took his place. During some moments he surveyed the spellbound audience with solemn eyes in which burned an uncanny light; then in a deep voice he said:

Families identify the dead, Crimea, 1942. Photograph by Dmitri Baltermants.

"I come from the throne—bearing a message from Almighty God!" The words smote the house with a shock; if the stranger perceived it, he gave no attention. "He has heard the prayer of His servant your shepherd and will grant it if such shall be your desire after I, His messenger, shall have explained to you its import—that is to say, its full import. For it is like unto many of the prayers of men, in that it asks for more than he who utters it is aware of—except he pause and think.

> For every state, war is always incessant and lifelong against every other state. For what most men call "peace," this is really only a name—in truth, all states by their very nature are always engaged in an informal war against all other states. —Plato, c. 350 BC

"God's servant and yours has prayed his prayer. Has he paused and taken thought? Is it one prayer? No, it is two—one uttered, the other not. Both have reached the ear of Him Who heareth all supplications, the spoken and the unspoken. Ponder this—keep it in mind. If you would beseech a blessing upon yourself, beware! Lest without intent you invoke a curse upon a neighbor at the same time. If you pray for the blessing of rain upon your crop which needs it, by that act you are possibly praying for a curse upon some neighbor's crop which may not need rain and can be injured by it.

"You have heard your servant's prayer—the uttered part of it. I am commissioned of God to put into words the other part of it—that part which the pastor, and also you in your hearts, fervently prayed silently. And ignorantly and unthinkingly? God grant that it was so! You heard these words: 'Grant us the victory, O Lord our God!' That is sufficient. The *whole* of the uttered prayer is compact into those pregnant words. Elaborations were not necessary. When you have prayed for victory, you have prayed for many unmentioned results which follow victory—*must* follow it, cannot help but follow it. Upon the listening spirit of

God the Father fell also the unspoken part of the prayer. He commandeth me to put it into words. Listen!

"O Lord our Father, our young patriots, idols of our hearts, go forth to battle—be Thou near them! With them, in spirit, we also go forth from the sweet peace of our beloved firesides to smite the foe. O Lord our God, help us to tear their soldiers to bloody shreds with our shells; help us to cover their smiling fields with the pale forms of their patriot dead; help us to drown the thunder of the guns with the shrieks of their wounded, writhing in pain; help us to lay waste their humble homes with a hurricane of fire; help us to wring the hearts of their unoffending widows with unavailing grief; help us to turn them out roofless with little children to wander unfriended the wastes of their desolated land in rags and hunger and thirst, sports of the sun flames of summer and the icy winds of winter, broken in spirit, worn with travail, imploring Thee for the refuge of the grave and denied it— for our sakes who adore Thee, Lord, blast their hopes, blight their lives, protract their bitter pilgrimage, make heavy their steps, water their way with their tears, stain the white snow with the blood of their wounded feet! We ask it, in the spirit of love, of Him Who is the source of love, and Who is the ever faithful refuge and friend of all that are sore, beset and seek His aid with humble and contrite hearts. Amen.

(After a pause.) "Ye have prayed it; if ye still desire it, speak! The messenger of the Most High waits!"

It was believed afterward that the man was a lunatic, because there was no sense in what he said.

Mark Twain. *The editors to whom Twain offered this manuscript in 1905 thought it "unsuitable for publication" at a moment of high and patriotic feeling. Twain was the vice president of the American Anti-Imperialist League and strongly opposed to the McKinley Administration's occupation of the Philippines subsequent to the Spanish-American War. The story didn't appear in print until 1923, thirteen years after Twain's death.*

1947: Washington

At no time, from 1941 to 1945, did I ever hear it suggested by the president, or by any other responsible member of the government, that atomic energy should not be used in the war. All of us of course understood the terrible responsibility involved in our attempt to unlock the doors to such a devastating weapon; President Roosevelt particularly spoke to me many times of his own awareness of the catastrophic potentialities of our work. But we were at war, and the work must be done. I therefore emphasize that it was our common objective, throughout the war, to be the first to produce an atomic weapon and use it.

Japan, in July 1945, had been seriously weakened by our increasingly violent attacks. It was known to us that she had gone so far as to make tentative proposals to the Soviet government, hoping to use the Russians as mediators in a negotiated peace. These vague proposals contemplated the retention by Japan of important conquered areas and were therefore not considered seriously. There was as yet no indication of any weakening in the Japanese determination to fight rather than accept unconditional surrender. If she should persist in her fight to the end, she had still a great military force.

My chief purpose was to end the war in victory with the least possible cost in the lives of the men in the armies which I had helped to raise. In the light of the alternatives which, on a fair estimate, were open to us, I believe that no man, in our position and subject to our responsibilities, holding in his hands a weapon of such possibilities for accomplishing this purpose and saving those lives, could have failed to use it and afterwards looked his countrymen in the face.

What I have written in this year of peace may have a harsh and unfeeling sound. It would perhaps be possible to say the same things and say them more gently. But I do not think it would be wise. As I look back over the five years of my service as Secretary of War, I see too many stern and heartrending decisions to be willing to pretend that war is anything else than what it is. The face of war is the face of death; death is an inevitable part of every order that a wartime leader gives. The decision to use the atomic bomb was a decision that brought death to over a hundred thousand Japanese. No explanation can change that fact, and I do not wish to gloss it over. But this deliberate, premeditated destruction was our least abhorrent choice. The destruction of Hiroshima and Nagasaki put an end to the Japanese war. It stopped the fire raids and the strangling blockade; it ended the ghastly specter of a clash of great land armies.

In this last great action of the Second World War, we were given final proof that war is death. War in the twentieth century has grown steadily more barbarous, more destructive, more debased in all its aspects. Now, with the release of atomic energy, man's ability to destroy himself is very nearly complete. The bombs dropped on Hiroshima and Nagasaki ended a war. They also made it wholly clear that we must never have another war. This is the lesson men and leaders everywhere must learn, and I believe that when they learn it, they will find a way to lasting peace.

From "The Decision to Use the Atomic Bomb," Harper's Magazine, *February 1947. Stimson was President Harry Truman's Secretary of War, persuasive in his arguments to deploy the bomb. The result provoked a good deal of angry disagreement in the American press. Eighteen months after the fact, Stimson defended the decision as the least abhorrent choice.*

The Battle of Valmy September 10th, 1792, by Jean Baptiste Mauzaisse, 1835, after H. Vernet.

48 BC: Pharsalus

FAREWELL TO THE ROMAN REPUBLIC

Wrong it would be, when a world was dying, to squander regrets on
Single deaths, and to follow the fate of this man or that man,
Giving details of who had his body transfixed by a sword lunge,
Who was disemboweled and staggered about on his entrails,
Who took a sword in the throat and drove it out by the force of
One last gasp. There were some who were struck and fell in an instant;
Some were shorn of their arms, but continued standing; a missile
Traversed the chest of some clean through, while others a spear thrust
Pinned to the ground; sometimes men's veins were pierced, and the blood came
Spurting out and bespattered the arms of their enemies; one man
Pierced his brother's heart and, to stay undetected in stripping
Such a close-kindred body, he cut off the head and hurled it
Out of sight, while another was hacking away at his father,
Hoping that people would think from his very rage that it could not
Possibly be his parent. No single death has a claim to
Special lament. No time to mourn individual victims.
This was a battle unique, not sharing the features of other,
Past defeats. For in those Rome's loss could be reckoned in people,
Here in nations; there you would speak of the death of a soldier,
Here the death of a race. Here flowed the blood of Achaeans,
Pontics, Assyrians—but that was nothing; it vanished
Swept from the field by the torrent that poured from the veins of the Romans.
Nor was this worldwide wound confined to the times of Pharsalia;
More was lost than lives and the right to existence; for all time
Ever to come we were laid prostrate. This battle established
Permanent servitude for every age of the future.
What did we, we sons and grandsons of Romans who fought there,
What did we do to deserve to be born to a tyranny? Were we
Guilty of cowardice, of saving our skins in the fighting?
No, but the penalty for the craven conduct of others
Rests like a yoke on our necks. We were born long after the battle;
Fortune, if she had wanted to saddle us with a master,
Ought to have given us also the chance of fighting for freedom.

> **Lucan,** *from* Pharsalia. *Cast in the form of an epic poem, Lucan's account of Rome's civil wars in the first century BC attributes the death of the republic to the murderous rivalry between Pompey and Julius Caesar. In 65, Emperor Nero ordered the poet, then age twenty-five, to commit suicide, and the poem did not appear in full until after Lucan's death.*

1812: Moscow

LET WAR BE WAR AND NOT A GAME

"So you think that we shall win a victory tomorrow?" asked Pierre.

"Yes, yes," answered Prince Andrei absently. "One thing I would do if I had the power," he began again. "I would not take prisoners. What sense is there in taking prisoners? It's playing knights of old. The French have destroyed my home and are on their way to destroy Moscow; and they have outraged and are outraging me every moment. They are my enemies. In my opinion they are all criminals, and that expresses the feeling of Timohin and the whole army with him. They must be put to death. Since they are my enemies, they cannot be my friends, whatever was said at Tilsit."

"Oh yes," murmured Pierre, looking with shining eyes at Prince Andrei. "I entirely agree with you!"

The question that had worried Pierre on the Mozhaisk hill and all that day now seemed to him quite clear and fully solved. He now realized all the import and all the gravity of this war and the impending battle. All he had seen that day, all the significant, stern expressions on the faces he had seen in passing, appeared to him in a new light now. The latent heat (as they say in physics) of patriotism which was present in all these men he had seen was now intelligible to him, and explained the composure and almost lightheartedness with which they were all preparing for death.

"Not to take prisoners," Prince Andrei continued. "That by itself would transform the whole aspect of war and make it less cruel. As

Upright shields. From the *Bellifortis* manuscript, fifteenth century.

it is, we have been playing at war—that's what's vile! We play at being magnanimous and all the rest of it. Such magnanimity and sensibility are like the magnanimity and sensibility of the lady who faints at the sight of a calf being killed: She is so tenderhearted that she can't look at blood—but *fricassée* of veal she will eat with gusto. They prate about the rules of warfare, of chivalry, of flags of truce, and humanity to the wounded, and so on. All fiddlesticks. I saw chivalry and flags of truce in 1805; they humbugged us and we humbugged them. They plunder people's homes, circulate false paper money, and, worst of all, they kill our children and our fathers, and then talk of the rules of warfare and generosity to a fallen foe. No quarter, I say, but kill and be killed! Anyone who has reached this conclusion through the same suffering as I have…"

Prince Andrei, who had believed it was a matter of indifference to him whether they took Moscow as they had taken Smolensk, was unexpectedly pulled up in his argument by a sudden cramp in his throat. He walked to and fro a few times in silence, but his eyes glittered feverishly and his lips quivered as he began to speak again.

"If there were none of this magnanimity business in warfare, we should never go to war, except for something worth facing certain death for, as now. Then there would not be wars because Paul Ivanich had given offense to Mihail Ivanich. And when there was a war, like this present one, it would be war! And then the

spirit and determination of the fighting men would be something quite different. All these Westphalians and Hessians that Napoleon has dragged at his heels would never have come to Russia, and we should not have gone fighting in Austria and Prussia without knowing why. War is not a polite recreation but the vilest thing in life, and we ought to understand that and not play at war. Our attitude towards the fearful necessity of war ought to be stern and serious. It boils down to this: We should have done with humbug, and let war be war and not a game. Otherwise, war is a favorite pastime of the idle and frivolous… there is no profession held in higher esteem than the military. And what is war? What makes for success in warfare? What are the morals of the military world? The aim and end of war is murder; the weapons employed in war are espionage, treachery and the encouragement of treachery, the ruining of a country, the plundering and robbing of its inhabitants for the maintenance of the army, and trickery and lying, which all appear under the heading of the art of war. The military world is characterized by the absence of freedom—in other words, a rigorous discipline—enforced inactivity, ignorance, cruelty, debauchery, and drunkenness. And yet this is the highest caste in society, respected by all. Every monarch in the world, except the Emperor of China, wears a military uniform, and bestows the greatest rewards on the man who kills the greatest number of his fellow creatures. Tens of thousands of men meet—as they will tomorrow—to massacre one another: to kill and maim, and then they will offer up thanksgiving services for having slain such vast numbers (they even exaggerate the number) and proclaim a victory, supposing that the more men they have slaughtered the more credit to them. Think of God looking down and listening to them!" cried Prince Andrei in a shrill, piercing voice.

"Death Gratuity"

U.S. Military Condolence Reimbursements:

1908-1956: six months' pay, based on rank

1956-1991: $800-$3,000, based on rank

1991-2003: $6,000, half-taxed

2003-2005: $12,000, tax-free

2005: $12,420, tax-free

2005-present: $100,000, tax-free

Leo Tolstoy, *from* War and Peace. *The conversation takes place on the evening before the Battle of Borodino, September 7, 1812. Napoleon's army won the battle at the cost of thirty thousand dead; the Russian army commanded by Marshal M. I. Kutuzov contributed another forty-five thousand dead.*

c. 1918: Flanders

DULCE ET DECORUM EST

Bent double, like old beggars under sacks,
Knock-kneed, coughing like hags, we cursed through sludge,
Till on the haunting flares we turned our backs
And towards our distant rest began to trudge.
Men marched asleep. Many had lost their boots
But limped on, blood-shod. All went lame; all blind;
Drunk with fatigue; deaf even to the hoots
Of tired, outstripped Five-Nines that dropped behind.

Gas! GAS! Quick, boys!—An ecstasy of fumbling,
Fitting the clumsy helmets just in time;
But someone still was yelling out and stumbling
And flound'ring like a man in fire or lime…
Dim, through the misty panes and thick green light,
As under a green sea, I saw him drowning.

In all my dreams, before my helpless sight,
He plunges at me, guttering, choking, drowning.

If in some smothering dreams you too could pace
Behind the wagon that we flung him in,
And watch the white eyes writhing in his face,
His hanging face, like a devil's sick of sin;
If you could hear, at every jolt, the blood
Come gargling from the froth-corrupted lungs,
Obscene as cancer, bitter as the cud
Of vile, incurable sores on innocent tongues—
My friend, you would not tell with such high zest
To children ardent for some desperate glory,
The old Lie: Dulce et decorum est
Pro patria mori.

> **Wilfred Owen.** *The last lines ("It is sweet and becoming to die
> for one's country") Owen borrowed from the Roman poet Horace.
> Enlisted in the British army in 1915 at age twenty-two, Owen was
> promoted to the rank of full lieutenant and awarded the Military
> Cross. He was killed at the Sambre-Oise Canal on November 4,
> 1918, seven days before the signing of the Armistice.*

1983: New York

CURE FOR AN ADDICTION

I am not an alcoholic. If I was, I would go before the nearest A.A. meeting and say, "My name is Kurt Vonnegut. I am an alcoholic." God willing, that might be my first step down the long, hard road back to sobriety.

The A.A. scheme, which requires a confession like that, is the first to have any measurable success in dealing with the tendency of some human beings, perhaps 10 percent of any population sample anyone might care to choose, to become addicted to substances that give them brief spasms of pleasure but in the long term transmute their lives and the lives of those around them into ultimate ghastliness.

The A.A. scheme, which, again, can work only if the addicts regularly admit that this or that chemical is poisonous to them, is now proving its effectiveness with compulsive gamblers, who are not dependent on chemicals from a distillery or a pharmaceutical laboratory. This is no paradox. Gamblers, in effect, manufacture their own dangerous substances. God help them, they produce chemicals that elate them whenever they place a bet on simply anything.

If I was a compulsive gambler, which I am not, I would be well advised to stand up before the nearest meeting of Gamblers Anonymous and declare, "My name is Kurt Vonnegut. I am a compulsive gambler."

Whether I was standing before a meeting of Gamblers Anonymous or Alcoholics Anonymous, I would be encouraged to testify as to how the chemicals I had generated within myself or swallowed had alienated my friends and relatives, cost me jobs and houses, and deprived me of my last shred of self-respect.

I now wish to call attention to another form of addiction, which has not been previously identified. It is more like gambling than drinking, since the people afflicted are ravenous for situations that will cause their bodies to release exciting chemicals into their bloodstreams. I am persuaded that there are among us people who are tragically hooked on preparations for war.

Tell people with that disease that war is coming and we have to get ready for it, and for a few minutes there, they will be as happy as a drunk with his martini breakfast or a compulsive gambler with his paycheck bet on the Super Bowl.

Let us recognize how sick such people are. From now on, when a national leader, or even just a neighbor, starts talking about some new weapons system which is going to cost us a mere $29 billion, we should speak up. We should say something on the order of, "Honest to God, I couldn't be sorrier for you if I'd seen you wash down a fistful of black beauties with a pint of Southern Comfort."

I mean it. I am not joking. Compulsive preparers for World War III, in this country or any other, are as tragically and, yes, as repulsively addicted as any stockbroker passed out with his head in a toilet in the Port Authority Bus Terminal.

If we know a compulsive gambler who is dead broke, we can probably make him happy with a dollar to bet on who can spit farther than someone else. For us to give a compulsive war-preparer a fleeting moment of happiness, we may have to buy him three Trident submarines and a hundred intercontinental ballistic missiles mounted on choo-choo trains.

If Western Civilization were a person—

If Western Civilization, which blankets the world now, as far as I can tell, were a person—

If Western Civilizations, which surely now includes the Soviet Union and China and India and Pakistan and on and on, were a person—

If Western Civilization were a person, we would be directing it to the nearest meeting of War-Preparers Anonymous. We would be telling it to stand up before the meeting and say, "My name is Western Civilization. I am a compulsive war-preparer. I have lost everything I ever cared about. I should have come here long ago. I first hit bottom in World War I." Western Civilization cannot be represented by a single person, of course, but a single explanation for the catastrophic course it has followed during this bloody century is possible. We the people, because of our ignorance of the disease, have again and again entrusted power to people we did not know were sickies.

And let us not mock them now, any more than we would mock someone with syphilis or smallpox or leprosy or yaws or typhoid fever or any of the other diseases to which the flesh is heir. All we have to do is separate them from the levers of power, I think.

Most addictions start innocently enough in childhood, under agreeable, reputable auspices—a sip of champagne at a wedding, a game of poker for matchsticks on a rainy afternoon. Compulsive war-preparers may have been encouraged as infants to clap their hands with glee at a campfire or a Fourth of July parade.

Not every child gets hooked. Not every child so tempted grows up to be a drunk or a gambler or a babbler about knocking down the incoming missiles of the Evil Empire with laser beams. When I identify the war-preparers as addicts, I am not calling for the exclusion of children from all martial celebrations. I doubt that more than one child in a hundred, having seen fireworks, for example, will become an adult who wants us to stop squandering our substance on education and health and social justice and the arts and food and shelter and clothing for the needy, and so on—who wants us to blow it all on ammunition instead.

And please understand that the addiction I have identified is to *preparations* for war. I repeat: to *preparations* for war, addiction to the thrills of demothballing battleships and inventing weapons systems against which there cannot possibly be a defense, supposedly, and urging the citizenry to hate this part of humanity or that one, and knocking over little governments that might aid and abet an enemy someday, and so on. I am not talking about an addiction to war itself, which is a very different matter. A compulsive preparer for war wants to go to big-time war no more than an alcoholic stockbroker wants to pass out with his head in a toilet in the Port Authority Bus Terminal.

Should addicts of any sort hold high office

in this or any other country? Absolutely not, for their first priority will always be to satisfy their addiction, no matter how terrible the consequences may be—even to themselves.

Suppose we had an alcoholic president who still had not hit bottom and whose chief companions were drunks like himself. And suppose it were a fact, made absolutely clear to him, that if he took just one more drink, the whole planet would blow up.

Afghan war rug made by women fleeing the Soviet invasion of Afghanistan, 1979–88.

So he has all the liquor thrown out of the White House, including his Aqua Velva shaving lotion. So late at night he is terribly restless, crazy for a drink but proud of not drinking. So he opens the White House refrigerator, looking for a Tab or a Diet Pepsi, he tells himself. And there, half-hidden by a family-size jar of French's mustard, is an unopened can of Coors beer.

What do you think he'll do?

Kurt Vonnegut, *in* The Nation, *December 31, 1983. Vonnegut had served with the Army in Europe during World War II; captured and imprisoned in Dresden, he was present in that city when the Allied fire-bombing killed or cremated 35,000 of its inhabitants. He memorialized the occasion in his novel,* Slaughterhouse-Five.

1953: Washington

"HUMANITY HANGING FROM A CROSS OF IRON"

Today the hope of free men remains stubborn and brave, but it is sternly disciplined by experience. It shuns not only all crude counsel of despair, but also the self-deceit of easy illusion. It weighs the chance for peace with sure, clear knowledge of what happened to the vain hope of 1945.

In the spring of victory, the soldiers of the Western Allies met the soldiers of Russia in

> *Political power grows out of the barrel of a gun.*
> *—Mao Zedong, 1938*

the center of Europe. They were triumphant of building, in honor of their dead, the only fitting monument—an age of just peace. All these war-weary peoples shared, too, this concrete, decent purpose: to guard vigilantly against the domination ever again of the world by a single, unbridled aggressive power.

This common purpose lasted an instant—and perished. The nations of the world divided to follow two distinct roads.

The United States and our valued friends, the other free nations, chose one road.

The leaders of the Soviet Union chose another.

The free nations, most solemnly and repeatedly, have assured the Soviet Union that their firm association has never had any aggressive purpose whatsoever. Soviet leaders, however, have seemed to persuade themselves—or tried to persuade their people—otherwise.

And so came to pass that the Soviet Union itself has shared and suffered the very fears it has fostered in the rest of the world.

This has been the way of life forged by eight years of fear and force.

What can the world—or any nation in it—hope for if no turning is found on this dread road?

The worst to be feared and the best to be expected can be simply stated.

The worst is atomic war.

The best would be this: a life of perpetual fear and tension; a burden of arms draining the wealth and the labor of all peoples; a wasting of strength that defies the American system or the Soviet system or any system to achieve true abundance and happiness for the peoples of this earth.

Every gun that is made, every warship launched, every rocket fired signifies—in the final sense—a theft from those who hunger and are not fed, those who are cold and are not clothed.

This world in arms is not spending money alone.

It is spending the sweat of its laborers, the genius of its scientists, the hopes of its children.

The cost of one modern heavy bomber is this: a modern brick school in more than thirty cities.

It is: two electric power plants, each serving a town of sixty thousand population.

It is: two fine, fully equipped hospitals.

It is: some fifty miles of concrete highway.

We pay for a single fighter plane with a half million bushels of wheat.

We pay for a single destroyer with new homes that could have housed more than eight thousand people.

This—I repeat—is the best way of life to be found on the road the world has been taking.

This is not a way of life at all in any true sense. Under the cloud of threatening war, it is humanity hanging from a cross of iron.

These plain and cruel truths define the peril and point the hope that come with this spring of 1953.

This is one of those times in the affairs of nations when the gravest choices must be made if there is to be a turning toward a just and lasting peace.

It is a moment that calls upon the governments of the world to speak their intentions with simplicity and with honesty.

It calls upon them to answer the question that stirs the hearts of all sane men: Is there no other way the world may live?

This we do know: A world that begins to witness the rebirth of trust among nations can find its way to a peace that is neither partial nor punitive.

With all who will work in good faith toward such a peace, we are ready—with renewed resolve—to strive to redeem the near lost hopes of our day.

The fruit of success in all these tasks would present the world with the greatest task—and the greatest opportunity—of all. It is this: the dedication of the energies, the resources, and the imaginations of all peaceful nations to a new kind of war. This would be a declared, total war, not upon any human enemy, but upon the brute forces of poverty and need.

The peace we seek, founded upon decent trust and cooperative effort among nations, can be fortified—not by weapons of war—but by wheat and by cotton, by milk and by wool, by meat and by timber, and by rice.

These are words that translate into every language on earth.

These are needs that challenge this world in arms.

We are ready, in short, to dedicate our strength to serving the needs, rather than the fears, of the world. They conform to our firm faith that God created men to enjoy, not destroy, the fruits of the earth and of their own toil.

They aspire to this: the lifting from the backs and from the hearts of men of their burden of arms and of fears, so that they may find before them a golden age of freedom and of peace.

President **Dwight David Eisenhower**, *from a speech given to the American Society of Newspaper Editors holding their annual convention in Washington's Statler Hotel on April 16, 1953. Eight years later, delivering his farewell address to the American people in the winter of 1961, Eisenhower ascribed the exploitation of the country's wealth, intelligence, energies, and freedoms to what he had come to recognize as the "military-industrial complex."*

War ship from the Temple of Fortuna Primigenia at Praeneste, late first century.

1953: New York

W. H. AUDEN RECONFIGURES THE SHIELD OF ACHILLES

She looked over his shoulder
   For vines and olive trees,
Marble well-governed cities
   And ships upon untamed seas,
But there on the shining metal
   His hands had put instead
An artificial wilderness
   And a sky like lead.

A plain without a feature, bare and brown,
   No blade of grass, no sign of neighborhood,
Nothing to eat and nowhere to sit down,
   Yet, congregated on its blankness, stood
   An unintelligible multitude,
A million eyes, a million boots in line,
Without expression, waiting for a sign.

Out of the air a voice without a face
   Proved by statistics that some cause was just
In tones as dry and level as the place:
   No one was cheered and nothing was discussed;
   Column by column in a cloud of dust
They marched away enduring a belief
Whose logic brought them, somewhere else, to grief.

She looked over his shoulder
   For ritual pieties,
White flower-garlanded heifers,
   Libation and sacrifice,
But there on the shining metal
   Where the altar should have been,
She saw by his flickering forge-light
   Quite another scene.

Barbed wire enclosed an arbitrary spot
   Where bored officials lounged (one cracked a joke)
And sentries sweated for the day was hot:
   A crowd of ordinary decent folk
   Watched from without and neither moved nor spoke
As three pale figures were led forth and bound
To three posts driven upright in the ground.

The mass and majesty of this world, all
   That carries weight and always weighs the same
Lay in the hands of others; they were small
   And could not hope for help and no help came:
   What their foes like to do was done, their shame
Was all the worst could wish; they lost their pride
And died as men before their bodies died.

      She looked over his shoulder
         For athletes at their games,
      Men and women in a dance
         Moving their sweet limbs
      Quick, quick, to music,
         But there on the shining shield
      His hands had set no dancing-floor
         But a weed-choked field.

A ragged urchin, aimless and alone,
   Loitered about that vacancy; a bird
Flew up to safety from his well-aimed stone:
   That girls are raped, that two boys knife a third,
   Were axioms to him, who'd never heard
Of any world where promises were kept,
Or one could weep because another wept.

      The thin-lipped armorer,
         Hephaestos, hobbled away,
      Thetis of the shining breasts
         Cried out in dismay
      At what the god had wrought
         To please her son, the strong
      Iron-hearted man-slaying Achilles
         Who would not live long.

Auden's poem, "The Shield of Achilles," was published in 1955 in a book of the same title.

1865: Washington

"WITH MALICE TOWARD NONE"

At this second appearing to take the oath of the presidential office, there is less occasion for an extended address than there was at the first. Then a statement, somewhat in detail, of a course to be pursued, seemed fitting and proper. Now, at the expiration of four years, during which public declarations have been constantly called forth on every point and phase of the great contest which still absorbs the attention, and engrosses the energies of the nation, little that is new could be presented. The progress of our arms, upon which all else chiefly depends, is as well known to the public as to myself; and it is, I trust, reasonably satisfactory and encouraging to all. With high hope for the future, no prediction in regard to it is ventured.

On the occasion corresponding to this four years ago, all thoughts were anxiously directed to an impending civil war. All dreaded it—all sought to avert it. While the inaugural address was being delivered from this place, devoted altogether to *saving* the Union without war, insurgent agents were in the city seeking to *destroy* it without war—seeking to dissolve the Union, and divide effects, by negotiation. Both parties deprecated war; but one of them would *make* war rather than let the nation survive, and the other would *accept* war rather than let it perish. And the war came.

One eighth of the whole population were colored slaves, not distributed generally over the Union, but localized in the Southern part of it. These slaves constituted a peculiar and powerful interest. All knew that this interest was, somehow, the cause of the war. To strengthen, perpetuate, and extend this interest was the object for which the insurgents would rend the Union, even by war; while the government claimed no right to do more than to restrict the territorial enlargement of it. Neither party expected for the war, the magnitude, or the duration, which it has already attained. Neither anticipated that the *cause* of the conflict might cease with, or even before,

the conflict itself should cease. Each looked for an easier triumph and a result less fundamental and astounding. Both read the same Bible and pray to the same God; and each invokes His aid against the other. It may seem strange that any men should dare to ask a just God's assistance in wringing their bread from the sweat of other men's faces; but let us judge not that we be not judged. The prayers of both could not be answered; that of neither has been answered fully. The Almighty has His own purposes. "Woe unto the world because of offences! For it must needs be that offences come; but woe to that man by whom the offence cometh!" If we shall suppose that American slavery is one of those offences which, in the providence of God, must needs come, but which, having continued through His appointed time, He now wills to remove, and that He gives to both North and South this terrible war as the woe due to those by whom the offence came, shall we discern therein any departure from those divine attributes which the believers in a Living God always ascribe to Him? Fondly do we hope—fervently do we pray—that this mighty scourge of war may speedily pass away. Yet, if God wills that it continue, until all the wealth piled by the bondman's two hundred and fifty years of unrequited toil shall be sunk, and until every drop of blood drawn with the lash shall be paid by another drawn with the sword, as was said three thousand years ago, so still it must be said, "The judgments of the Lord are true and righteous altogether."

With malice toward none; with charity for all; with firmness in the right, as God gives us to see the right, let us strive on to finish the work we are in; to bind up the nation's wounds; to care for him who shall have borne the battle, and for his widow, and his orphan—to do all which may achieve and cherish a just and lasting peace among ourselves and with all nations.

President **Abraham Lincoln**, *Second Inaugural Address, March 4, 1865. The Washington correspondent for the* New York Times *thought it "a very faulty affair." Six weeks later, on April 14, Lincoln was assassinated.*

1965: Thermopylae

WILLIAM GOLDING RETURNS
TO THE ISTHMUS

Lamia central square was hot and dusty. The tables of the one restaurant spilled out on the pavement in the shade of some small trees. It was in these parts, in 480 BC, that the Persian army had been held up for a few days on its way to Athens. South of Lamia, the river Spercheios has cut a valley athwart the invasion route, and the road must crawl round the corner on the other side of the valley between the cliffs and the sea. Sitting beneath a tree, I thought about Athens and Persia, and the hot springs that bubble out of the cliff where the road is narrowest, so that the Greeks call it the Hot Gates. I thought of myself, too—dreaming for twenty years of coming here, poring over ancient maps, and now faced with the duty and necessity of trying to understand.

I had seen the valley of the Spercheios when I entered Lamia, had glimpsed the vast wall of rock five thousand feet high on the other side of the valley, which lay between me and Athens.

Athens was shining Athens, the Athens of history, shining in the mind. Yet when the Persian Xerxes, King of Kings, drove his army at her, she did not shine. At that time she was little but a thorn in his side, a small city which had insisted on running her own affairs—and had an odd knack of encouraging cities which ought to bow to the King of Kings to do the same.

Athens needed thirty years, and then she would shine as no city had shone before or has shone since. For all her faults she would take humanity with her a long, long step—but on that day she was nothing but a pain in the neck of the King of Kings, who had the greatest army in the world poised at her last gate.

I went back for my car and drove down into the little valley and across the plain. A new motor road lies across it and sweeps round the corner where the old Hot Gates had lain between the cliffs and the sea. The road was unsurfaced, and in the rearview mirror I saw the great white cloud of dust that hung in the air behind me until it settled on the crops.

The Hot Gates were deserted. I came to an avenue and then to a group of mean-looking

Confederate soldiers killed at Antietam, 1862. Photograph by Alexander Gardner.

buildings huddled among trees. I drove in, but of course there was no one about. It was a spa, I supposed, and as far as I was concerned, on that burning afternoon, anyone who wanted a hot bath—with native sulfur—was welcome to it. I sat in the car and considered that history has left not a trace of scar on this landscape.

At the time of the Persian invasion, when the sea came close to these cliffs, the narrow track had held seven thousand men—Spartans, Thebans, Locrians, Thespians, Phocians—who watched one another as much as they watched the enemy. Greece to the south was in a turmoil as the Persians marched toward it. What to do? Whom to trust? What to believe? The track that summer was thick with dusty messengers bearing appeals for help, or accusations, or denials, or prayers to the gods.

Was there no memorial left? I drove out of the avenue and found one man awake at last. He was a goatherd carrying a thumbstick and a whistle. His goats were a tumultuous jumble of horns, of black and brown fur with ruffs and edgings of white, and staring, yellow, libidinous eyes. You see these herds in Greece as you may see flocks of sheep on a country road in England. I asked him about the Hot Gates, and he pointed forward along the road. Then he turned aside with his goats and they began to file off and scatter up the side of the cliffs.

I drove on to the Hot Gates proper, where once there had been room for no more than one wagon at a time. Sure enough, there was a memorial, level with the place where that mixed force had once stood in the pass, a nineteenth century monument, grandiose and expensive. When the battle was fought, the place where the monument stands was out in the sea.

Nature has not done her best here for the story of that battle. The Vale of Tempe would have been in a better place, and there are a hundred haunted spots in Greece where the setting would be more striking and the drama more obvious. Quiet, crop-fledged fields lie between the cliffs and the sea, with the scar of the motor road on them. The slopes and cliffs, though sprinkled with shrubs and flowers, aromatic in the hot sun, are arid with outcroppings of rock.

U.S. soldiers, Kirkuk, Iraq, 2003. Photograph by Lynsey Addario.

There is dust everywhere. Little gullies leading back into the cliffs are marked with low stone walls that look ancient but are recent structures made by farmers and goatherds.

Just at the mouth of one of these gullies, I came across a mound. It was not very imposing to look at. But it was here, by this very mound, that the mixed force led by Leonidas and his three hundred Spartans came to hold the pass. I wondered what Leonidas made of it all. He was, like all the Spartans, a dedicated soldier. But what did he think? As he looked north, where Lamia now lies on the hills across the valley, he must have heard the sound of quarreling at his back. That is the one certain thing—the mixed force was quarreling.

You can imagine the sullen afternoon lengthening, the ribaldry, the sudden shouts, perhaps even the clash of arms, the mutter of men who had to do as they were told but knew better than their leaders, the cynical laughter of men who had no faith in anything because Greece behind the wall—Athens, Sparta, Thebes, and the rest—was at war not only with Persia but with itself.

Mark that Leonidas did not know how Athens needed thirty years to blossom. For him, Sparta, that dull, cruel city, shone brighter than Athens. But as the Persian army seeped down from a dozen pathways into the valley, and the mixed force fell silent at his back, it must have been some inarticulate and bitter passion for freedom as he knew it that kept him there, sullen and fiercely determined as he gazed across the plain.

No man had ever seen anything like this army before. It was patently unstoppable. It came along the neck of the hills on the banks of the Asopus, from the heights of the mountain and along the coastal track from Alope and Phalara. Lengthening rivers of men—Persians in fish-scale armor, turbaned Cissians, bronze-clad Assyrians, trousered Scythians, Indian bowmen, Caspians, Sarangians in bright cloth and high-heeled boots—came down and spread in a flood that filled the plain. Soon there was nothing to see but rising clouds of white dust, pierced and

Rationed during WWII

Bicycles
Tires
Gasoline
Shoes
Sugar
Meat
Cheese
Butter
Coffee
Cigarettes
Lard
Canned Fish

Items unavailable during WWII

Hair curlers
Wigs
Lawn mowers
Girdles
Nylon stockings
Corn poppers
Cast-iron skillets
Suspenders
Bronze caskets
Electric toasters
Waffle irons
Eggbeaters
Tin soldiers
Leather
Whiskey
Electric trains
Cooking tongs
Beer mugs
Spittoons
Cameras
Birdcages
Cocktail shakers
Sliced bread
Diapers

speckled with the flicker of steel. If each of the seven thousand Greeks should kill his ten men, there would be more than enough to press forward—and this was only the vanguard.

At their back, stretching for league after league by Mounts Pelion and Ossa, back through the narrow gorge of the Peneus to the wide plain beneath Olympus, marched the main body of the Persian war machine: Arabs in robes and Negroes in leopard skins; leather-clad Libyans, Thracians with head-dresses of foxpelt, Pisidians with their oxhide shields, Cabalians and Milyans, Moschians, Tibareni, Tacrones, and Mossynoeci; Marians, Colchians with their wooden helmets, Ala-rodians, Saspires, and Medes; and horses and oxen and mules. There were eighty thousand mounted bowmen and lancers, and chariots in a swarm no one could count. This was the army

that seeped and flooded into the valley all day and halted under its own dust before the narrow entrance of the Hot Gates.

Not a man in the pass could be sure that the rest of Greece really meant to fight. And if those panicky cities on the other side of the wall *did* combine, what could they do against such an army? And who could be sure that these lousy Thebans (or Thespians or Locrians, according to your own nationality) really meant to fight? Only the three hundred Spartans were calm, and even cheerful. They were soldiers, and nothing but soldiers, and this was what they were for.

Xerxes waited four days—and nothing happened. The men in the pass would not recognize the obvious. On the fifth day he sent forward a troop, and the result was a pushover for the Greeks. Every time the Persians thrust them back, the Greeks simply plugged the pass more

Fallen Shiite martyrs, seventh century. Safavid fresco, c. seventeenth century.

completely. He sent forward his own bodyguard, the Company of Immortals, his best troops. They were defeated. For two days the Persians attacked, and the Greeks held them.

And then, of course, the inevitable traitor appeared from the wings.

I moved back and peered up at the cliffs. The traitor had led a Persian force over those cliffs at night, so that with day they would appear in the rear of the seven thousand in the pass. For years I had promised myself that I would follow that track. But I should have come twenty years earlier, with knapsack, no money, and plenty of breath. Yet twenty years ago I was fighting, too, and in as bitter a war. If I could climb cliffs less easily now, it was possible that I could understand war better.

I put out my hand to steady myself on a rock, and snatched it back again, for a lizard lay there in the only patch of sunlight. I edged away, kicked loose a stone, disturbed another with my shoulder so that a rivulet of dust went smoking down under the bushes. The blinding sea, the snow mountains of Euboea were at my back, and the cliffs leaned out over me. I began to grope and slither down again.

I smiled wryly to myself. So much for the map, pored over in the lamplight of an English winter. I was not very high up, but I was high enough. I stayed there, clinging to a rock until the fierce hardness of its surface close to my eye had become familiar.

Suddenly, the years and the reading fused with the thing. I was clinging to Greece herself. Obscurely, and in part, I understood what it had meant to Leonidas when he looked up at these cliffs in the dawn light and saw that their fledgling of pines was not thick enough to hide the glitter of arms.

It was then—and by the double power of imagination and the touch of rock, I was certain of it—that the brooding and desperate thinking of Leonidas crystallized into one clear idea. The last pass was sold. If the rest of Greece beyond the wall did not unite and make its stand, the game was up. Leonidas knew now that he could make one last plea for that stand—a desperate plea, but

one which those dull, dedicated Spartans were eminently fitted to give. I clambered and sweated down the cliffside to the place where he made it. He sent away most of his army but moved the Spartans out into the open, where they could die properly and in due form. The Persians came at them like waves of the sea. The Spartans retreated to make their last stand on a little mound.

The King with half the East at heel is marched
from lands of morning;
Their fighters drink the rivers up, their shafts
benight the air,
And he that stands will die for nought, and
home there's no returning.
The Spartans on the sea-wet rock sat down and
combed their hair.
—A.E. Housman, 1922

To most of the Persian army, this must have meant nothing. There had been, after all, nothing but a small column of dust hanging under the cliffs in one corner of the plain. If you were a Persian, you could not know that this example would lead, next year, to the defeat and destruction of your whole army at the battle of Plataea, where the cities of Greece fought side by side.

The column of dust diminished. The King of Kings gave an order. The huge army shrugged itself upright and began the march forward into the Hot Gates, where the last of the Spartans were still fighting with nails and feet and teeth.

Climbing to the top of that mound by the uneven, winding path, I came on the epitaph, newly cut in stone. It is an ancient epitaph, though the stone is new. It is famous for its reticence and simplicity—has been translated a hundred times but can only be paraphrased:

"Stranger, tell the Spartans that we behaved as they would wish us to, and are buried here."

From The Hot Gates, 1965. *The story of the three hundred Spartans defending the pass at Thermopylae against the advance of tens of thousands of Persians was first told by Herodotus in the middle of the fifth century. Golding, author of* Lord of the Flies, *won the Nobel Prize for Literature in 1983.*

1704: Blenheim

'TWAS A FAMOUS VICTORY

It was a summer evening,
    Old Kaspar's work was done,
And he before his cottage door
    Was sitting in the sun,
And by him sported on the green
His little grandchild Wilhelmine.

She saw her brother Peterkin
    Roll something large and round,
Which he beside the rivulet
    In playing there had found;
He came to ask what he had found,
That was so large, and smooth, and round.

Old Kaspar took it from the boy,
    Who stood expectant by;
And then the old man shook his head
    And with a natural sigh,
" 'Tis some poor fellow's skull," said he,
"Who fell in the great victory.

"I find them in the garden,
    For there's many here about;
And often when I go to plough,
    The ploughshare turns them out!
For many thousand men," said he,
"Were slain in that great victory."

"Now tell us what 'twas all about,"
    Young Peterkin, he cries;
And little Wilhelmine looks up
    With wonder-waiting eyes;
"Now tell us all about the war,
And what they fought each other for."

"It was the English," Kaspar cried,
    "Who put the French to rout;
But what they fought each other for,
    I could not well make out;
But everybody said," quoth he,
"That 'twas a famous victory.

"My father lived at Blenheim then,
    Yon little stream hard by;
They burnt his dwelling to the ground,
    And he was forced to fly;
So with his wife and child he fled,
Nor had he where to rest his head.

"With fire and sword the country round
    Was wasted far and wide,
And many a childing mother then,
    And new-born baby died;
But things like that, you know, must be
At every famous victory.

"They said it was a shocking sight
    After the field was won;
For many thousand bodies here
    Lay rotting in the sun;
But things like that, you know, must be
After a famous victory.

"Great praise the Duke of Marlbro' won,
    And our good Prince Eugene."
"Why, 'twas a very wicked thing!"
    Said little Wilhelmine.
"Nay... nay... my little girl," quoth he,
"It was a famous victory."

"And everybody praised the Duke
    Who this great fight did win."
"But what good came of it at last?"
    Quoth little Peterkin.
"Why, that I cannot tell," said he,
"But 'twas a famous victory."

> **Robert Southey's** *poem recalls the Battle of Blenheim, a famous victory won by the Duke of Marlborough in 1704 over the army of Louis XIV in western Bavaria. The battle lasted a single day and decorated the countryside with more than twenty thousand splendidly uniformed corpses.*

Zapatista figurines, Chiapas, Mexico.

BAND OF BRIGANDS

The Criminality of Modern Warfare

by John Mueller

The combat experience has been aptly characterized as consisting of long periods of tedium punctuated by episodes of sheer terror, and the prosecution of a war requires the recruitment, retention, and motivation of men equal to both challenges. Some people actively enjoy violence; for them, it is something of a high. Some are drawn to it compulsively—serial killers, for example, or certain sadists, who continue to perform violent acts even though they know this enhances the likelihood that they will be apprehended. There are also those who are, or become, addicted to violence and who feel anxiety in its absence. They exult in the thrill of violence and spend a great deal of time anticipating it and seeking it out. We have in civilian life a name for such people—criminals—but the category would also encompass individuals popularly known as bullies, hooligans, goons, toughs, and thugs. Violent conflicts dominated by such people can be called criminal warfare, a form in which combatants are induced to wreak violence primarily for the fun and material profit they derive from the experience.

Europe at one time was probably the most warlike place in the world, and the recruitment process for national armies was singularly unselective: about all that the military normally required of recruiters was that they enlist boots on the ground. Frequently, it was possible for potential conscripts to buy (or bribe) their way out of service or to furnish substitutes in a process which guaranteed that the ranks of the soldiery would be manned disproportionately by criminals, as well as by vagabonds, misfits, social failures, beggars, derelicts, drunks, the unemployable, the idle poor, and the mentally disturbed. Taverns and brothels proved fertile recruiting grounds. So did jails. They housed men awaiting trial or sentencing, very often for capital offenses, for whom even the worst form of soldiering would have been an improvement. Their enlistment was especially attractive to recruiters dragooning participants into foreign

John Mueller, Woody Hayes Chair of National Security Studies and Professor of Political Science at Ohio State University, is the author of numerous books, including The Remnants of War *and, most recently,* Overblown.

armies because many of their fellow towns-people saw a welcome opportunity to banish criminals and other undesirables from the community quite likely forever. Some of the armies in the Hundred Years' War consisted of 2 to 12 percent convicted criminals, many of them murderers seeking royal pardons for their services. The French came to know such men as *écorcheurs*—scorchers of the earth.

The term could also describe the parasitic mercenary bands, or "companies of adventure," that plagued Italy during the fourteenth century.

chronicler, at once solving the dispute and pre-serving the nun's virginity. Since Hawkwood lived by war and would be out of business in peacetime, wrote one Italian novelist, "He man-aged his affairs so well, that there was little peace in Italy in his times."

Predatory militias like Hawkwood's, in fact, continue well into the present. As the dis-ciplined, conventional warfare witnessed in the twentieth century becomes comparatively rare, we are increasingly left with the often savage maneuvers of irregulars. The military historian

Abducting Horse, by Francisco de Goya y Lucientes. Plate 10 from *Proverbs,* 1819–23 (detail).

They operated under fanciful, self-infatuated names like the Company of the Star, the Com-pany of the Hook, and the Company of the Hat, and proudly promulgated graffiti-like slo-gans such as, "Enemy of God, Pity, and Mercy." Their camps reminded one observer of "brothels of harlots and the taverns and bistros of glut-tons." One of the most destructive and effective of these bands was led by John Hawkwood, "an Italianized Englishman" famous for his solution to a problem that arose during the plundering of a monastery. While two of his men argued over which would get to ravish a beautiful young nun, Hawkwood plunged a dagger into her heart, thereby, observed an admiring

Martin van Creveld has suggested that war has become "transformed" as we enter a "new era, not of peaceful competition between trad-ing blocs, but of warfare between ethnic and religious groups," waged not "by armies but by groups whom we today call terrorists, gueril-las, bandits, and robbers." Virtually all of the world's armed conflicts that remain are civil or primarily civil. And most of these, as it hap-pens, are essentially ancient forms of criminal banditry in which what have been called "en-trepreneurs of violence" engage in warfare in much the same way as their forebears did in medieval and early modern Europe; that is, as mercenaries recruited by desperate state governments or as warlord and brigand gangs arising within failed or weak states.

The recent wars in the former Yugoslavia illustrate the mercenary principle. The violence erupting there in the early 1990s didn't derive from a paroxysm of societal angst or from a frenzy of nationalism, whether ancient or newly aroused. Instead, it derived principally from the actions of newly empowered and unpoliced thugs. Politicians may have started the wars, and they may have whipped up a fair amount of hatred, but the killing wasn't done by hordes of ordinary citizens released from their ethnic repression and incited to commit violence against their neighbors.

Even the Serbian (or Yugoslav) army substantially disintegrated early in the hostilities. After years of supposedly influential media propaganda and centuries of allegedly pent-up ethnic and societal antagonism, ordinary Serb soldiers were finally given an opportunity to express these proclivities through government-sanctioned violence. They responded to the opportunity by pointedly declining to embrace it. Observing that they did not know why they were fighting, they often mutinied or deserted en masse—a turn of events vividly illustrated in the experience of General Slavko Lisica. The general attempted to shame Serb conscripts in Croatia by declaring that all those who were not prepared to "defend the glory of the Serbian nation" should lay down their arms and take off their uniforms. To his astonishment, "They all did, including their commanding officer." Furious, the general shouted at them "to remove everything including their underpants, and, with the exception of one man, they all removed their military-issue underpants and marched off completely naked." Later, he said, the recruits commandeered a cannon and used it to shell his headquarters.

Like many of the lords and kings of medieval Europe, the politicians soon opted to recruit criminals and hooligans to populate their armies. Thousands of prison inmates, promised shortened sentences and enticed by the prospect of abundant booty, were released in Serbia for the war effort. The most dynamic (and murderous) Serbian units, then, were composed not of committed nationalists or ideologues, but of common thugs recruited for the task as mercenaries. Some of them bolstered what remained of the Yugoslav army. Others joined semicoherent paramilitary groups such as Vojislav Šešelj's Chetniks and Arkan's Tigers, organizations already heavily composed of criminal adventurers and, in the case of the Tigers, soccer hooligans. For their part, the Bosnian Muslims were protected by paramilitary bands led by Ćelo, a convicted rapist, and by Juka, a former mob boss, racketeer, and underworld thug. The Croats had Tuta, a former protection racketeer.

Those in the right positions quickly discovered an especially lucrative opportunity: weaponry, ammunition, fuel, and goods worth

Those who condemn the profession or art of soldiery smell rank of Anabaptism and Quakery. —Sir James Turner, 1683

hundreds of millions of Deutschmarks could be traded with the enemy. The Serbs in Bosnia inherited large stores of weaponry from the Yugoslav national army, and, once the war settled down a bit, many went looking for— and found—buyers nearby: The Croats and the Bosnian Muslims were eager for weapons with which to attack the Serbs in Croatia and Bosnia (and, for a time, each other). There were opportunities in the other direction as well, and the speaker of the Bosnian Serb assembly made millions buying fuel from Croatia and then selling it to Croatia's Serb enemies in Bosnia. Croats could sometimes rent tanks from their Serbian enemies at a going rate of around $670 per day. Whether they had to pay extra for insurance is not recorded.

Ethnicity was important in all this as an organizational or predictive device, not as a crucial motivating force. It was the human characteristic around which the perpetrators and politicians happened to have arrayed themselves, and it furnished their militias with a degree of predictability. If you were a member of the opposite group, you could be sure they would persecute you, but if you were a member of their group, they would more or less protect you (at least initially), as long as you seemed to be reasonably loyal. That is, they may have been thugs, but they were not *random* thugs.

The same sort of dynamic would have held if the thugs' organizational principle had been class or ideological allegiance—or, for that matter, loyalty to a specific soccer team. If they had taken control in a town and were determined to cleanse it violently of, say, supporters of an opposing team, those in that group would have quickly found it in their interest to leave. Meanwhile, fans of the thug-favored team would have, often reluctantly, come to recognize that the thugs had become their only protection against revenge-seeking goons of the other group.

Similarly, during the Rwandan genocide of 1994, much of the reporting gives the impression that the conflict was one of all against all, friends against friends, neighbors against neighbors, even Cain against Abel. Friends and neighbors (and even brothers, perhaps) did kill each other,

but it seems that by far the greatest damage, as in the former Yugoslavia, stemmed from the rampages of murderous criminals guided by the government and performing as mercenaries.

The conflict was far from a spontaneous eruption in that the basic elements of the genocidal process had been planned for years by Hutu extremists who were substantially in charge of the ruling party, the government bureaucracy, the army, and the police. A civil war between Hutu military forces and the Tutsi-dominated Rwanda Patriotic Front (RPF) was going badly for the Hutus, and a power-sharing agreement was brokered. Rather than let this agreement take effect though, the fanatics, seizing an opportunity when a plane carrying the country's president was shot down, ordered the murder of all Tutsis in the country.

Initially, the killings were of politically unreliable Hutus and of carefully selected Tutsis known to be in opposition to the Hutu extremists. The scale of the killing quickly expanded as Hutu government leaders and local administrators responded to orders to carry out the genocide throughout the country. The Presidential Guard probably engaged in the most focused and systematic of the killings. It was organized by the Hutu army, the *Forces Armées Rwandaises* (FAR), most of whose members had been hastily recruited in the previous few years from landless peasants, the urban unemployed, and foreign drifters guaranteed food and drink (each man was entitled to two bottles of beer a day, a luxury by Rwandan standards), as well as the opportunity to loot. Finally, there was the *interahamwe*, militia bands trained by Hutu extremists. As Philip Gourevitch has pointed out, the *interahamwe* had their genesis in soccer fan clubs, and they recruited jobless young men who were "wasting in idleness and its attendant resentments." Extremist youth leaders sped around on motorbikes and sported "pop hairstyles, dark glasses, and flamboyantly colored pajama suits and robes, preached ethnic solidarity and civil defense." At *interahamwe* rallies, "alcohol usually flowed freely... and paramilitary drills were conducted like the latest hot dance moves."

Noms de Guerre in the Liberian Civil War, 1999-2003:

Captain Mission Impossible

Major Trouble

Young Colonel Killer

Colonel Action

Colonel Evil Killer

General Murder

General Jungle King

General Monster

General War Boss III

General Jesus

General Rambo

General Butt Naked

It seems reasonable to suggest that there might have been some fifty thousand hardcore *genocidaires*—some 2 percent of the male Hutu population older than thirteen. Although it is conceivable that 200,000 participated in the massacres, this high figure would include people who did nothing more than point out where local Tutsis lived or simply manned roadblocks under orders. Even this larger number would represent only about 9 percent of the Hutu male population over the age of thirteen.

In some sense, these are very high—astoundingly high—figures, and they demonstrate how extraordinary the event was. In a normal year, by comparison, the proportion of males over thirteen who committed murder in Rwanda was probably something like 1 in 1,000. Nonetheless, a situation in which more than 90 percent of Hutu males over thirteen did not participate in the killing hardly seems to justify the notion that the situation was one of all against all or neighbor against neighbor.

Distinct from the mercenary principle at work in Rwanda and the former Yugoslavia, organized banditry can also look like conventional warfare, particularly in countries whose governments are so weak that crimes of extortion, kidnapping, and murder become commonplace. Bill Berkeley has described the phenomenon in his book *The Graves Are Not Yet Full*, noting that "Africa's warring factions are best understood not as 'tribes' but as racketeering enterprises." Samuel Doe, a master sergeant who seized control of Liberia in 1980, ruled through Cold War largess supplied largely by the United States and through a violently corrupt patronage network. In late 1989, after the United States—no longer so concerned about the Cold War—cut off its funding in disgust, Doe's weakened rule was threatened by an armed group of about a hundred led by Charles Taylor, an accused embezzler and jail-break artist, and by a somewhat larger group that had spun off from Taylor's led by a psychopathic, hymn-singing drunk named Prince Yormi Johnson. The rebels quickly gained adherents in large measure because of the excessive and arbitrary retaliation of Doe's forces.

The country was soon dominated by some seven warlord bands that engaged in occasional battles over turf but were mostly involved in looting, rape, torture, occasional cannibalism, and the selling of commodities like iron ore, timber, rubber, gold, diamonds, and drugs on the international market. Berkeley describes the soldiers as "orphans bent on revenge, illiterate teenage peasants and school dropouts seizing the main chance, and unemployed street toughs known as 'grunah boys' [grown-up boys]." He cites UN estimates that there

War is the child of pride, and pride the daughter of riches. —*Jonathan Swift, 1697*

were eventually "sixty thousand Liberians under arms, of whom no more than a handful had received any form of formal military training." Carnivals of looting and pillaging took place, as well as occasional massacres. With amazing frankness, Taylor's final offensive against Monrovia was labeled Operation Pay Yourself. Combatants routinely styled themselves after heroes in violent American action movies like the *Rambo* and *Terminator* series. In the early years, rebels decked themselves out in bizarre, even lunatic, costumes: women's dresses, wigs, and pantyhose; painted fingernails and decorations composed of human bones. The combatants were routinely intoxicated with alcohol and narcotics, and it is estimated that 25 to 30 percent of them emerged from the war with serious drug problems.

In search of further profit, Charles Taylor looked to the diamond areas in neighboring Sierra Leone. When fighting broke out there in 1991, he threw his support behind a rebel group in that country under the control of a former corporal in the Sierra Leonean army. The government, already characterized by hopeless ineptitude, then predictably made a disastrous decision: It rapidly expanded its not very good army of three thousand into a really terrible army of fourteen thousand. This ragtag force, consisting mostly of "dropouts and robbers," according to a prominent Sierra Leonean human rights campaigner, was sent—underpaid, undertrained, and underfed—into combat under commanders who had a distinct preference for leading from the rear. Instead of confronting the rebels, the troops fragmented into bandit gangs, many of them composed of children who routinely drank blood mixed with drugs. They raped, killed, pillaged, extorted, looted, destroyed, and mutilated. As an aid worker put it, "By fighting, you get a lot of money and excitement and see the country. You're going from nothing in a village to being Rambo." Before sending their charges off to what passed for battle, rebel commanders often showed them *Rambo* films.

Chris Hedges has referred to Africa's civil wars as "Hobbesian playgrounds," and Michael Ignatieff has compared the conditions that prevailed in the former Yugoslavia to a Hobbesian state of nature. Although the adjective is often evoked for many post-Cold War civil conflicts, experience suggests that the reference to Hobbes is wrong. Hobbes was obsessed by the chaos and calamity of the English Civil War of 1642-1649, which took place during his lifetime, and his important book, *Leviathan*, was, he notes, "occasioned by the disorders of the present time." He viewed the conflict as essentially one of competing ideas—religious ideas rather than nationalist, ideological, or ethnic ones. Like Ignatieff on Yugoslavia, he envisioned the conditions as a descent into a base state of nature, a "kingdom of darkness" and a "confederacy of deceivers" in which "force and fraud" become "the two cardinal virtues," where "every man is an enemy of every man," and where life, as he famously put it, becomes "solitary, poor, nasty, brutish, and short." The modern civil wars in Africa and Yugoslavia call his summation into question. Although there was plenty of deception, force, and fraud in those conflicts, the population did not descend into the war of all against all that Hobbes so ardently and influentially described. The conditions of deep insecurity certainly resembled a Hobbesian state of nature, but they came about not because people generally succumbed to barbarism, but because they came under the arbitrary sway of bands—often remarkably small ones—of armed and murderous thugs and fanatics.

Through the mid-1990s, the increased number of civil wars was due mostly to a process of accumulation—not just because new wars were starting, but because old wars were not ending. In recent years, this process seems to have reversed itself. Many of the wars—or competitive criminal enterprises—have exhausted themselves, and new ones have failed to take their places. The reason seems to lie with the development of competent governments increasingly able to police domestic conflicts rather than inadvertently (or actively) exacerbating them.

The war in Iraq is a blend of the criminal and the noncriminal and often resembles the civil war in Lebanon that raged from 1975 to 1990. Some of the combat in that lengthy conflict could be considered disciplined: Forces stood and fought—for cause or sect or revenge—against each other or against foreign occupiers, sometimes risking death or committing suicide in the process. Much of the violence, however, followed the brigand pattern as private armies, militias, or bandit gangs engaged in racketeering, looting, kidnappings for ransom, rape, extortion, and a bewildering array of shifting turf wars.

Journalists and some cautious politicians have become comfortable describing the violence engulfing Iraq as a civil war, a notion often skewed to absolve the United States of any role in its creation. However, the American invasion, carried out by forces sufficient to run over Saddam Hussein's pathetic army but insufficient to maintain civil order, managed to create, almost instantly, a failed state. What began with opportunistic looting has generated a truly massive increase in criminality. If some of the statistics coming out of Baghdad are correct, the criminal homicide rate there may have reached historic proportions. As usual, the losers are the masses of civilians whose chief form of defense, if they cannot flee, is to ally themselves with comparatively congenial thugs, to endure, and to hope for eventual salvation.

Detail from a sculpture of Darius I with defeated rebels. Photograph by Roger Wood.

THE PERSIAN
WAY OF WAR

by Tom Holland

History, like poetry, began with war. In around 440 BC, some three centuries after Homer, singing the wrath of Achilles, composed the *Iliad*, a Greek by the name of Herodotus embarked upon a project no less epic. His goal was to explain what would now be termed "the clash of civilizations," the inability of the peoples of East and West to live together in peace. Asiatics, so Herodotus reported, "believe that the Greeks will always be their enemies." But why they should have come to this conclusion

in the first place was, he acknowledged, a puzzle. Perhaps the kidnapping of a princess or two by Greek pirates had been to blame? Or the burning of Troy? "That, at any rate, is what many nations of Asia argue—but who can say for sure if they are right?" As Herodotus well knew, the world was an infinite place, and one man's truth might easily be another man's lie. Yet if the origins of the conflict between East and West appeared lost in myth, then not so its effects. These, at least, had been made all too recently

Tom Holland writes fiction and nonfiction. His works include Rubicon: The Last Years of the Roman Republic *and most recently,* Persian Fire: The First World Empire and the Battle for the West.

and tragically clear. Difference had bred suspicion—and suspicion had bred war.

A war like no other. In 480 BC, some forty years before Herodotus began his history, Xerxes, the King of Persia, had led an invasion of Greece. Military adventures of this kind had long been a speciality of the Persian people. Victory—rapid, spectacular victory—had for decades seemed to be their birthright. As a result of his predecessors' triumphs, Xerxes had ruled as the most powerful man on the planet. The resources at his disposal were so stupefying

> *There is more of misery inflicted upon mankind by one year of war than by all the civil peculations and oppressions in a century. Yet it is a state into which the mass of mankind rush with a greatest avidity, hailing official murderers, in scarlet, gold, and cock's feathers, as the greatest and most glorious of human creatures.*
> —Sydney Smith, 1813

as to appear virtually limitless. Europe was not to witness another invasion force to rival his until World War II and the summer of D-Day.

Set against this unprecedented juggernaut, the Greeks were few in numbers and hopelessly divided. Even the two leading Greek powers, the nascent democracy of Athens and the sternly militarized state of Sparta, appeared ill-equipped to put up an effective resistance. With the Persian King resolved to pacify once and for all the fractious and peculiar people on the western margin of his great empire, the result seemed to most a foregone conclusion. And yet somehow, astonishingly, against the largest expeditionary force ever assembled, the Greeks held out. The invaders were turned back. Greece remained free.

The story of how they had taken on a superpower and, unbelievably, defeated it, appeared to the Greeks themselves the most astounding achievement of all time. How precisely had the victory been won? And why? And what might have caused the invasion to be launched in the first place? Not lacking in significance even

four decades later, these questions prompted Herodotus into a momentously novel style of investigation. For the first time, a chronicler set out to trace the origins of a conflict—not to a past so remote as to be utterly fabulous, nor to the whims and wishes of some god, nor to a people's claim to a manifest destiny, but rather to explanations that he could verify for himself. Herodotus' term for the task he set himself was "inquiries"—*historia*. "And I set them down here," he declared, in the first sentence of the first work of history ever written, "so that the record of human achievement may be spared the ravages of time, and so that everything significant and astounding, all those exploits by which Greeks and non-Greeks alike have made a mark, can be kept in the public eye—and additionally, and most importantly, so that I can trace the steps that led them into conflict."

What gave added urgency to this project was the fact that, as Herodotus well knew, "the ravages of time" were already serving to erase the marks of the war. Anyone who doubted this had only to visit Athens and look up at the Acropolis, the mighty rock that dominated the city. For centuries, this had served as the storehouse of Athenian memories—an incomparable repository of shrines, statues, and trophies—until in 480 BC, during the course of the great invasion, Xerxes' armies occupied the city, captured the Acropolis, and put it to the torch. All its treasures were incinerated. Some months later, shortly before the climactic battle of Plataea in which the Persian threat was ended once and for all, the Greek allies—the Athenians, of course, prominent among them—had sworn a solemn oath, that any "ground zero," any temple burned by the invaders, was to be left permanently as a ruin, "to serve as a witness for generations yet to come." So it was for thirty years that the summit of the Acropolis had been left a blackened pile of rubble—until the Athenian people, repenting of their vow, voted to redevelop the sacred rock.

Their goal in doing so was quite consciously to rewrite history. The role of the Athenians in the great victory over Persia was to be blazoned;

that of their allies, and of the Spartans in particular, put thoroughly in the shade. So it was, for instance, that the most sumptuous and celebrated of all the new *grands projets*, the temple that subsequent ages would call the Parthenon, was raised on the foundations of an older, unfinished building, one that had been begun in the 480s BC as a celebration of the victory won by the Athenians, and the Athenians alone, at Marathon. So it was too that by the entranceway to the Acropolis, a colossal statue of Athena was raised, its eyes turned serenely westward, toward the straits of Salamis where the lead in sinking the Persian battle-fleet had been taken, of course, by none other than the Athenians. The whole spectacular makeover, that entire extraordinary array of monuments which remains to this day the very symbol of classical Greece, was designed to serve above all as a war memorial—to the dead, yes, but also to the deathless glory that they had won in battle for their city.

Etruscan plate, war elephant.

How, then, could the Spartans, originally the allies of the Athenians against the Persian king, but now their bitterest rivals, possibly compete with the Parthenon? Not by raising monuments of their own, to be sure, for it was their custom to scorn masonry as pompous and marble as frivolous. It did not necessarily require great architecture, however, to commemorate a victory—or even a defeat. "Go tell them in Sparta, O passer-by / That here, in obedience to their orders, we lie." These lines, carved on a simple stone memorial, were to be read on the site of the most famous engagement of the entire Persian Wars, an engagement that had ended, not in triumph, but in heroic failure. Teeming hordes of Asiatics, driven forward into battle by the whip; a Spartan king, Leonidas, resolved to fight or die an exemplary death, as he and some three hundred of his countrymen made a suicidal last stand—the story of Thermopylae had it all. Already, even as Herodotus embarked upon his researches, it had begun to take on the force of myth. Some evidence suggests that the historian, when he came to write his account of Thermopylae, was consciously attempting to avoid sensationalizing it and to purge it of Spartan spin. If so, he did not altogether succeed. His description of the battle has an indisputably epic, even Homeric, glow. Describing the aftermath of Leonidas' death, for instance, Herodotus has the Spartans and the Persians fight over the corpse, precisely as though they were combatants on the plain of Troy. So strong is the force of his narrative that even today, two and a half millennia after Leonidas fell, Thermopylae stands supreme as the paragon of heroism in war. When Hollywood wishes to dramatize the Persian invasions, it is not to Marathon or to Salamis, those incomparable victories, that it turns. If glory, as the Greeks believed, is the truest immortality, then it is the Spartans who have had the last laugh.

But if the Athenians would be infuriated to

know this, then how much more so, of course, would be the Persians. As the outraged response in Iran to the movie *300* suggests, sensitivities about Thermopylae can still run high. And well they might, for the battle eulogized by the Spartans as a defeat so splendid as to outshine many a victory would no doubt have appeared to the Persians as a truly thumping military success. To flush out a pass held by heavy infantry, to take a mere two and a half days to achieve it, and to kill a Spartan king—these, by any reckoning, were splendid achievements. Doubtless a Persian would have been quick to point out as much. Except that no Persian is known to have written about the battle. Indeed, no Persian is known even so much as to have mentioned the invasion of Greece. Revisionists have deduced from this silence that perhaps the war which the Greeks themselves regarded as the most momentous of all time was seen by their opponents in a slightly less dramatic light, as a peripheral border skirmish, nothing more. Maybe. Yet it is important not to mistake the nature of the evidence. That the Persian sources opted to ignore a defeat is hardly surprising, but that they are no less silent about all their empire's many glorious victories does appear truly astounding. And this not least because chronicling the triumphs of imperial warlords was a venerable tradition in the ancient Near East. Scribes at the Assyrian court, in particular, had competed with one another to describe the gallons of blood shed by the their royal masters, the cities stormed, the palaces looted, the prisoners enslaved or impaled. Yet the Persian kings, who in almost every other respect were assiduous borrowers from the traditions of Mesoptamia, chose not to borrow from the example of these sanguinary chronicles. Far from broadcasting the details of all their many victories, they seem rather to have turned their backs upon the very subject of war.

COALITION(S) OF THE WILLING

Nations enlisted for the mission to liberate Baghdad,
then (401 BC) and now (2003)

Under Cyrus the Younger:

Achaea
Ainianes
Arcadia
Boeotia
Crete
Dolopes
Egypt
Megara
Miletus
Olynthus
Persia
Sparta
Stymphalia
Syracuse
Thessaly
Thrace

Under George W. Bush:

Afghanistan	Japan
Albania	South Korea
Australia	Latvia
Azerbaijan	Lithuania
Bulgaria	Macedonia
Colombia	Netherlands
Czech Republic	Nicaragua
Denmark	Philippines
El Salvador	Poland
Eritrea	Romania
Estonia	Slovakia
Ethiopia	Spain
Georgia	Turkey
Hungary	United Kingdom
Italy	Uzbekistan

Why? Any attempt to answer this intriguing and suggestive question must draw upon the single exception that proves the rule. One narrative of a Persian king's campaigns does exist, carved into a mountain in western Iran, on a sheer cliff face overlooking what is today the main road between Baghdad and Tehran. Bisitun was a place holy to the ancients, but that was not the only reason why Darius the Great, in 521 BC, ordered a massive inscription carved there, its huge blocks of cuneiform, as the travel writer Robert Byron put it, "cut like the pages of a book on the blood-colored rock." To Darius, the site had a political as well as a spiritual significance. In 522 BC, a year before work on the inscription began, he and a group of six coconspirators had ridden past Bisitun on their way to a nearby fortress, where Bardiya, the King of Persia, had installed himself for the summer. Coming upon their royal lord as he lay in bed with a concubine, the assassins hacked him to death, and Darius seized the throne. It was an act of bloody treachery, plain and simple.

Or was it? The Bisitun inscription served to give the story a very different spin. According to Darius' account, the victim of the assassination squad had not in fact been Bardiya at all. The true Bardiya was long dead. Taking his place upon the throne, unsuspected by anyone save for Darius himself, there had snaked a magus by the name of Gaumata, skilled in all the arts of blackest necromancy. The "Bardiya" killed by Darius, in short, had been a doppelgänger: a fake, a fraud, a liar. Which in turn, of course, was to cast Darius himself, not as a murderer, not as a usurper, but as a defender of truth. No more honorable role could possibly have been imagined, for the Persians knew, as more benighted peoples did not, that a universe without truth would be one undone and lost to perpetual night. Back in the beginning of time, when Ahura Mazda, greatest of the gods, first summoned creation into being, he had engendered Arta—Truth—to give order to existence. Without it, the universe would have lacked all form and value and beauty. Yet the work of Arta was never done—for perpetually it was shadowed by

its opposite, Drauga, the Lie. Two orders—one of perfection, the other of falsehood, each the image of the other—were coiled in a conflict as ancient as time. What else could Darius worthily have done, then, but take the side of Arta against Drauga, Truth against the Lie, lest the universe itself should totter and fail?

So it was that he came to justify his usurpation by means of an innovative and fateful claim: that he, and he alone, was the appointed lieutenant of Ahura Mazda on earth. The global dominion of which he made himself the master

> To this war of every man against every man, this also is consequent: that nothing can be unjust. The notions of right and wrong, justice and injustice, have there no place. Where there is no common power, there is no law; where no law, no injustice. Force and fraud are in war the cardinal virtues. —Thomas Hobbes, 1651

was henceforward to be regarded as nothing less than a sacral image of the order of the universe, a beacon of truth and order lit to illumine all the world. Here was a formulation no less profitable than it was original, for what it provided, in effect, was a license to engage in conquest without limit. If it was indeed the god-given destiny of Darius to bring peace to a bleeding world, then what could those who opposed him be reckoned, if not the agents of anarchy and darkness—of an axis of evil? In 520 BC, when an ever fractious people named the Elamites rose for a third time in revolt, Darius, driven to fury, anathematized them in new and startling terms. "Those Elamites were faithless," he ordered it proclaimed on the cliff face of Bisitun. "They failed to worship Ahura Mazda." The condemnation of a people for their neglect of a religion not their own was something wholly remarkable. So too was Darius' declaration that those sent to war against the rebels might expect "divine blessings—both in their lives, and after death." The manifesto, novel though it was, proved thoroughly inspiring. The Elamites were crushed with a peremptory, almost dismissive, speed. Never again would they dare to challenge the awful might of the Persian king. Such was the devastating effect of the world's first holy war.

Yet Darius, unlike the kings of Assyria or Babylon, had no interest in dwelling upon the specifics of his victory. What mattered to him was not the war, but the fact that the war had been won; not the bloodshed, but the fact that the blood had dried, and that an eternal age of peace had dawned. To be sure, the victory over Gaumata and his supporters had been a great and a terrible one, and because it proved

I had often before this said that if the Indians should come, I should choose rather to be killed by them than taken alive, but when it came to the trial, my mind changed; their glittering weapons so daunted my spirit, that I chose rather to go along with those (as I may say) ravenous bears, than that moment to end my days. —Mary Rowlandson, 1675

that Darius was indeed the champion of Ahura Mazda—the great truth on which he founded his empire—the new king had ordered its details to be recorded and proclaimed. Never again, however, would he permit himself to be shown enclosed within mere events. Just as the Lord Mazda dwelt beyond the rhythms of the world, so did his proxy, the King of Persia, transcend space and time.

Which is why, essentially, there were no war correspondents at the court of the King of Kings, no chroniclers of all his many victorious campaigns. From the point of view of Darius—and of his son and heir, Xerxes—history had been brought to a glorious close. The empire of the Persians was both its end and its summation— for what else could a dominion be that contained within itself all the limits of the horizon, if not the bulwark of a truly cosmic order? Such a monarchy, redeemed as it had been from the Lie, surely could be expected to endure for all time, infinite, unshakable, the watchtower of the Truth. The King of Kings did not dwell upon diurnal banalities such as battles.

And yet there was an irony. A vision as imperious as that formulated by Darius naturally needed to be broadcast to the entire globe—and what better way to do that than by leading the empire to war? Thus, in the judgment of Xerxes, Greece had to be invaded. To shrink from risk, to confess that Persian power might be susceptible to overstretch, to abandon to the Lie the terrorist states of Athens and Sparta and the continent beyond them would constitute an abject betrayal of Darius and, even more unforgivably, of Ahura Mazda. Xerxes, as he prepared to conquer the West, aimed to triumph not merely as the King of Persia, but as the agent of Arta, of truth and order. So it was, in defiance, it seems, of his military advisers, who had urged him to lead a strike force composed only of elite units, that he insisted upon summoning the peoples of even the obscurest frontiers to pay him the tribute of their sons: a grand and extravagant coalition of the unwilling. Strategic folly it might have been, but war, for the King of Kings, had long ceased to be simply a matter of strategy. Rather, it served him as a vehicle of propaganda, as a means of flaunting his global mastery.

The result, of course, was catastrophe. Bogged down in a remote and inhospitable backwater, the King of Kings was forced, humiliatingly, to cut his losses and run. To the victorious Greeks, Xerxes' name would forever after serve as a byword for folly and arrogance. The legend of Thermopylae and the beauty of the Parthenon stood—and would continue to stand—as glorious memorials to the victorious character of what has been termed by some "the Western way of war." In matters of combat and strategy, as in so much else, we in the West certainly remain proud to consider ourselves the heirs of the Greeks. Yet "the Persian way of war," despite its rebuffs at Marathon and Salamis, was destined to cast a no less momentous shadow over the succeeding millennia. Jihads and crusades, wars fought in defense of democracy, UN resolutions, even human rights; all, in the end, and however indirectly, owe something to it. Perhaps the future of human conflict, after all, is no less Persian than it is Greek.

The Battle of San Romano, by Paolo Uccello, c. 1456.

IMPERIAL HUBRIS

A German Tale

by Fritz Stern

All happy families are alike; each unhappy family is unhappy in its own way.　　—*Leo Tolstoy*

The great French historian and resistance martyr, Marc Bloch, is supposed to have said that history was like a knife: You can cut bread with it, but you could also kill. This is even more true of historical derivatives like analogies; they can provide either illumination or poisonous polemic. The first requirement for an acceptable historical analogy is plausibility; the two situations compared must have striking similarities, and the image of the historic ante-cedent must be as clearly understood as possible. This becomes an unlikely presupposition when the analogy is proposed by partisans working in an age of stunning historical ignorance. Nowadays, politicians and partisans use analogies instead of arguments, convenient shorthand for their defenses of dubious policies.

It was beneficial that President Kennedy was conscious of historical analogies. During the Cuban Missile Crisis of 1962, he remembered

Fritz Stern is University Professor Emeritus at Columbia University and the author of several books, including The Politics of Cultural Despair, Gold and Iron: Bismarck, Bleichroder, and the Building of the German Empire, *and most recently,* Five Germanies I Have Known.

how easily nations had slipped into World War I in 1914, and how important it was to give an adversary a chance to back down while saving face. When the invasion of Cuba was being considered, he noted to Robert McNamara, "It seems to me we could end up bogged down. I think we should keep constantly in mind the British in the Boer War, the Russians in the last war with the Finnish, and our own experience with the North Koreans." But it was dangerously misleading in 2003 to brandish comparison of the Allied occupations of Germany and Japan in 1945 with the American occupation of Iraq solely in order to suggest the ease of establishing democracy by force of arms.

The Devil and the good man may cite Scripture—for opposite purposes. This is true for analogies as well. Some historic moments or persons may be unique—try to find another Abraham Lincoln, for example. Even Iagos are hard to come by. It may be proper to recall Jacob Burckhardt's warning-cum-aspiration: Our study of history will not make us clever for the next time but should make us wise forever.

The United States, with its frequent claim of exceptionalism, should be free of historical analogies, and at the time of the American Revolution, the struggle to establish a constitutional republic was without modern parallel. But as the nation became a world power and, finally, the world power, its boast of exceptionalism began to sound hollow, and comparisons with the fate of earlier empires became common.

Frontline Luxuries

Prostitutes (French, 1810–1950s)

Absinthe (French, 1844–1847)

Saunas   (Finns, 1939)

Espresso (Italians, 1940–1943)

Cigarettes (Americans, 1917–1918, 1941–1945)

Fast Food (Americans, 2003–present)

With the defeat of the Axis powers in 1945, the United States emerged as the leading power of the West, and was thereafter confronted by imperial responsibilities and temptations. At home, the "Red Scare" became a powerful political-psychological force. Abroad, the successive burdens of Korea and Vietnam, which demanded the sacrifice of American lives and fortunes, were followed by the rise of an altogether new challenge, international terrorism, with the United States as its principal target.

A nation puzzled and divided by American ascendancy following World War II was attuned to the many analogues that politicians and partisan scholars offered. It is no wonder many of these analogies focused on the most dramatic and recent world-historical disaster—the rise and fall of Hitler and his empire. In the early 1950s, left-wing alarmists saw in Senator McCarthy a Hitler and in Eisenhower, a Hindenburg. At the time, I thought this an invidious and dangerous comparison in that American political culture was fundamentally different from that of Germany. But German has been the language of politics *in extremis*, Weimar the symbol of democratic self-destruction, Hitler the reminder of the all-powerful, enthralling tyrant—and appeasement of him as the road to war.

Perhaps no single analogy has been so often and so perniciously invoked as "Munich." (How many remember what actually happened?) The Munich Conference of September 1938 was the culmination of Anglo-French attempts to anticipate or accept Hitler's demands, to recognize the "injustices" visited upon Germany at Versailles, and to make efforts above all to avoid another war. Some proponents of appeasement—members of the ruling classes, ill-guided conservatives who hoped to preserve their own power—may have had a sneaking admiration for the decisive leader as the great anti-Bolshevik shield. Meanwhile, the European left and a few realistic conservatives (Winston Churchill is the heroic example) insisted that Hitler aimed for European hegemony and that only resolute will and the threat of force could stop him. To label American critics of an escalating involvement in Vietnam or Iraq as "appeasers" or proponents of "Munich" is dangerous nonsense, all the more so because the analogy may obscure the actual dangers that confront the United States.

I have been struck recently by an altogether different analogy from the drama of German history, namely the disaster and political fatality of German leadership during World War I, epitomized by the supreme leader of the time, Kaiser Wilhelm II. The Kaiser came to the throne in 1888 at the age of twenty-nine, his liberal father having reigned—voicelessly—for ninety-nine days before succumbing to cancer of the throat. The young Kaiser's grandfather, Wilhelm I, a true Prussian monarch, had presided over the military victories that had enabled Bismarck to create the unified Reich in 1871. Within two years of his ascension to the throne, Wilhelm II dismissed Bismarck—the nation's later idol, a prudent diplomat in European affairs, and a fierce enemy of democratic reform at home.

Wilhelm II became the leader of a country that was on the cusp of European mastery. By the 1890s imperial Germany had become the strongest power on the continent, strongest in economic and military terms and equal or superior to all in scientific and technological advances. But power generates opposition, and Germany's neighbors, alarmed at this unpredictable upstart, began to form defensive alliances against it. Supreme prudence would have been required on Germany's part to meet these challenges, but Wilhelm sought to incarnate that power in his person and to concentrate it within his conflicted self. He appeared on the world stage as a boisterous and threatening leader, while at home he flaunted his absolute power, believing that it had been divinely ordained. He had contempt for a parliament whose tightly circumscribed powers were set forth in a constitution he boasted of never having read. He was intelligent, perhaps even gifted, and impressed by technological progress, but untutored and impulsive. He reveled in the trappings of power and delighted in uniforms (at times he changed them daily). In his ostentation and ex-

travagance, he was deeply un-Prussian. He was the perfect parvenu of ancient plumage, and he both reflected and reinforced the proud, ambitious, yet fearful character of his subjects. Given his position in Europe—not nearly as hemmed in politically as his royal cousin in Britain, King George V, and not nearly so absolute in his rule as his Russian cousin, Tsar Nicholas II, over a far less developed country—he was unique, and hence his deeply complicated character is an attractive object for historians. Recently published evidence derived from wartime diaries and let-

> *To lead an uninstructed people to war, is to throw them away.*
>
> —*Confucius, sixth century* BC

ters of his closest associates powerfully amplify our picture of the emperor and his private flaws that so decisively deformed his public policy.

He was given to bombastic speeches, once warning newly sworn-in recruits that, if ordered by him, they would have to shoot their parents. He gave astounding orders to departing soldiers at the time of the Boxer Rebellion that they should arouse fear as had the Huns of yore. He detested liberal critics. And he spoke disparagingly of foreign nations, especially of Great Britain. Some of this had to do with his Anglophobia; he totally distrusted his mother, the daughter of Queen Victoria. Worse, though, than his arrogant, bombastic statements, he supported ministers and military personnel who called for an ever greater German army— and, most ominously—for a high seas fleet that would eventually be strong enough to defeat the British navy. The details of government he shunned, for they interfered with his diversions. He wanted to reign, and he enjoyed his huge court—over two thousand subordinates from generals to servants to gardeners, whom he would at times affront with crude jokes and offensive pranks.

From the beginning, members of his entourage and some cognoscenti worried about his volatility and mental health. He had suffered an extremely complicated birth, and moments of oxygen deprivation may have damaged his brain. As a youth, he contracted a chronic middle-ear infection that some people wrongly thought could induce mental imbalance. Others saw mere tactlessness bolstered by boundless vanity. Some of his immediate subordinates made harsher judgments. Thus Admiral Tirpitz—fateful champion of the all-powerful navy—thought that Wilhelm compensated for his inner uncertainty and insecurity with pomp and militant rhetoric. Brutal virility was

> *The nation that makes a great distinction between its scholars and its warriors will have its thinking done by cowards, and its fighting done by fools.* —*Thucydides, fifth century* BC

a central feature of Wilhelm's persona. In 1903, Tirpitz further noted, "The sad and worrisome thing about this talented monarch is that for him appearance trumps substance."

German foreign policy from 1890 to 1914, for which the Kaiser bore formal and—intermittently—actual responsibility, culminated in a series of failures and setbacks. Many blamed these gratuitous blunders on Wilhelm's capriciousness and desire for prestige, his concern for dynastic and personal vanity, and his failure to assess Germany's true national interests. A strident militaristic tone prevailed, supported by well-organized interests who saw economic benefits in greater armaments. These "lobbyists" thought foreign triumphs a protection against democratic political reforms at home, which posed an ominous threat to the anachronistic power of what has often been called an agrarian-industrial-military complex. Max Weber, a passionate advocate of Germany's worldwide ambitions and responsibilities, noted in 1906, "The degree of contempt that our nation increasingly encounters abroad (Italy, America, everywhere!)—and with justice—is the decisive issue. Our submission to *this* regime of *this* man is gradually becoming a power issue of 'world' importance to us....We are becom-

ing 'isolated' because this man rules us in this way *and because we tolerate it and make excuses for it.*" [Emphasis added.] This was not an uncommon view among true conservatives, although in Weber's case, it was voiced only in private correspondence, becoming public only after a particularly egregious interview the Kaiser gave to the *Daily Telegraph* in 1908.

And yet they were wrong, at least in part. Wilhelm's rule was not absolute, as Germany's conduct during World War I made clear. In early July 1914, after the murder of the Austrian archduke, the Kaiser egged on the Austrians. By the end of the month, he couldn't restrain his own subordinates from beginning a war according to the dictates of military strategy—the famed Schlieffen Plan—rather than political rationale. Once war had started, Wilhelm became Supreme War Lord, and his chief function should have been to adjudicate among rival elements in his government. Instead, the civilian-military conflict deepened. The German army always had a state-within-a-state mentality, and, in this case, both the military and the civilian leaders were divided among themselves.

After a proclamation exalting national unity—rallying the innocent nation in the face of foreign attacks—Wilhelm established himself at Supreme Headquarters away from Berlin. Although geographically closer to the front, he was comfortably distant in every other respect. He was more than ever dependent on the heads of his military and civilian cabinets. (Their diaries and letters have been published recently.) By the end of September 1914, after the First Battle of the Marne and the failure of the Schlieffen Plan, some of his advisers realized that the chances for a military victory were slim and argued the need for a negotiated peace. But by that time, even the civilian chancellor had committed to extravagant war aims that made hopes for a negotiated peace illusory. The head of the military cabinet, the ultraloyal General Hans Georg von Plessen, noted that, "The Kaiser was again at lowest point with his nerves, without faith in the future, without self-confidence."

From then on, the Kaiser's ever shifting

mental state became a dominant issue in the conduct of the war. Publicly he enunciated his faith in total victory, but privately, he suffered moments of distressed indecision. Publicly he proclaimed the nation's innocence while privately he condoned German atrocities committed in Belgium. Portentous decisions had to be made, including whether to declare unrestricted submarine warfare, thereby insuring the entry of the United States into the war. Although the fate of his country (and of Europe) depended on how he made these decisions, the Kaiser was only intermittently informed, as his advisers systematically shielded him from bad news. In June 1917, General Plessen noted, "Everything unpleasant is repressed and everything propitious is enormously exaggerated. This ostrich style he calls optimism, and anyone who doesn't cooperate in this self-deception, he calls a pessimist. Never once during this entire war did he ask even with a syllable about our own losses." At the same time, the Kaiser regarded the war as a struggle between good and evil, light against darkness: "God wants this struggle and we are His instruments," he said.

After three years of unimaginable carnage, Wilhelm had been reduced to an instrument of a military dictatorship run by Field Marshal Paul von Hindenburg and Quartermaster General Erich Ludendorff, whom he had been forced to appoint and whose virtually unlimited power rested on their ever present threats of resignation. They enjoyed the confidence of Germany's ruling classes and were determined to reject all compromise, always putting their faith in one more push that would deliver the ever elusive goal of total victory. Moderate conservatives were ardent in their concern for their country, whose people grew ever hungrier and ever more desperate for an end to the slaugh-

ter. A new political force, the Fatherland Party, clamored loudly and successfully for total victory, while thundering at the same time against "internal enemies." They vilified critics of wartime policies as subversives aiding the enemy. Among such blatant jingoism, anti-Semitism grew exponentially. The Social Democrats were split between the old, stolid group that still hoped for

The Meeting of Cortés and Moctezuma II at Tenochtitlán, 8 November 1519.

gradual political reform and the newly formed "Independent Socialists" who demanded an immediate end to the imperialist war.

Meanwhile the Kaiser, the putative Almighty or *Allerhöchster*, as he was called, continued to be shielded from the truth and became further estranged from reality because his immediate circle feared his nervous collapse. As General Plessen framed it, "The Emperor needs the sun." And so he was protected as much as possible from all darkness, a feat facilitated by his own faith in his infallibility; after all, he was God's instrument, so providence exculpated him. In this, too, he epitomized his nation; though Wilhelm's self-delusion was *sui generis*, the delusion of his people was carefully controlled by official mendacity and repression, the more effective for being largely concealed. All the belligerent nations trimmed the truth, but none as devastatingly successfully as Germany under Hindenburg and Ludendorff.

For the Kaiser, diversions would at times take the place of reality. The ever-loyal chief of the military cabinet, Moritz Freiherr von Lyncker, noted in May 1917, "It is unfortunately true that he disconnects himself from many things and prefers his comfort to all else. He has always been like this, even before the war. He is, after all, very weak, and strong only in protecting his personal private interests, above all an easy and as much as possible undisturbed existence... He isn't up to the great task—neither with his nerves nor with his intellect."

For a fleeting moment in the spring of 1918, after the Bolsheviks had signed a German-dictated Carthaginian peace, a German victory seemed as possible as it had in August 1914. But by August 1918, Allied forces had broken through German lines, and a stunned Ludendorff, fearing a sudden collapse of his army, demanded that the newly constituted civilian government send an immediate request to President Woodrow Wilson for an armistice. Wilson responded that the Allies wouldn't negotiate with the Kaiser. Negotiations dragged on while the hungry, war-weary Germans began to demand the Kaiser's abdication. At first he refused. "I have no intention of abandoning my throne because of a few hundred Jews, a few thousand workers," he said on November 3, 1918, as Germans took to the streets in pent-up fury.

The Kaiser finally went into exile in the Netherlands—not by his will, but because the army leaders insisted that he go. As he left, he blamed "Ludendorff, Bethmann, and Tirpitz for having lost the war," a triumvirate itself consumed by hatred of one another. Until his death in exile in 1941, the Kaiser spread venomous poison where he could: The Jews were to blame, as were the socialists—he alone was right. Reflecting and encouraging the sentiments of all too many Germans, he saw in Hitler the new man chosen by providence, a savior after the treachery that had caused Germany's defeat.

The Kaiser, long the Allies' favorite symbol for German arrogance and aggression—as he was for many Germans—came to be regarded as the chief villain of the Great War. British Prime Minister David Lloyd George waged his 1918 election campaign with the slogan "Hang the Kaiser." Wilhelm had his terrifying flaws, and he operated at the head of a deeply flawed political system. But ultimately his chief failure had been to abandon his responsibility and to yield power to military and civilian hawks—wrongly called conservatives, for their vision was a radical reordering of Europe's state system. The true villains, Ludendorff and his Pan-German allies, aimed at nothing less than world hegemony while Wilhelm became almost an alibi for men who were even blinder than he yet possessed greater power. In his astonishing book about Germany's collapse published in 1924, Charles de Gaulle enumerated "the defects common to these eminent men: the characteristic taste for immoderate undertakings; the passion to expand their personal power at any cost; the contempt for the limits marked out by human experience, common sense, and the law." But beneath them was an all too accommodating German bourgeoisie, whom Max Weber, in a phrase that resonates across the decades, urged to throw off "the cowardly will to impotence."

Our nation is not like imperial Germany, and great as our dangers are, they can't be compared to the horrors of that earlier time. But there may be a distant lesson from a country whose rulers in war, quarrelling among themselves, inflicted unimaginable harm to their people and to the world with their mendacity, secrecy, and paranoia. The consequences of their leadership—bolstered as it had been by claims of divine guidance, shrouded in chauvinism, and fortified by the cunning manipulation of pervasive fear—became fully manifest only later, as the people of an aggrieved nation turned against each other, almost reveling in their deep political and moral divisions and hatreds. It took a worse catastrophe, a world-historical scourge, to teach a lesson to these affected people. By distant analogy, we too might learn a lesson about the dangers and follies of imperial hubris.

Christ's Descent into Limbo, by Hieronymus Bosch.

STORM WARNING

by Caleb Carr

An American failure in Iraq may well be the prelude to a type of conflict that has very rarely been seen, not merely during the last century or few centuries, but during the last fifteen hundred years. Even the World Wars, with their horrifying death tolls and political as well as economic costs, may pale in comparison to the unraveling of the post-World War II international order—possibly the first result of the consistent inability of current American leaders to grasp in a timely fashion what has actually been taking place, not only in Iraq, Afghanistan, and the Muslim world generally, but in every arena of global affairs. Like any other war, the American struggle against Islamist extremism is not occurring in a vacuum. Other forces are bearing down on the United States that may fatally erode not only American, but global security and cohesion, aggravating the destructive potential of an expanded Western-Muslim confrontation, and in turn being aggravated by such a widened conflict.

The first of these larger forces is population migration. At the moment, we are witnessing very rare movements of entire communities and even populations throughout the world, nearly all of them driven by the repeated failures of various national economies, as well as by political

Caleb Carr is a novelist and historian, the author of The Lessons of Terror: A History of Warfare Against Civilians *and* The Alienist. *He teaches military studies at Bard College.*

corruption and religious intolerance. In the Western Hemisphere, for example, the pervasive inefficiency and corruption of governments in nations ranging from Mexico to Argentina—aggravated, as always by the exploitative, even predatory practices of U.S. multinational corporations—is fueling what the news media has termed an "immigration crisis" in America.

The planetary environment, meanwhile, long under assault by agricultural and industrial practices that have been woefully short-sighted and mercenary, is causing physical disasters—ruined harvests, hurricanes and other catastrophic storm systems, mudslides, and wildfires. America has been responsible for much of the atmospheric poisoning that, it is now generally agreed among scientific experts, is seriously and perhaps fatally accelerating those already bizarre shifts in climatic cycles that have contributed so heavily to such natural disasters abroad and at home.

At this moment, when we are challenged by a potentially destabilizing war in the Middle East, population shifts on every continent, and severe environmental deviations throughout the world, it may be time to look for similarly cataclysmic historical moments in global history in order to see if mankind met them any more successfully in the past; or, if it did not, to determine what circumstances might have been changed to effect a happier outcome.

Should the worst-case scenario concerning our Iraq invasion actually materialize; that is, should the entire Middle East become destabilized as increasing parts of the Muslim world are seized by extremist religious regimes, all of whom band together to pursue the forceful establishment of an expansionist Islamic caliphate throughout the world (which was, as most experts who minimize the current Islamist-jihadist threat tend to forget, the goal of the original Muslim armies in the seventh and eighth centuries—a goal they came within one or two decisive battles of achieving), then it would represent a shift in global power and populations such as we have not seen since the fourth and fifth centuries, the era of "The Invasion of Europe by the Barbarians," as the famous early-twentieth-century Anglo-Irish scholar of the period, J. B. Bury, pronounced it.

It is in this example—Europe at the outset of the Barbarian Age—that we encounter a shift in global power, a mass migration of populations, and, quite probably, a series of environmental crises (and even pandemics) that fully echo the present historical moment. Taken together, these factors changed the world in much the manner that stands to happen today if our radical Islamist enemies will not or cannot reach a mutually satisfactory compromise with the West and the rest of the developed world. For their parts, should the industrialized and polluting states of the world—led by America, China, and India—refuse to undertake measures to allow the atmosphere of our planet to begin to heal, and if the increasing economic inequity that accompanies the phenomenon known as globalization is not brought under control, we could very easily enter a new international dark age, one characterized by massive exterminations of life and the breakdown of what is left of international economic and political order.

Cullen Murphy, in his insightful study *Are We Rome?*, warns of both the dangers of repeating many of Rome's mistakes and of over-identifying our own position with that empire's. "Are we Rome?" he ultimately asks. "In important ways, we just might be.... But the antidote is everywhere. The antidote is being American." Before we can conclude whether or not "being American" is in fact an adequate or even a possible solution to our current international and environmental dilemmas, it would behoove us to note the important ways in which we are not like the Rome that found itself on the losing end of the fourth- and fifth-century barbarian invasions. Not only does the United States exert more types of influence throughout the actual world than Rome did over what its leaders considered the "known" world, but Rome was a dramatically more brutal state than is America. There are also more countries today that claim they are ready to step in and ensure Western political stability and security—should the

United States undergo a Rome-like collapse—than there were kingdoms ready to assume the full obligations of Roman imperial power in the fifth century.

Many of these objections are wise and well-founded, yet no historical comparison can ever achieve precision; and the fact remains that, should the United States suddenly become a second- or third-tier global power (a very real possibility, if it cannot resolve the ills that currently plague both it and the world over which it exerts such influence), there is every chance that those nations of Europe who claim the ability to take the lead in the West, assuming they have not already suffered the same fate as the United States, will experience just such crises largely *because* of our decline. Either way, tyranny, religious

Aeneas wounded and attended by a doctor. Detail of fresco, Pompeii, first century.

fundamentalism of all varieties, and would-be usurpers of regional power around the world will all receive enormous shots in the arm.

Yet this may actually pose less of a long-term threat to the economic, military, and environmental stability of the world than would several other consequences of a critically weakened America: economic crisis in China caused by a heavy reduction in demand for manufactured goods on the part of its principal trading partner; the emboldening of post-Soviet Russia, which is currently displaying dangerous signs that it is reverting to the brutal, warlike authoritarianism and international unreliability of the

tsarist Russian Empire; and the intensification of population fluctuations, including genocidal ethnic cleansings such as the one we are currently witnessing in the Darfur province of Sudan.

There are further reasons to take seriously a comparison between a prospective modern American decline and that of the western region of the Roman empire of the fourth and fifth centuries. These reasons are far more substantive and manifold than have been indicated by the popularized, clichéd notions about inevitable American "imperial decline" that have been kicking around for most of the last forty years. These more serious comparisons go beyond the shared pressures of unwise military adventures and large-scale population migrations on both U.S. and Roman borders. There are crises of *internal* strength and order to be considered as well, and—perhaps even more importantly—there are similarities between the calamitous state of the global physical environment during the two periods.

As in late imperial Rome, the upper classes of today's America have virtually divorced themselves (with some noteworthy exceptions) from the actual dirty work of preserving and projecting American economic and military power abroad.

Service in the U.S. military, voluntary since the end of the Vietnam War, now attracts the children of very few educated, upper-middle-

and upper-class American families. Similarly, young Romans of those same classes had ceased, by the time of the western portion of the empire's collapse, to view military service as especially incumbent upon them. The reasons for this latter condition have often been debated, with some analysts saying it was facilitated by the increased participation of barbarian auxiliary troops and officers, and others arguing that it was the degeneracy of those same upper class Roman youths that made them avoid such service. Whatever the case, the empire's upper classes, once a source of its most vigorous leaders, had become largely useless and parasitic by the late fourth century, and the empire's armies were filled out by foreigners who not only achieved citizenship through their service, but who also rose to high ranks. Indeed, in its twilight, the greatest generals of Rome were almost all "barbarians" by birth or descent.

The parallels here with the modern United States are more than academically amusing. As America increasingly treats first- and second-generation immigrants—some of them illegal and receiving a fast track to citizenship through their military service—as a deep and reliable pool of military recruits, and while the children of well-to-do American families who have been here for generations go on failing, year after year, to gain even basic historical competence in secondary schools and colleges, the analogy

Marine Armaments at the WWII Battle of Guadalcanal, 1942

WWI leggings

WWI cartridge belts

WWI Browning machine-guns

WWI mortars

Stored ammunition from WWI

1,093 bolt-action, single shot Springfield rifles

becomes genuinely alarming. The attitude of those privileged young people, who, given their privileged status, we have every right to expect to form the next generation of American leaders, continues to deteriorate into hollow echoes of the radicalism of the 1960s at best and unabashed hedonism at worst, thereby reinforcing the comparison with fourth-century western Rome to a point where it is nearly precise, in both its essential characteristics and its effects on the rest of the world.

This consideration of the paths that, on the one hand, legal and illegal immigrant youths in the United States are taking toward advancement, contrasted with how native, privileged youths are choosing to enter adult society may seem trivial, perhaps even laughably dismissible, to some; it is anything but. Many of the barbarian tribesmen who sought first a place and then advancement in the Roman legions did so out of both practical need and out of a genuine desire to belong to what they had always perceived, from the perspective of the far banks of the Rhine and Danube rivers, to be a great and functional state, one that could protect them from the vagaries of tribal existence, in which they were at the mercy of radically capricious weather patterns and the migration of new, almost nihilistically destructive tribes heading their way from eastern Asia, particularly but not exclusively the Huns. There were, however, other barbarian recruits who had future mischief against Rome on their minds when they went looking for a military education in the legions. Once they achieved rank and power within those imperial units, not a few of these foreign auxiliaries either turned on their masters, inciting mass mutinies, or returned home to teach their own tribesmen how to fight their way into Roman lands in order to set up new communities and kingdoms, thus eroding imperial borders irrevocably.

In considering these various activities of desperate foreigners on Roman borders in the late imperial period, what may be most important for the United States is the misperception that the Romans themselves formed about the nature of the tribes they faced and about what those tribes wanted from them. Because the tribes could, ever since the legendary uprising of Arminius (a Germanic tribesman-turned-Roman officer-turned-insurgent leader), cause serious military problems for Rome, the historians of the empire began to compose rhapsodic but highly speculative myths about the nature and origins of the "barbarian hordes"—especially the Germanic hordes, and particularly the Goths, who were said to have originated in Scandinavia, to have spent hundreds of years migrating and fighting their way south to the Black Sea, and thence into Europe, eventually populating all that continent's principal regions, outside of the young kingdom, and later republic, of Rome.

The great problem with this tale—which would become pseudohagiography in Victorian Europe, especially among admiring British authors and German historians and politicians seeking a definitive cultural identity for their new empire—is that it may well be largely fiction, created as something of a rationalization. The Romans fought the various Germanic tribes, especially the several Gothic peoples, and found them to be enemies so formidable that Julius Caesar himself advised leaving them alone in their wildernesses east of the Rhine and north of the Danube. There had to be a reason for this singular failure of the Roman legions, and the tale of world-wandering, virile tribes fit the need nicely. Roman vanity needed the barbarian hordes to be so legendarily powerful as to be able to wander about western Asia and Europe almost at will; Roman authors simply created the myth that they were and did. However there is now much evidence to support a new theory, most recently and capably advanced by the historian Michael Kulikowski in his study of Romano-Gothic history. The truth may well be that the tribes that the Romans encountered in their generally futile (although sometimes partially successful) efforts to subdue portions of Germania were not migratory at all, but were longtime inhabitants of the region who simply happened to be better and more committed warriors than could be fielded by imperial Rome—particularly in the empire's latter years.

Why should the explosion of a myth concern anyone save classical historians? Because the United States, in its modern wars, has shown a similar tendency to elevate the deadliness of some enemies (most notably the Soviet Union, which the Central Intelligence Agency reported, during the 1980s, was reaching a new peak of power, when in fact the Berlin Wall and the Soviet state itself were about to collapse), while downplaying the danger of others. At the same time that the CIA was warning of the heightening danger of the dying Soviet Union

If McClellan is not using the army, I should like to borrow it for a while.
—*Abraham Lincoln, 1862*

in the 1980s, for example, it and other U.S. government agencies were downplaying the nascent threat of Islamist terrorism. Indeed, as is now widely known, the CIA, pursuing a policy established by Zbigniew Brzezinski, Jimmy Carter's National Security Adviser in the late 1970s, was aiding and heavily arming some of the same Afghan Islamist warriors who would later give refuge to Osama bin Laden and his Al Qaeda terrorists.

The prostitution of national security concerns to propagandistic or profiteering schemes (there was, after all, very little money to be made in the low-tech counterterrorism tactics of the 1980s, whereas the perpetuation of large conventional weapons systems indeed preserved the breathtaking profitability of what President Eisenhower called the military-industrial complex), or, on a more basic level, the desire to satisfy the virile fantasies of a weakening society are, in the cases of late imperial Rome and the modern United States, of a piece, as such misdirected ventures almost inevitably lead to conflict, whether at the farthest frontiers of power or along the domestic borders of the home nation.

Consider only the extent to which the Bush administration, by continuing its calls for the liberalization of immigration laws (laws that are important to keeping large American agricultural and other industries functioning at a windfall-profit pace), along with the Senate, with its vehement and often paranoid opposition to such reform, have raised tempers on both sides of southern America's border to the boiling point, and left the most vital portion of the debate—the establishment and enforcement of just labor standards throughout the Western Hemisphere, as was promised by sponsors of the North American Free Trade Agreement—very nearly out of the quarrel altogether. Can anyone seriously doubt that the very great deal of misdirection on both sides of this argument will only further erode American national security by perpetuating the basic hemispheric ills that are generating the crisis? The other main example of the magnification by the Bush administra-

Two sets of hussars' armor, Poland, c. late seventeenth century.

tion of an external threat—that of terrorism—has not been a matter of degree (for the administration has rightly rated the possibility of future terrorist action as high), but rather one concerning the proliferation of terrorism's probable methods, a useful ratcheting up of domestic fear that has served to justify such measures as the more extreme portions of the PATRIOT Act and the establishment of the Guantánamo Bay detention facility. Mischaracterization of the enemy, then, is an ancient practice still very useful to political leaders.

Not surprisingly, it is among the denizens of the boardrooms of those same American corporations that are pushing for liberalized immigration laws, and especially of those multinational corporations most involved in advancing the several aspects of globalization that especially infuriate many potential terrorists in Muslim countries and elsewhere, that we find the most startling parallel to late imperial Rome. There is little if any evidence that, say, the executives who run the infamous octopus called Halliburton (well-known as Vice President Dick Cheney's former employer) and its former subsidiary KBR, the corrupt contractor in Iraq, have ever really placed the interests of the United States above those of internationalist capitalism, or that they have ever even conceived of "nationalism" in the manner that the soldiers who have died and are continuing to die in Iraq and Afghanistan do. Parsons, another Iraq contractor (which had been hired to refurbish Iraqi hospitals, a vital part of any security and stability program), was eventually revealed as so larcenous that the U.S. Army was forced to cancel contracts with the company, but not before Parsons robbed the American people of hundreds of millions, and perhaps billions, of dollars. Thus, corruption that eats at the very security of the United States can be found at every level of our governmental system, as well as outside our borders.

Thus, we have the first two components necessary to complete the analogy between Rome in the fourth and fifth centuries and the United States today: military corrosion and dramatic population shifts caused not by the naked aggression of wild-eyed foreigners (although it was and is portrayed that way) but by the same desperation to feed and clothe their families that drove the barbarian tribes who had long lived north and east of Rome across the frozen Danube and Rhine rivers, in order to gain access to more plentiful resources and avoid the ruthless "displacement" dealt out by such genuinely barbaric tribes as the Huns, the Alans, the Sarmatians, and, later, the Slavs. In fact, the "invasion" of the barbarian tribes (particularly, again, the Goths), far from accelerating the death of Rome, actually prolonged the empire's life (as illegal immigration has actually helped the American economy to function and kept the ranks of the military full). When the Huns were finally checked at the Battle of Châlons (451), they were faced by a half-Scythian Roman commander, Flavius Aëtius, who was supported by the great Visigoth king, Theodoric (who died in the battle), and by numerous other barbarian units.

But what of the further component of what we have postulated as the necessary conditions for drawing a parallel between the position of the contemporary United States and Rome, generalized environmental catastrophe?

Here, again, accounts from the late Roman/barbarian period are not always reliable, but we do know a few facts. For reasons yet to be definitively determined, Europe's fertile farming lands, especially in the north, were stricken with every manner of misfortune, during the late fourth, fifth, and sixth centuries. Droughts, bitter winters, prolonged frosts (even during summer), blights, and the crop failures and the food shortages that accompany them, along with the heightened susceptibility to disease and starvation that characterize human populations as a result of such malnourishment, were remarkably persistent in most of the "known" world. Indeed, it was the relentlessness of these phenomena (along with the pressing terror of the Huns and their allies) that made the tribes northeast of Rome bold enough to launch the first of their migrations south across the fro-

zen Danube, after which they soon conducted overwhelmingly successful military operations against the Roman emperor Valens and his forces at Adrianople in 378. Soon thereafter, in 406, the tribes to the west, driven by the same motives, crossed the frozen Rhine. Throughout this era, pestilences—sometimes mistaken for the bubonic plague—broke out periodically, until finally the plague itself did strike in 541. Many theories concerning climate shift have been offered for these terrible changes in environmental conditions in Roman Europe.

In 2004, two undergraduate students at the University of Cardiff discovered evidence that a relatively small comet impacted the Earth in the early sixth century, creating conditions similar to a nuclear winter. They said that the conditions created by the comet's impact led to a long series of failed harvests and bitterly cold conditions that, along with starvation, so weakened the peoples of Europe that they eventually became particularly susceptible to the outbreak of the plague, which occurred shortly thereafter. Yet similar, if somewhat less severe, conditions had been anecdotally reported a century or so earlier; indeed, it has often been claimed that the barbarian crossing of the Rhine in 406 was only made possible by the worst in a long series of terrible winters, which froze that mighty river so solid that entire human tribes—really nascent barbarian nations—could cross it in a relatively short period of time. Did the earth suffer some similar cosmic event at that time? Whatever the case, the Dark Ages, or at least much of that infamous era, appear to have gained their name for reasons more complex than the simple paucity of historical documentation. For generations and centuries on end, the European environment was repeatedly stricken by unusual and unusually catastrophic conditions that claimed untold lives through starvation and pestilence.

There are still scientists in the West and particularly in America who are attempting to tell the world that the phenomenon we call "global warming" is in fact a perfectly normal, if rare, cyclical event. Perhaps this is true, and perhaps that cycle simply wound around to brutal cold and endemic blight during the Dark Ages, and it is in the process of doing so again now. It seems far more certain, however, that a specific trigger caused the bizarre phenomena associated with the early Dark Ages, just as it seems more likely that the steady degradation of the Earth's atmosphere during the Industrial Age is behind our current bizarre weather patterns, which are producing many of the same results evident a millennium and a half ago: periods of severe cold (during winters, but at other times as well), crop failures, droughts, pandemics, and, once again, the migration of whole communities toward areas where these problems are less prevalent (or are at least perceived to be less prevalent).

We can form as tight an historical analogy between the period of the barbarian "invasions"—really a series of desperate migrations—of imperial Roman territory and our own era as it is reasonable to expect to find between any two periods separated by so large a gap in time. This leads, then, to the last and most fatal question of all pragmatic counterfactual history: Is there anything that either the Romans or their barbar-

ian neighbors could have done differently in order to have staved off the centuries of suffering, starvation, ignorance, political disintegration, religious tumult, and warfare that is generally conceded as beginning with the Gothic crossing of the Danube at the end of the fourth century?

Unfortunately, this question brings us to the least amusing of possible counterfactual answers, one that has harrowing implications for the contemporary world. In all likelihood, conditions in the Roman Empire and on its frontiers had so deteriorated by the time of the Danube and Rhine crossings that, even had Rome undergone a renaissance of civic and military commitment by its own most prosperous citizens, or had the tribes of northeastern Europe somehow found a way to slow the Hunnish advance into their lands and counterbalance the effects of environmental devastation by making new trade agreements with Rome, both sides would only have been borrowing time, and—if the disastrous conditions on the continent really were caused as much by a natural catastrophe such as a comet's collision with the earth as by

Detail of a study for *The Battle of Anghiari*, by Leonardo da Vinci.

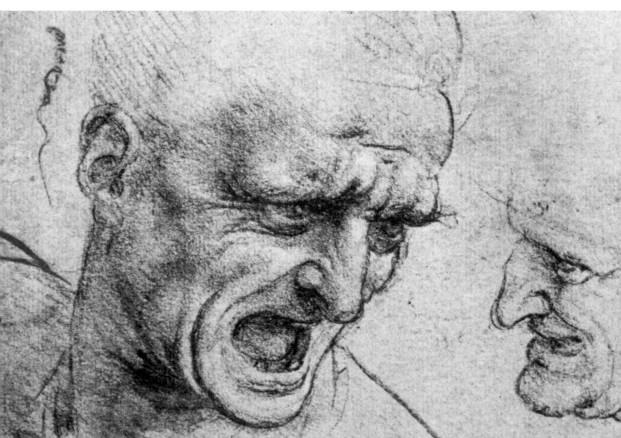

human folly—then even borrowing time would likely not have been a sustainable policy for very long. If environmental factors badly damaged continental food supplies, triggering famines, diseases, and demographic movements of critical magnitude, the fending off of which was beyond the power of any empire or tribe, then curing political arrogance and stupidity, replacing foolish leaders with wise ones, winning rather than losing important battles—none of it could have counteracted the awesome effects of what had happened to the earth.

The parallels to our own situation are self-evident. We have been warned time and again, in recent decades, by the vast majority of responsible scientists specializing in the field, that climatic shift (or global warming) is almost certainly the result of human foolishness, and that it will soon reach—if, indeed, it has not already reached—irreversible proportions. Should such be the case, then it makes little real difference whether George W. Bush withdraws Americans from Iraq in the near or the far term, or if American immigration laws are tightened or liberalized, or whether any other political and military measures are taken. Earth science trumps all human endeavors, and perhaps many Americans are wise to spend as much of their time as frivolously as they do and to ignore history to the extent they have. Perhaps those of us who seek solutions to problems such as the Iraq War and international terrorism really are just rearranging the deck chairs on a ship very much larger than the *Titanic*. Perhaps the only people whose lives matter right now are those groups of scientists who are busily trying to determine if the ultimate effects of climate shift can be avoided.

This much, at least, can be said: By the time the Romans realized that many of the barbarian tribes on their frontiers were not the frightful demons they took them for and decided to make some common cause with them in the effort to defend Europe from the Huns and their followers, the moment for effective action had already passed. The Huns were checked at Châlons, although they did not depart Europe until they were ready. Their readiness was no doubt assisted by the fact that what they found in Europe was not a united, well-fed, well-supplied enemy, but a continent still torn by civil strife and sinking ever faster into starvation, chaos, war, disease, and religious fervor. It is scant wonder that such plundering nomads as the Huns ultimately decided to turn their horde eastward again and head for the open steppes of Asia.

And in this sense, counterfactual history has, at the last, one piece of advice to offer us: Environmental devastation may be coming—indeed, may be upon us—and that fact may be irreversible. But a planet riven with religious intolerance, political disunity, and avoidable wars will fall prey to the worst effects of that devastation far more quickly and to a far greater extent than will a planet that has at long last decided to make common cause for the mutual good. Europe in the early Dark Ages did not learn this lesson, and it is arguable, again, that—given the centuries-old ways of warlike or merely dissolute life that had been developing among the barbarian tribes and the Romans—any single event can be chosen, the reversal of which would have forestalled the horrors to come, or that any one leader can be selected, whose survival (or death) would have meant a similarly changed set of ensuing circumstances. Hard times were approaching, and could not be stopped; but had they been faced together, could their effects at least have been mitigated? Can they, in the modern era?

It is worth returning, in this context, to Cullen Murphy's notion that "being American" is the "antidote" for being Rome: a deceptively simple idea, but one which turns out to have important implications. Consider the similarly deceptive simplicity of the approach that Franklin Roosevelt brought to bear on the seemingly intractable problem of the Great Depression: "It is common sense to take a method and try it," FDR said. "If it fails, admit it frankly and try another. But above all, try something." This is a line of thinking that has been painfully absent among American leaders of late; but it may be the only way to stem and finally turn the tide of international catastrophes of every stripe that are bearing down on us.

War: The Fringe Benefits

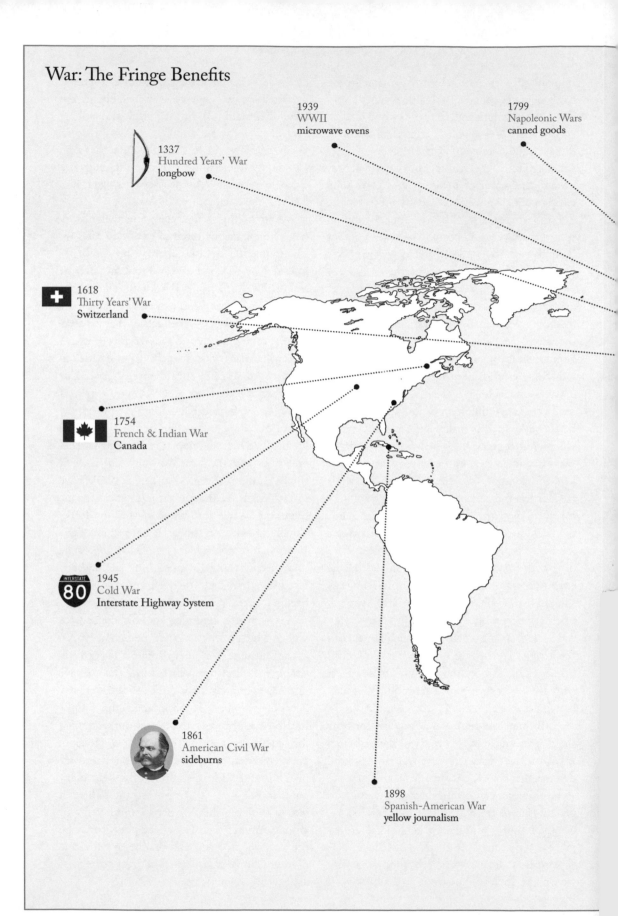

1939
WWII
microwave ovens

1799
Napoleonic Wars
canned goods

1337
Hundred Years' War
longbow

1618
Thirty Years' War
Switzerland

1754
French & Indian War
Canada

1945
Cold War
Interstate Highway System

1861
American Civil War
sideburns

1898
Spanish-American War
yellow journalism

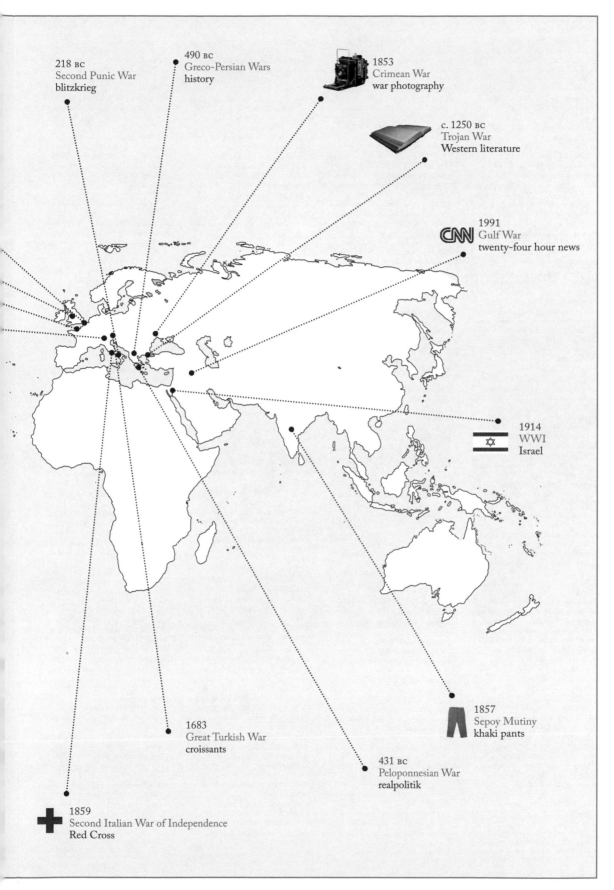

218 BC
Second Punic War
blitzkrieg

490 BC
Greco-Persian Wars
history

1853
Crimean War
war photography

c. 1250 BC
Trojan War
Western literature

1991
Gulf War
twenty-four hour news

1914
WWI
Israel

1683
Great Turkish War
croissants

431 BC
Peloponnesian War
realpolitik

1857
Sepoy Mutiny
khaki pants

1859
Second Italian War of Independence
Red Cross

Sources

p. 19, Kuwait Collins, Tim. "U.K. Troops Told: Be Just and Strong." *BBC News*, 20 March 2003, http://news.bbc.co.uk/1/hi/uk/2866581.stm (accessed 20 September 2007).

p. 20, Baghdad Maude, Sir Stanley. "The Proclamation of Baghdad." *Harper's Magazine*, May 2003.

p. 21, Clermont Munro, Dana Carleton, A. M., ed. *Translations and Reprints from the Original Sources of European History*, 3rd ed. Vol. 1, No. 2, *Urban and the Crusaders*. Philadelphia: Department of History of the University of Pennsylvania, 1901.

p. 23, Troy Homer. *The Iliad*. Translated by Robert Fagles. New York: Viking Penguin, 1990. Copyright © 1990 by Robert Fagles. Used by permission of Viking Penguin, a division of Penguin Group (USA), Inc.

p. 24, East Anglia Patton, George S. "Speech to the Third Army," delivered in England, 5 June 1944. U.S. Army Heritage and Education Center, Department of the Army.

p. 25, Paris Léon, Pauline. "Petition to the National Assembly on Women's Right to Bear Arms," in *Women in Revolutionary Paris, 1789–1795*, Darline Gay Levy, Harriet Branson Applewhite, and Mary Durham Johnson, eds. and trans. Urbana, Ill.: University of Illinois Press, 1979. Copyright © 1979 by the Board of Trustees of the University of Illinois. Used with permission of the editors and the University of Illinois Press.

p. 27, Hautefort Goldin, Frederick, trans. *Lyrics of the Troubadours and Trouveres: An Anthology and a History*. Garden City, N.Y.: Anchor Books, 1973. Reprint, Gloucester, Mass.: Peter Smith, 1983. Copyright © 1973 by Frederick Goldin. Used by permission of Doubleday, a division of Random House, Inc.

p. 28, Woolwich Ruskin, John. *The Crown of Wild Olive*. Philadelphia: Henry Altemus, 1895.

p. 30, Allston Holmes Jr., Oliver Wendell, "The Soldier's Faith," in *The Essential Holmes*, Richard A. Posner, ed. Chicago: University of Chicago Press, 1992. Reprint, 1996.

p. 32, Petrograd Lenin, V. I. "Hanging Order," *Revelations from the Russian Archives: Collectivization and Industrialization*. Washington: Library of Congress, 1997.

p. 34, Istanbul Sultan Selim I. "Sultan Selim's Letter to Shah Isma'il, 1514," in *The Muslim World on the Eve of Europe's Expansion*, John J. Saunders, ed. and trans. Englewood Cliffs, N.J.: Prentice-Hall, 1966. Copyright © 1966 by Prentice-Hall, Inc. All rights reserved. Reprinted with the permission of Simon & Schuster Adult Publishing Group.

p. 36, Hippo Schaff, Philip, ed. *A Select Library of the Nicene and Post-Nicene Fathers of the Christian Church*. Vol. 1, *The Confessions and Letters of St. Augustine, with a Sketch of His Life and Work*. Buffalo: The Christian Literature Company, 1886.

p. 37, Afghanistan bin Laden, Osama, Ayman al-Zawahiri, Abu-Yasir Rifa'I Ahmad Taha, Shaykh Mir Hamzah, and Fazlur Rahman. "Jihad Against Jews and Crusaders." Translated by the Federation of American Scientists. Federation of American Scientists, 23 February 1998, http://www.fas.org/irp/world/para/docs/980223-fatwa.htm (accessed 21 September 2007).

p. 38, Berlin Goebbels, Joseph. "Nation Rise Up, and Let the Storm Break Loose," trans. Randall Bytwerk. Grand Rapids, Mich.: Calvin College German

Propaganda Archive, 1998. Used by permission.

p. 40, St. Petersburg/Berlin Tsar Nicholas II and Kaiser Wilhelm II. *The Kaiser's Letters to the Tsar, Copied from the Government Archives in Petrograd, and Brought from Russia*. Edited by Isaac Don Levine. London: Hodder and Stoughton Ltd., 1920.

p. 42, Washington Wilson, Woodrow. "Necessity of War Against Germany," in *Selected Addresses and Public Papers of Woodrow Wilson*, Albert Bushnell Hart, ed. New York: The Modern Library, 1918.

p. 46, India Miller, Barbara Stoler, trans. *The Bhagavad-Gita*. New York: Bantam Classics, 1986. Copyright © 1986 by Barbara Stoler Miller. Used by permission of Bantam Books, a division of Random House, Inc.

p. 48, Tilbury Elizabeth I, "Speech to the Troops at Tilbury," in *The Norton Anthology of English Literature*, 6th ed, M. H. Abrams, ed. Vol. 1. New York: W. W. Norton & Company, 1993.

p. 49, Boston Howe, Julia Ward. "The Battle Hymn of the Republic," *The Bookman* 32 (Sept. 1910–Feb. 1911): 10–11.

p. 49, Tenochtitlán Galeano, Eduardo. *Memory of Fire*, Vol. 1, *Genesis*. Translated by Cedric Belfrage. New York: Pantheon Books, 1985. Reprint, New York: W. W. Norton, 1998. Copyright © 1985 by Cedric Belfrage. Used by permission of Pantheon Books, a division of Random House, Inc.

p. 50, Washington 2002 State of the Union Address, delivered in Washington, 29 January 2002. Library of Congress, Washington.

p. 52, Caledonia Tacitus. *The Agricola and the Germania*. Translated by H. Mattingly; translation revised by S. A. Handford. Baltimore: Penguin Books, 1948. Reprint, 1970. Copyright © the Estate of H. Mattingly, 1948, 1970. Copyright © S.A. Handford, pp. 80–83.

p. 53, Mississippi Territory Tecumseh. "Sleep Not Longer, O Choctaws and Chickasaws," in *Indian Oratory: Famous Speeches by Noted Indian Chieftans*, W. C. Vanderwerth, ed. Norman, Okla.: University of Oklahoma Press, 1971.

p. 55, Harfleur Shakespeare, William. *The Life of King Henry V*, in *William Shakespeare: The Complete Works*, Alfred Harbage, ed. Baltimore: Penguin Books, 1969. Reprint, 1971.

p. 57, Haditha Langewiesche, William. "Rules of Engagement," *Vanity Fair*, November 2006. Reprinted with permission.

p. 59, Rhineland Freytag, Gustav. *Pictures of German Life*. Translated by Mrs. Malcolm. London: Chapman and Hall, 1862.

p. 60, New Carthage Polybius. *The Histories*, Vol. 4, W. R. Patton, trans. Cambridge, Mass.: Harvard University Press, 1925. Reprint, 1960. Reprinted by permission of the publishers and the Trustees of the Loeb Classical Library from *Polybius: The Histories*, Loeb Classical Library Vol. 159, translated by W.R. Paton, 137, 139, 141. Cambridge, Mass.: Harvard University Press, © 1960, by the President and Fellows of Harvard College. The Loeb Classical Library ® is a registered trademark of the President and Fellows of Harvard College.

p. 61, Rwanda Hatzfeld, Jean. *Machete Season: The Killers in Rwanda Speak*. Translated by Linda Coverdale. New York: Picador, 2005. Translation copyright © 2005 by Farrar, Straus and Giroux, LLC.

Reprinted by permission of Farrar, Straus and Giroux, LLC.

p. 64, Washington Nixon, Richard, and Henry Kissinger. "White House Tape Conversation." National Archives EOB 332-35, April 25, 1972.

p. 64, Thérouanne "Truce for the Bishopric of Thérouanne," in Thatcher, Oliver J. and Edgar Holmes McNeal, eds., *A Source Book for Mediaeval History*. New York: Charles Scribner's Sons, 1905.

p. 65, Poitiers Froissart, Jean. *The Chronicles of Jean Froissart*, Gillian Anderson and William Anderson, eds. Carbondale, Ill.: Southern Illinois University Press, 1963.

p. 66, Japan "Leaflet dropped on the Japanese, August 6, 1945." Harry S. Truman Library, Miscellaneous Historical Documents Collection.

p. 66, Cairo Ayalon, David. *Gunpowder and Firearms in the Mamluk Kingdom: A Challenge to a Mediaeval Society*. London: Vallentine, Mitchell, 1956. Copyright © 1956, Vallentine, Mitchell. Reproduced by permission of Taylor & Francis Books UK.

p. 68, London Gilbert, Martin. *Road to Victory*. London: Guild Publishing, 1986.

p. 69, Atlanta Sherman, William T. *Memoirs of General William T. Sherman*. New York: D. Appleton and Company, 1875.

p. 72, China Sun Tzu. "The Nine Situations," in *The Art of War*, Dallas Galvin, ed. and Lionel Giles, trans. New York: Barnes & Noble Classics, 2003.

p. 73, Rafah "In the Zone." *Harper's Magazine*, May 2005.

p. 74, Japan Yamamoto Tsunetomo. *Hagakure: The Book of the Samurai*. Translated by William Scott Wilson. New York: Kodansha, 1979. Reprint, 1983.

p. 75, Guatemala City "A Study of Assassination." National Security Archive at George Washington University. August 1997.

p. 78, Washington "Harass Cuba Memo." National Archives, College Park, Md.

p. 79, Tegucigalpa Ryszard Kupuściński. "The Soccer Game." *Harper's Magazine*, June 1986. Copyright © 1986, 1990 by Ryszard Kupuściński. Used by permission of Alfred A. Knopf, a division of Random House, Inc.

p. 79, Rome Vegetius. *De Re Militari*. Translated by Lt. John Clarke, 1767.

p. 81, Ukraine Malaparte, Curzio. *Kaputt*. Translated by Cesare Foligno. New York: New York Review Books, 2005.

p. 86, Potsdam Truman, Harry S. "Potsdam Declaration July 26, 1945." UCLA Asia Institute, Los Angeles.

p. 88, Tennessee Grant, Ulysses S. *Personal Memoirs of U.S. Grant*. New York: Charles L. Webster & Company, 1885.

p. 89, Pianosa Heller, Joseph. *Catch-22*. New York: Simon & Schuster Paperbacks, 2004. Copyright © 1955, 1961 by Joseph Heller. Copyright renewed © 1989 by Joseph Heller. Reprinted by permission of Simon & Schuster, Inc., N.Y.

p. 90, Melos Thucydides. *The History of the Peloponnesian War, Book Five*. Edited by Sir Richard Livingstone and translated by Robert Crawley. London: Oxford University Press, 1943. Reprint, 1972. Reprinted with permission of Oxford University Press.

p. 93, Vietnam O'Brien, Tim. "The Man I Killed," in *The Things They Carried*. New York: Broadway Books, 1990. Copyright © 1990 by Tim O'Brien. Reprinted by permission of Houghton Mifflin Company. All rights reserved.

p. 96, Constantinople Gibbon, Edward. *The History of the Decline and Fall of the Roman Empire*, Vol. 6. Edited by David Womersley. New York: Penguin Classics, 1995.

p. 100, Troy Virgil. *The Aeneid*. Translated by Robert Fagles. New York: Viking, 2006. Copyright © 2006 by Robert Fagles. Used by permission of Viking Penguin, a division of Penguin Group (USA), Inc.

p. 104, B-24 Liberator Jarrell, Randall. "The Death of the Ball Turrett Gunner," in *Selected Poems*, William H. Pritchard, ed. New York: Noonday Press, 1990. Copyright © 1969, renewed 1997 by Mary von S. Jarrell. Reprinted by permission of Farrar, Straus and Giroux, LLC.

p. 104, Catalonia Orwell, George. *Homage to Catalonia*. New York: Harcourt Brace Jovanovich, 1980. Copyright © 1952 and renewed 1980 by Sonia Brownell Orwell, reprinted by permission of Harcourt, Inc.

p. 106, Tolbiac Gregory of Tours. *The History of the Franks*. Translated by Lewis Thorpe. New York: Penguin, 1974. Copyright © Lew Thorpe, 1974.

p. 107, Ypres Céline, Louis-Ferdinand. *Journey to the End of the Night*. Translated by Ralph Manheim. New York: New Directions, 1983. Copyright © 1934, 1952 by Louis-Ferdinand Céline, Translation © 1983 Ralph Manheim. Reprinted by permission of New Directions Publishing Corp.

p. 111, Balaclava Woodham-Smith, Cecil. *The Reason Why*. New York: Penguin, 1958. Copyright © Cecil Woodham-Smith, 1953. Reprinted by permission of A.M. Heath & Co., Ltd.

p. 115, Adrianople Ammianus Marcellinus. *The Later Roman Empire*. Selected and translated by Walter Hamilton. New York: Penguin Books, 1986. Translation copyright © Walter Hamilton, 1986. Introduction and Notes copyright © Andrew Wallace-Hadrill, 1986.

p. 116, Rome Guicciardini, Luigi. *The Sack of Rome*. Translated by James H. McGregor. New York: Italica Press, 1993. Copyright © 1993 by Italica Press. Used by permission.

p. 119, New England Saltonstall, Nathaniel. "A True but Brief Account of Our Losses Sustained Since This Cruel and Mischievous War Began," in *Original Narratives of Early American History*, J. Franklin Jameson, ed. *Narratives of the Indian Wars*, Charles H. Lincoln, ed. New York: Charles Scribner's Sons, 1913.

p. 120, Jerusalem Josephus. *The Jewish War*. Translated by G. A. Williamson. Revised with an introduction, notes and appendixes by E. Mary Smallwood. New York: Penguin, 1959; revised, 1981. Copyright © G. A. Williamson, 1959, 1969. Introduction and editorial matter copyright © E. M. Smallwood, 1981.

p. 122, Hispaniola De las Casas, Bartolomé. *A Short Account of the Destruction of the Indies*. Edited and translated by Nigel Griffin, introduction by Anthony Pagden. New York: Penguin Classics, 1992. The Translation and Notes copyright © Nigel Griffin, 1992. Introduction copyright © Anthon Pagden 1992.

p. 124, Pennsylvania Frontier Seaver, James Everett. *A Narrative of the Life of Mary Jemison*. New York: The American Scenic & Historic Preservation Society, 1918.

p. 127, Scythia Herodotus. *The Histories*. Translated by Aubrey de Sélincourt, revised with introduction and notes by

A.R. Burn. Baltimore: Penguin Books, 1954; revised, 1972. Copyright © the Estates of Aubrey de Sélincourt, 1954. Copyright © A.R. Burn, 1972.

p. 128, Agincourt Keegan, John. *The Face of Battle.* New York: Viking, 1976; Penguin Books, 1978.

p. 132, Peleliu Sledge, E. B. *With the Old Breed at Peleliu and Okinawa.* Novato, Cal.: Presidio Press, 1981. Copyright © 1990 by E.B. Sledge. Used by permission of Presidio Press, an imprint of The Ballantine Publishing Group, a division of Random House, Inc.

p. 135, Hindenburg Trench Sassoon, Siegfried. "Memoirs of an Infantry Officer," in *The Memoirs of George Sherston.* Garden City, N.Y.: Doubleday, Doran & Company, 1937.

p. 139, My Lai Ridenhour, Ron. "Memorandum for Lieutenant General William R. Peers." Department of the Army, 1969.

p. 141, Virginia Whitman, Walt. *Specimen Days in America.* London: Walter Scott, 1887.

p. 142, Cape Trafalgar Howarth, David. *Trafalgar: The Nelson Touch.* New York: Atheneum, 1969. Reproduced with permission of Curtis Brown Group Ltd., London, on behalf of the Estate of David Armine Howarth. Copyright © David Armine Howarth 1955.

p. 143, Majdanek Grossman, Vasily. *Life and Fate.* Translated by Robert Chandler. London: Collins Harvill, 1985; New York Review Books, 2006. Copyright © 1980 by Editions L'Age d'Homme. Translation copyright © 1985 by Collins Harvill. Introduction copyright © 1985, 2006 by Robert Chandler.

p. 147, Nagasaki Laurence, William L. "Atomic Bombing of Nagasaki Told by Flight Member," *The New York Times,* 9 September 1945. Used by permission.

p. 151, Washington Jessica Lynch. Testimony of Jessica Lynch. House Committee on Oversight and Government Reform, April 24, 2007.

p. 154, Arlington Dos Passos, John. *1919,* in *U.S.A.* New York: Library of America, 1996. Copyright © 1932, and renewed 1959 by John Dos Passos. Reprinted by permission of Houghton Mifflin Company. All rights reserved.

p. 157, New York Cummings, E. E. *Complete Poems: 1904–1962, by E. E. Cummings.* Edited by George J. Firmage. Copyright 1952, © 1980, 1991 by the Trustees for the E.E. Cummings Trust. Used by permission of the Liveright Publishing Company.

p. 158, Paris Voltaire. *Philosophical Dictionary.* Edited and translated by Theodore Besterman. New York: Penguin, 1972. Reprinted by permission.

p. 161, Paris/Vienna Einstein, Albert, and Sigmund Freud. *Einstein on Peace.* Edited by Otto Nathan and Heinz Norden. New York: Simon and Schuster, 1960.

p. 164, Stanford James, William. "The Moral Equivalent of War," in *Memories and Studies.* New York: Longmans, Green, and Co., 1917.

p. 168, Western Front Remarque, Erich Maria. *All Quiet on the Western Front.* Translated by A. W. Wheen. New York: Random House, 1982. "Im Westen Nichts Neues", copyright 1928 by Ullstein A.G.; Copyright renewed © 1956 by Erich Maria Remarque. "All Quiet on the Western Front", copyright 1929, 1930 by Little, Brown and Company; Copyright renewed © 1957, 1958 by Erich Maria Remarque. All Rights reserved.

p. 170, New York Twain, Mark. *The Portable Mark Twain.* Edited by Bernard DeVoto. New York: Viking Press, 1946. Reprinted, 1965.

p. 173, Washington Stimson, Henry L. "The Decision to Use the Atomic Bomb." *Harper's Magazine,* February 1947.

p. 174, Pharsalus Lucan. *Lucan's Civil War.* Translated by P. F. Widdows. Bloomington, Ind.: Indiana University Press, 1988.

p. 175, Moscow Tolstoy, Leo. *War and Peace.* Translated with an introduction by Rosemary Edmonds. (First published in Penguin Classics in two volumes 1957, reprinted with revisions 1978). New York: Penguin, 1957. Reprint, 1978. Copyright © Rosemary Edmunds 1957, 1978.

p. 177, Flanders Owen, Wilfred. "Dulce Et Decorum Est," in *The Collected Poems of Wilfred Owen,* C. Day Lewis, ed. New York: New Directions, 1965. Copyright © 1963 by Chatto & Windus, Ltd. Reprinted by permission of New Directions Publishing Corp. SALES TERRITORY: U.S./Canadian rights only.

p. 178, New York Vonnegut, Kurt. *Fates Worse Than Death.* New York: G. P. Putnam's Sons, 1991. Copyright © 1991 by Kurt Vonnegut. Used by permission of G. P. Putnam's sons, a division of Penguin Group (USA), Inc.

p. 180, Washington Eisenhower, Dwight David. "Peace in the World: Acts, Not Rhetoric, Needed," in *Selected Speeches of Dwight David Eisenhower, 34ᵗʰ President of the United States.* Washington: Government Printing Office, 1970.

p. 182, New York Auden, W. H. "The Shield of Achilles," in *Collected Poems by W. H. Auden.* Edited by Edward Mendelson. New York: Random House, 1976; Vintage International, 1991.

p. 184, Washington Lincoln, Abraham. "Second Inaugural Address," in *Selected Speeches and Writings.* New York: Vintage/Library of America, 1992.

p. 185, Thermopylae Golding, William. *The Hot Gates and Other Occasional Pieces.* New York: Harcourt, Brace & World, Inc.: 1966.

p. 190, Blenheim Southey, Robert. *A Choice of Robert Southey's Verse.* Edited by Geoffrey Grigson. London: Faber and Faber, 1970.

Art

Front cover, © Scala/Art Resource, NY.

IFC, © ullstein bild/The Granger Collection, New York.

pp. 4–5, © The Granger Collection, New York.

p. 8, © The Granger Collection, New York.

p. 8, © Museo Archeologico Nazionale, Naples, Italy/The Bridgeman Art Library.

p. 8, © Stapleton Collection, UK/The Bridgeman Art Library.

p. 8, © The Granger Collection, New York.

p. 8, © Reuters/CORBIS.

p. 8, © Private Collection/The Bridgeman Art Library.

p. 8, © The Granger Collection, New York.

p. 8, © Private Collection/The Bridgeman Art Library.

p. 9, © Private Collection/The Bridgeman Art Library.

p. 9, © The Art Archive/Musée du Louvre, Paris/Gianni Dagli Orti.

p. 9, © Scala/Art Resource, NY; Image Reference: ART189438.

p. 9, © Bettmann/CORBIS.

p. 9, © The Granger Collection, New York.

p. 9, Private Collection/© Philip Mould Ltd., London/The Bridgeman Art Library.

p. 9, © The Granger Collection, New York.

p. 9, © The Granger Collection, New York.

p. 10, © Erich Lessing/Art Resource, NY.

p. 13, © Bibliotheque Nationale, Paris/The Bridgeman Art Library.

pp. 16–17, Reprinted by permission, Edward R. Tufte, The Visual Display of Quantitative Information (Cheshire, Connecticut, Graphics Press LLC, 1983, 2001).

p. 18, © The Granger Collection, New York.

p. 20, © The Granger Collection, New York.

p. 22, © ullstein bild/The Granger Collection, New York.

p. 25, © The Granger Collection, New York.

p. 26, © The Granger Collection, New York.

p. 29, Photograph by Tim A. Hetherington © Panos Pictures.

p. 31, © The Granger Collection, New York.

p. 33, © The Granger Collection, New York.

p. 34, © Adoc-photos/Art Resource, NY.

p. 37, Photograph by Roger Fenton © CORBIS.

p. 39, (L) © Rue des Archives/The Granger Collection, New York.

p. 39, (C) © The Granger Collection, New York.

p. 39, (R) Photograph by Heinrich Hoffmann/Getty Images.

p. 45, Photograph © Chris Hondros/Getty Images.

p. 47, © The Granger Collection, New York.

p. 48, © The Granger Collection, New York.

p. 50, © The Granger Collection, New York.

p. 53, (L) © Smithsonian American Art Museum, Washington, DC/Art Resource, NY.

p. 53, (C) © Smithsonian American Art Museum, Washington, DC/Art Resource, NY.

p. 53, (R) © Smithsonian American Art Museum, Washington, DC/Art Resource, NY.

p. 56, © Erich Lessing/Art Resource, NY.

p. 60, © Erich Lessing/Art Resource, NY.

p. 62, © The Art Archive/British Library.

p. 67, © Erich Lessing/Art Resource, NY.

p. 69, © The Granger Collection, New York.

pp. 70–71, © Musée de la Tapisserie, Bayeux, France/The City of Bayeux/Giraudon/The Bridgeman Art Library.

p. 75, © Erich Lessing/Art Resource, NY.

p. 76, © The Granger Collection, New York.

p. 81, © Réunion des Musées Nationaux/Art Resource, NY.

p. 83, © The Granger Collection, New York.

p. 89, © The Granger Collection, New York.

p. 92, © Scala/Art Resource, NY.

p. 96, Photograph by Andrew Testa © Panos Pictures.

p. 98, © Erich Lessing/Art Resource, NY.

p. 101, © Alinari/Art Resource, NY.

p. 105, © HIP/Art Resource, NY.

p. 106, Photograph by Andrew Testa © Panos Pictures.

p. 108, © Erich Lessing/Art Resource, NY.

p. 110, © The Granger Collection, New York.

p. 113, © Erich Lessing/Art Resource, NY.

p. 116, © The Granger Collection, New York.

p. 119, © The Granger Collection, New York.

p. 121, © Lynsey Addario/CORBIS.

p. 123, © The Granger Collection, New York.

p. 124, © Werner Forman/Art Resource, NY.

p. 127, © Giraudon/Art Resource, NY.

p. 128, © Werner Forman/Art Resource, NY.

p. 132, © The Granger Collection, New York.

p. 137, © Erich Lessing/Art Resource, NY.

p. 138, © ullstein bild/The Granger Collection, New York.

p. 140, © Clore Collection, Tate Gallery, London/Art Resource, NY.

p. 142, © The Art Archive/Musée Archéologique Naples/Alfredo Dagli Orti.

p. 147, The Art Archive / Museo di Capodimonte, Naples / Gianni Dagli Orti.

p. 148, © Rue des Archives/The Granger Collection, New York.

p. 150, © ullstein bild/The Granger Collection, New York.

p. 155, © Lynsey Addario/CORBIS.

p. 159, © Scala/Art Resource, NY.

p. 162, © Erich Lessing/Art Resource, NY.

p. 165, © David Turnley/CORBIS.

p. 166, © Bill Ross/CORBIS.

p. 168, Photo © Erich Lessing/Art Resource, NY.

p. 171, © Dmitri Baltermants/The Dmitri Baltermants Collection/CORBIS.

p. 173, © The Granger Collection, New York.

p. 175, © Erich Lessing/Art Resource, NY.

p. 179, The Art Archive/John Meek.

p. 181, © Scala/Art Resource, NY.

p. 185, © The Granger Collection, New York.

p. 186, © Lynsey Addario/CORBIS SABA.

p. 188, © SEF/Art Resource, NY.

p. 192, © The Art Archive/Gianni Dagli Orti.

p. 194, © Private Collection/Index/The Bridgeman Art Library.

p. 199, Photograph © Roger Wood/CORBIS. Photographed November 1, 1968.

p. 201, © Scala/Art Resource, NY.

p. 205, © Erich Lessing/Art Resource, NY.

p. 209, © The Granger Collection, New York.

p. 211, © Bildarchiv Preussischer Kulturbesitz/Art Resource, NY.

p. 213, © Erich Lessing/Art Resource, NY.

p. 216, © Erich Lessing/Art Resource, NY.

p. 218, © Scala/Art Resource, NY

IBC, © Getty Images.

LAPHAM'S
QUARTERLY

You'll pretend you were men instead of babies, and you'll be played in the movies by Frank Sinatra and John Wayne or some of those other glamorous, war-loving, dirty old men. And war will look just wonderful, so we'll have a lot more of them, and they'll be fought by babies like the babies upstairs. —Kurt Vonnegut, 1969

A uniformed child joins forty thousand teenage Fascists at Rome's Place du Peuple, 1932.